Careers in International Affairs

Careers in International Affairs

Seventh Edition

MARIA PINTO CARLAND
LISA A. GIHRING
Editors

GEORGETOWN UNIVERSITY PRESS / WASHINGTON, D.C.

Georgetown University Press, Washington, D.C.
© 2003 by Georgetown University Press. All rights reserved.
Printed in the United States of America

10 9 8 7 6 5 4 3 2 1   2003

This volume is printed on acid-free offset book paper.

Library of Congress Cataloging-in-Publication Data

Careers in international affairs / Maria Pinto Carland, Lisa A. Gihring,
editors.—7th ed.
        p. cm.
Includes bibliographical references and index.
  ISBN 0-87840-391-4 (pbk. : alk. paper)
  1. International relations—Vocational guidance—United States. 2.
International economic relations—Vocational guidance—United States.
I. Carland, Maria Pinto, 1944- II. Gihring, Lisa A.
  JZ1238.U6 C37 2003

                                                    2002013807

Contents

Preface

The seventh edition of *Careers in International Affairs* is the essence of what we at the School of Foreign Service at Georgetown University believe a career guide should be. It is compiled by a career counselor and a student. Alumni share their career experiences in its pages, and friends of the School and employers of our graduates offer advice and insights about the international job situation. These individuals make up the kind of network necessary to inform and support every young person seeking an international career in the twenty-first century.

Our intention here is to prepare students for positions in business, government, world organizations, or nongovernmental organizations where they will serve and represent their country or the international community. And from their first positions, we assume that graduates of international affairs programs will move easily in and out of the public, private, and nonprofit sectors. *Careers in International Affairs* is designed to provoke thought about possibilities and the means to translate those possibilities into realities. It offers an introduction to and an overview of a wide variety of employment opportunities around the world, and it provides

- basic understanding of international career fields and what they offer,
- insights into the skills and requirements employers find necessary for success,
- heightened awareness of career options,
- broad guidelines for future career decisions.

In this edition, our aim is to help international affairs graduates use their education to inform and contribute to international affairs in all walks of life. We intend to emphasize the interpersonal dynamics of the job search. Everyone knows the essential elements of preparation for that international job search: education, internships, resumé and cover letter writing, interviewing, and contacts. However, twenty years of observing students move through these phases toward an

Chapter 1

THE INTERNATIONAL JOB MARKET

The International Affairs Job Market

MARIA PINTO CARLAND

O n a Tuesday morning in 2001, we suddenly understood that advanced technology would not protect us from or prepare us for the complex requirements of the twenty-first century. Despite our best intentions and interests in international education, we had not gone far enough in our exploration of what was foreign to us. Our fascination and success with technology had lulled us into the safe, satisfied notion that new-wave technology and English language skills were all that we would need in the next century. We assumed our language and technology would be not only imitated but welcomed around the world. Technology bloomed in our classrooms. Computer skills suddenly seemed much more practical than studying languages and cultures.

We are now learning, to our dismay, that dangerous gaps exist in our understanding of the world and its people and that we need to focus on those gaps—and fill them—now. We must insist that students acquire knowledge of foreign societies—their histories, norms, values, aspirations, capacities, and perceptions—and the requisite language abilities to understand and reach them. This knowledge will come from an interdisciplinary, intercultural, and

---

Maria Pinto Carland is Associate Director of the Master of Science in Foreign Service program in the School of Foreign Service at Georgetown University. Prior to joining the School, she was an administrator at the Patterson School of Diplomacy and International Commerce and the University of Toronto Graduate History Department. She has also been a curatorial assistant at the Metropolitan Museum, the Art Gallery of Ontario, and the University of Kentucky Art Museum, and a program officer at the United Nations Association and the Foreign Policy Association. She is also a career counselor for men and women of color at the annual International Career Advancement Program in Aspen, which works to bring greater diversity to the staffing of senior management and policymaking positions in international public and nonprofit careers. Ms. Carland holds an M.A. from Georgetown University.

multilingual education, all critical elements for communication and collaboration in the international arena. Vast communication technologies are worthless unless we can apply them creatively and effectively in regions of the world we understand poorly, or not at all. Our responsibility in the twenty-first century is to provide an education that prepares young people to communicate across cultures and to do so over the course of several careers.

Professional schools of international affairs are no longer the only institutions with international curricula. They have been joined by schools of medicine, law, business, and public policy, all of which offer courses with a global perspective. Today, bright students of international affairs demand an education that will allow them several concentrations and multiple options. They want to integrate foreign policy and business, law and economics, medicine, and human rights. They see themselves not only combining disciplines but preparing to move at one time or another in and out of sectors and specialities. And they are right. Creative combinations of courses are more and more common. The joint degree—international relations and law, international relations and business, international relations and medicine—is extremely popular. The interest in and need for cross-cultural studies is as important as, if not more so than, ever.

Education and Experience
Information about careers has become such an integral part of the American educational system that even many children in elementary schools have a day set aside to learn what firefighters and farmers do. We are a can-do country, and we are urged early in our lives to discover what we want to do, and whether we have what it takes— in terms of interest, skills, education, and experience. To this end, effective career guidance and employment services are essential. Most educational institutions recognize this and offer students preparation and training, insights and advice, opportunities and contacts, as well as encouragement and assistance. What they don't offer is jobs. Indeed, experience at the School of Foreign Service shows that our students' achievements are supported by our career services, but their accomplishments come through their own efforts. We believe that career achievement is the result of interaction between a student's character and our curriculum, a student's intelligence and our instructors, and a student's skills and our services.

It is crucial that you realize the responsibility for finding a job is yours. It is also critical that you understand that the most difficult part of any job search—and of life in general—is knowing who you are and what you want. The answers to these questions will assist you in choosing a sector, will help you explain why you want to join a particular organization, and will enable you to convince others that you have something to contribute to the field. *You* must create and seize opportunities for yourself. *You* must be able to present yourself as an asset to potential employers and to those whose placement assistance you seek.

Preparation for the Entry Level: Education
Today it is no longer sufficient, or satisfying, to study a single discipline in isolation. Just as the line between domestic and international has blurred, so too the lines between disciplines are disappearing. Historians must understand economics and science; political scientists must appreciate budgets and finance. Furthermore, educated individuals must be able to combine technical and cultural skills, not only to expand their knowledge, but to apply it. In the future, we will assume that the physical and behavioral sciences, the humanities and cultural and ethical studies will be part of every person's body of knowledge. Studies reveal that employers place the highest value on skills not usually associated with specific training: generic cognitive skills and social skills. Nonacademic training and experience are rated as highly as the knowledge, principles, and practices of a particular academic discipline or trade. Cross-cultural competence is the critical new human resource requirement created by the global environment.

This integrative approach of interdisciplinary, intercultural, and multilingual education will soon infiltrate and inform all the traditional fields. However, a number of enduring requirements continue to stand out:
- knowledge of history and an awareness of patterns in international relations,
- thorough grasp of what determines foreign policy priorities and realities,
- solid grounding in economics and an understanding of international business,
- familiarity with basic business and accounting skills,
- well-developed computer skills and a high comfort level with technology,
- understanding of policy development and implementation,
- clarity and accuracy in speaking and writing,
- self-awareness: comprehension of leadership and teamwork skills,

- logic and objectivity in thinking, particularly the abilities to identify issues, to detail alternative courses of action, and to establish and act on criteria for making choices,
- ability to project possible future consequences of present decisions,
- talent for time management,
- poise, humor, imagination, compassion, intellectual curiosity, bal-
  anced judgment, and openness to new ideas,
- awareness of and commitment to ethical standards and personal
  values.

The utility of specialization is perhaps one of the more common questions posed with regard to educational requirements and concerns. Specialization and sophistication of knowledge and analytical techniques can be crucial to the knowledge and work of the international professional. However, the isolation essential for scientific study or specialist investigation is a severe handicap in policy prescription and in the successful implementation of a given strategy. Coping in policy situations with the multidimensional interactions that characterize international affairs requires a holistic, conceptual approach. The requirements of a new era in international affairs demand "generalists" capable of understanding the work of specialists and able to synthesize knowledge from various fields. Thus the liberally educated generalist is prepared to wrestle with complex issues, sort them out, and produce logical and responsive conclusions.

Practitioners of international affairs must recognize the importance of interpersonal relations in effecting the outcome of any deci-
sion-making situation. The circulation of knowledge will be the most significant aspect of the twenty-first century. The ability to communicate is the essence of international relations. Students will need experience in both theory and practice of international affairs in order to be able to communicate and collaborate across disciplines; it is the capacity to resolve communication difficulties among special-
ists that distinguishes the international policymaker. Students eager to prepare themselves for the twenty-first century must understand that although practical training will help them land their first job, it is their theoretical training that will ensure promotion and a long and successful career.

Preparation for the Entry Level: Internships

Most entry-level job seekers in the international field face an "expe-
rience" dilemma: They need a job in order to gain experience but cannot get a job without experience. One solution is to find a job

for a few years between undergraduate and graduate school. This is an ideal time to explore the world of work, travel, make mistakes, test yourself, and then return to the classroom. However, if this is not possible, there is a middle way: internships. Many students obtain an internship while in school. The term *internship* loosely refers to a part-time or temporary position (paid, unpaid, or for credit) involving some relevant professional experience. Ideally, an internship should be a training experience that involves mutual learning and screening by both the intern and the employer. It should be an occasion for the student to take academic knowledge out of the classroom and apply it in the professional world and use real-world experience to complement academic courses.

Internships offer several advantages:
- insights into and an understanding of a particular career field,
- exposure to and experience in a professional environment, enabling the intern to make contacts and get a feel for the working world,
- the potential for an inside track to an unadvertised full-time position.

An internship's major disadvantage is the risk that off-campus involvement during the academic year may undermine academic performance, given the tendency of employers to emphasize their priorities over the intern's. The ability to handle an internship depends on the ability to manage one's time. In seeking an internship, there are several points worth considering:
- Consult a variety of sources for leads. It pays to cast a wide net, but be discriminating—don't apply for every opportunity.
- It takes time to arrange an internship, because they are not high on the list of an employer's priorities. Be persistent. Be patient.
- You may be able to take on more responsibility than an internship description would first indicate. Many employers will want to test you on the job before rewarding you with pay or substantive responsibilities. Remember that if you have a particular interest you can sometimes convince an employer to create an internship where none exists.

The Employment Search

Job hunting is a testing, matching process. What makes it challenging and stimulating is the way you use your self-knowledge and your knowledge about the world of work. It is especially important that you do the necessary preparation or homework to acquire this knowledge. Your goal should be to learn about a career field and about your capabilities and interests in that area. Generally, the most successful job seekers are those who have researched various job sectors, who have done a good deal of reading, who have made many contacts, phone calls, and consultations, and who have skillfully used their academic base. They have done considerable internal preparation, self-assessment, and thinking. They know their personal characteristics, their desired job environment, their long-range goals, and what they can offer an employer. How do you go about this?

There are two kinds of preparation: internal and external. Internal preparation involves some soul-searching about who you are, what you have accomplished, what you do well, and what makes you happy. Career guidance and testing will help you here, as will workshops on resumé and cover letter writing. The process of putting together your resumé will help you define your accomplishments and experience. Be honest with yourself about who you are and what you want.

External preparation involves investigating career fields in general, and firms and agencies in particular. You already possess the tools necessary—by virtue of your education you are a researcher and analyst. You should approach career planning in the same way as you approach your studies. Just as you attend classes, attend workshops offered by your school's career office. Just as you use the library and the Internet for research, consult them for information on career planning. In the same way you strive to write clear and concise prose, you should learn how to prepare an impressive resumé and write a targeted cover letter. Just as you may interview various individuals for term papers and other projects, interview them for career information. Just as you expend considerable effort analyzing competing worldviews, historical interpretations, or philosophical tomes, analyze your own aspirations, skills, and credentials.

You may also wish to consult one of the many books that have appeared in recent years covering the mechanics of locating a job. Although there are many witty and engaging manuals on the techniques of job seeking, the basic components of the employment process can be reduced to the following:

- Identify your interests.
- Prepare an effective resumé.
- Develop leads and contacts.
- Prepare for interviews.

Resumés

Resumés are useful for one purpose only—to get an interview. Job-hunting manuals all have sections on the preparation of a resumé, but the form and content vary significantly. There is no standard way to do a resumé, but for young people, a chronological approach is ideal. It is critical to keep it brief (one page) and neat and make sure that an employer can easily discover your assets and skills. Your resumé should be technically perfect—no errors, no typos, and in an easy-to-read font that can be easily scanned into a computer database. Although the resumé is important, you can waste much time by reworking it. A properly worded cover letter, carefully targeted (with resumé enclosed) can be just as effective. The time best spent is in honing your interview skills. In the end, the resumé can only convey to the employer a sense of where you've been and what you've done. It is in the interview that you must explain what you've learned and what you are capable of doing.

Your cover letter should be more specific. It should emphasize why you wish to join that particular organization instead of another, what it is about that organization that attracted you, and why your skills and knowledge would be a good match.

Contacts

An overwhelming majority of jobs—85 percent—are never advertised. Additionally, many companies have decided that on-campus recruiting is an inefficient use of resources. An incredible number of employment opportunities are passed on only by word of mouth. Thus, it is important to establish a wide circle of acquaintances who know your interests and abilities, so that when they hear of a position, they will think of you. Only by consulting with a variety of people of different ages and experience who are willing to help you (e.g., faculty or university staff members, alumni/ae of your school, family friends, relations, interviewees for past research projects) can you expect to tap into the "hidden job" network.

Networking is an overused word but with good reason. Networking is often the most important component in a job search. However, do not overuse your network—contacts are a valuable yet delicate and perishable resource. You need to cultivate them carefully. Be appreciative, be reasonable, and be courteous—particularly about their time. Most people you will meet and speak with have full-time jobs, which require their attention and energy. They are doing you a favor by giving you some of that attention. Never request an information interview with a contact if you intend to ask for a job. Honesty and forthrightness are essential elements in maintaining this valuable access. Contacts, used properly, can provide you with excellent information about their own and other organizations. They may suggest job search strategies that will assist you, they may share stories about what they did right or wrong with their education and their career decisions, and they may even find you a job or refer you to one. Remember, an information interview provides a showcase for your ability. Use it wisely.

We believe that a critical component of networking is a mentoring relationship, and we have included a brief chapter on what such relationships involve, how to find mentors, and how to work with them.

Interviews

Interviews are the key to receiving employment offers. Thoughtful preparation and participation are keys to a successful interview. Despite the lengthy and sometimes convoluted path that an interview may follow, there are really only three essential questions posed: Why are you interested in our organization? What can you offer this organization? What type of a person are you? If you cannot answer these questions, you shouldn't be there. If you cannot give specific examples to support and illustrate your answers, you won't be convincing. The next chapter is devoted exclusively to preparing and participating in an interview.

The Realities of Seeking a Job

Carefully consider the following advice:

- Take the time to evaluate your education, experience, and abilities. Although you may be short on experience, perhaps you are long on the ability to analyze issues and make judgments in an intense, competitive atmosphere. You probably know how to organize your time, meet deadlines, and define and defend your ideas and interests orally and in writing. In a tight job market, you must present your assets intelligently and distinguish yourself.
- Employers may ask what have you done, but they really want to know *what you can do for them*. Make sure you prepare examples that illustrate what you can do for them.
- Job search manuals, university career offices, and college deans all emphasize the value of focusing interests. This doesn't mean closing doors to other opportunities, but rather choosing which door

to open first. You must be focused. That doesn't mean your focus can never change. You can still keep your options open.

- The overwhelming majority of people who fail in their careers do so as a result of personality, not skill, problems. You can master most jobs. The way you handle interpersonal dynamics, however, will make all the difference between an acceptable and a superior performance.
- Remember that one of the most highly valued experiences these days is teamwork. Make sure you can cite experiences—in the classroom, as a volunteer, or on the job—in which you served a meaningful role on a team. Be prepared to explain the results of that teamwork, not only in terms of success or failure, but in terms of what you learned about yourself and the situation.
- At the entry level, be willing to pay your dues (i.e., accept the small projects and do them well so as to earn recognition and greater responsibility). It's simply a way to demonstrate not only ability but an appreciation for the on-the-job culture.
- There is no forward movement if risks are not taken. You are young. You can afford to take calculated risks—don't just apply for jobs you know you can do without effort.

Apply for the jobs that will make you stretch.

We hope that the international career information that follows will give you a fuller understanding of the opportunities available and facilitate your career campaign. You will soon find that there are unlimited opportunities for those whose international, interdisciplinary education has prepared them for the twenty-first century.

Chapter 2

INTERVIEWING
AND FINDING A MENTOR

Two Crucial Components of International Careers

MARIA PINTO CARLAND

This essay is designed to make you think about interviewing and its elements: about how to present yourself, who you are, what you want, why you're interviewing, and where you want to go. You must think about and know these things because, in an interview, you choose what to reveal; you are the source of all information about yourself.

You need to be clear about the purpose of the interview, how it's structured, what to expect, how to prepare, and how to participate. The ability to interview well must be learned, needs to be practiced, and can always be improved.

Just as in your favorite seminar, in the best interview you listen, you share what you know, you ask questions, you learn, and you strive to make a good impression. What occurred in that favorite seminar to make it work? Everyone was at ease with themselves, comfortable with one another, glad to be there, familiar with the topic, and, ideally, interested in and enthusiastic about the discussion. A successful interview requires the presence of those very same elements.

To arrive at this happy juncture, you need to be clear about the purpose of the interview, how it's structured, what to expect, how to prepare, and how to participate. The ability to interview well must be learned, needs to be practiced, and can always be improved.

Two categories of interviews exist—informational interviews and job interviews—but we focus here on the job interview. There are various kinds:
- a meeting between an interviewer and a candidate,
- a succession of meetings with different interviewers and a single candidate,
- a meeting between a single interviewer and a group of interviewees,

• a meeting with a panel of interviewers and a single candidate.

Although participation in each is different, the preparation for all of them is the same.

Preparation

Interview preparation requires the completion of two distinct tasks: a personal assessment of yourself and a professional assessment of the organization you are approaching. A word of advice before you even begin: Everything you read and everyone you speak to will emphasize the value of focusing your interests. However, doing so doesn't mean closing doors to other opportunities. Rather, it requires choosing which door to open first. Count on it, you will be able to open the other doors later. And remember, being focused doesn't mean that your focus will never change. Opportunities will arise that you aren't even aware of at this stage in your life. Think of the doctor from Tennessee who is now a U.S. senator!

Personal Assessment

Do you know who you are? Do you know what you want? Are you comfortable talking about yourself? You've given presentations and spoken up in class and can respond without hesitation to questions about current events. However, to your surprise, you may find yourself hesitating when asked to provide answers to questions about yourself. Although the questions may seem simple, you need to answer such questions in polished, thoughtful sentences. For example: Why did you choose your university? What was your most significant accomplishment during your last job? Who was your best boss? An interviewer might use these questions to discover not only how you make decisions, what your priorities are, and what your work style is, but also to determine your ability to clearly articulate your ideas. You don't want to find yourself searching for the answers during the interview. You need to start formulating and polishing those ideas and answers now.

To do so, you must become aware of and structure the ongoing self-assessment you've been participating in all your life. What are you capable of, and where do you want your education and experience to take you? Start with your resumé. It outlines the professional facts about your life. Familiarize yourself with it, as if it described someone else. You should be able to produce three sentences about any fact on your resumé. For example, what your undergraduate thesis was and what you learned from it, why you were made captain of the tennis team, where you traveled as a backpacker and how it influenced you. In addition, you should be able to identify a consistent theme that runs through your education and experience and leads toward your goal. Be sure that your resumé emphasizes those things most pertinent to the career you intend to pursue. Review projects you initiated and problems you solved. Make certain you understand how your course work, internships, and jobs interconnect, and how they all relate to your goals. Know what you have been responsible for and what you have achieved. Be able to quantify your accomplishments. Be able to relate your achievements to the needs of the organization to which you are applying and focus on what you have to offer that organization.

Take time to actually imagine yourself working:

- Do you know your work style? Do you value routine, prefer flexibility, or some combination of the two? Do you prefer to work alone or in a group, or are you comfortable in both situations? Do you want to be at the front desk or in the library alone?
- Reflect on your last job or internship—what did you enjoy most? Did anything about the experience bother you—the way the office was managed? The training or lack of it? The work itself?
- Are you able to cite your strengths and weaknesses clearly and professionally? If you don't enjoy writing or don't do it well, you should be prepared to say that you are working on improving it and how.
- Have you developed a sense of the kind of work culture you prefer and the colleagues with whom you are most compatible?
- What are your priorities and values? If you care deeply about the environment, the opportunity to manage a lumber camp in the Amazon may not be for you. The interview is not the time to suddenly wonder what your opinion is on an issue or on some aspect of your experience and education. "Eureka!" moments ideally should occur before the interview.

Remember that no matter how sympathetic your interviewer, she is not your career counselor! This is not the time to detail your anguish over whether you should work with refugees or use your accounting skills to enter an investment house on Wall Street. Your interviewer expects you to be focused, like a laser, on the job being offered. Otherwise, why are you there?

After reviewing your resumé several times, get together with a friend. With his or her help, formulate statements about your ideas and opinions regarding your experience and education. Remember, an actor can always learn lines but won't succeed unless she rehearses them as well. Once you have clarified your ideas and opinions and become comfortable with the appropriate vocabulary and phrasing to describe them, you are ready to articulate them to an interviewer. Not all of the questions you prepare for will arise in your interviews. But knowing answers to them will inform and enhance all your responses. The process will produce a bonus: you will have created a menu of responses to hold you in good stead in a variety of circumstances.

Professional Assessment

When you identify an organization you wish to become part of and are given an opportunity to interview there, you need to make a professional assessment of the organization. Now you utilize the skills every good student has mastered: research and analysis. Find out what you can about the organization. The most common complaint from interviewers is that the interviewees have not done their homework. Interviewers have been describing their organization for years and may be tired of doing so. They will always welcome an interviewee who is clearly familiar with the company and has already targeted areas of interest within it. Furthermore, studies show that nearly 70 percent of an interview tends to be spent describing the company and only 30 percent on the interviewee. Change that so more interview time is focused on you and what you have to offer. And of course, if the company is making a presentation or a representative of the organization speaks on a career panel in your area, be sure to attend. At your interview, they may ask if you were there, or you can volunteer that information. It makes a good impression.

Your research can start at the organization's website—find out about the organization's philosophy and objectives, products or projects, subsidiaries or alliances, growth plans, board members, and so on. But go beyond the website. Conduct a wider search online or in the reference room of your library to see what has been written about the company. (If you can refer to an article you've read recently about the company, you will make a strong impression.) Read the relevant journals so that you are familiar with the major issues in the field. Speak to friends or alumni who work in the organization or in that field. You will want to know what the firm or agency's reputation is, not just what its employees say about it. An informational interview with an alumnus or friend knowledgeable about the organization can give you insight into how it is set up, as well as what the various jobs involve, what the typical new-hire profile looks like, and the salary range. If you can arrange a site visit, even better—you'll see how the office is laid out, what employees wear, and how they interact.

Next, you need to prepare your questions. There are many ways to discover what you need to know without being overly blunt or obvious, and if an alumnus or a friend will answer them, you will be ahead of the game. If not, prepare similar questions for the interviewer.

- If you want to know what the career ladder is like, ask where your predecessor is—if you are told he was fired after the third day or retired after thirty-five years or was promoted, you've learned something. If you hear that there were six people in the job in the last year, you've learned something.

- If you are concerned about quality of life (and you should be!), ask about a typical day, and if you are told there are none (which says something about routine), ask about any one day. Ask the interviewer to start with when she arrives at work. Does she come in early or right at 9:00 A.M.? Does she travel a great deal? Does she delegate? Are there training sessions to attend? Does she eat lunch at her desk or with clients or with colleagues? Is she expected to entertain clients after 5:00 P.M.? Does she stay late, how often does she speak to the boss, and how are decisions made?

These questions may elicit useful data about attitudes, culture, and responsibilities—all things you need to know before you make a decision about the company. With this information, you can plan how to articulate and illustrate your interest in the job. If the organization is an aggressive investment bank, you need to demonstrate that you are a can-do type. If the company is very structured, you need to be able to give examples of how you work within a system.

Finally, you need to consider how you present yourself. Ask for feedback from professors and friends about your presentation style. You must be able to look people in the eye and give a firm handshake (sound like a cliché?—you'd be amazed how many people still haven't mastered that simple social exchange!) Your voice should be firm and clear—do you lower your voice when you speak? Does your voice trail off at the end of the sentence or rise as if you are asking a question? Identify and correct any idiosyncrasies that interfere with your ability to look, sound, and act confident, competent, and professional.

The next step is to put together what you intend to bring with you. First, always bring extra copies of your resumé. Inevitably, another staff member will stop by or be called in, and will ask for another copy. Have it ready. You can also bring an extra copy of your transcript and writing samples, as well as a neatly typed list of references.

A note here: if you are planning to use someone as a reference, have the correct name, title, and address, of course, but even more importantly, send them a copy of your latest resumé and ask permission to use their name and *ask if they feel able to give you a good reference*. If they agree, be sure you keep them up to date on what you're applying for and why so that they can sound informed and in touch when the interviewers call. And make no mistake, the interviewer will *call*. It's the best way to elicit an immediate, unrehearsed response.

Take a small notebook and a pen with you, in case you are required to make notes during the interview. Put all this is a neat, professional-looking briefcase or portfolio. And of course, be sure you have a good suit, shirt and tie or blouse, shined shoes, clean hair and hands, and a nice briefcase or handbag ready for the interview so that you look prepared, polished, and appropriate. At this point, you are about to move beyond preparation to participation.

Participation

The communication tools you'll use to arrange the interview will be the telephone and/or e-mail. The first thing to remember is that no one can see you when you use the phone or send e-mail, *so use notes!* Before you pick up the phone, create an outline of what you wish to convey. That way, whether your make the call or receive the call, you'll sound precise and professional. If you find you must leave a voice-mail message, with the notes in front of you, you will be succinct and coherent. Say who you are, why you called, how and when you will call again, and/or where the person you are calling can reach you. And with your notes, you won't leave out anything important or find yourself hesitating or, worse, repeating yourself!

When you call, be formal—that way, if there are any adjustments to be made—that is, from addressing someone as "Mr. Smith" to calling them "John"—the change can be seen as a compliment to you, not a correction. If you use e-mail, be as formal as if you were writing a business letter. Begin with "Dear Mr. Smith" and give your name, home address, and e-mail address. Be brief. Make every effort to keep your message within the space of a single screen. In a busy office, no one has time to read more. This is a good rule of thumb, as it forces you to edit your letters and demonstrates that you know their time is valuable and, by extension, so is yours. Remember, the organization's assessment of you begins the minute they receive something from you: your resumé, your first call, your e-mail.

When a firm returns your call to invite you to a job interview, be sure you are clear about all the details, and if you aren't, ask: when, where, with whom, what (if anything) should you bring, and how to get there.

Plan your schedule so that on the day of the interview you are rested and alert. Be prompt—even if it means arriving early—and allow plenty of time for the unexpected (e.g., a rainy day and no cabs, long delays to get through building security, confusion about which floor your interview is on). You want to be on time and unflustered. Take your coat off in the reception area, and leave it there if possible. You don't want to arrive with your arms full, and you do want to be ready to shake hands and perhaps accept a packet of material. Smile, repeat the name of the individual aloud so you get it right, look them in the eye, and give a firm handshake. The strongest impression you make is usually in the first thirty seconds. In spite of this, don't be nervous or nonchalant.

Never underestimate the interviewer. Assume she has a reason for all of the questions asked. Even if she is not a human resources professional, she has no doubt interviewed many men and women, and has developed an eye and a method for determining character, skills, and abilities. In other words, she can learn, and intends to learn, from everything you say and do.

Be prepared for stress. Experiencing stress before and during an interview is only natural. You are putting yourself and your abilities on the line before a complete stranger who may or may not offer you something you want. Definitely a stressful situation! On the other hand, it can be exciting and interesting if you are comfortable enough to allow your enthusiasm to shine through. Keep your sense of humor. No one wants to hire someone who comes unglued over small incidents. If you spill your coffee, mop it up, apologize for the interruption, laugh about it, and keep talking. You'll be the person they want on their team when things are difficult, as well as when everything is going smoothly. Think of it as an opportunity to demonstrate grace under pressure!

We have suggested earlier the importance of having prepared responses regarding your resumé. You don't want to sound canned, so pause and think before you speak. Ask for clarification if you need it. Provide examples of your skills rather than simply stating them. If you cannot give specific examples to support and illustrate your answers, you won't be convincing. Never respond_by simply saying "yes" or "no." If they ask whether you are good with statistics, say "Yes," and go on: tell them about a class you took that prepared you for a project and how that project contributed to obtaining an internship, and you will present the image of someone competent, interesting, and well prepared. Or, say "No, but . . ." Or, agree and qualify. For example, if you are told you are "too young, too inexperienced," respond diplomatically. Acknowledge the remark, and then provide additional information:

> *Yes, that's true. However, when I was twenty-one, I spent a summer interning at an American Embassy abroad. Most of the staff were taking vacations, and I was given the work and responsibilities of a junior foreign service officer. I wrote cables and interviewed visa applicants and learned a great deal about making judgments, articulating my opinion and defending it in a fast-moving, high-powered environment.*

The trick is to juggle several notions at the same time: you don't want to brag, you don't want to appear uninterested, and you don't want to drone on about yourself! Keep it short and honest and be realistic with yourself. Be sure you can do the job, even if it's a stretch, because once you're hired, you'll have to perform and produce!

You can almost assume that certain questions will be asked in a first interview. This session, often called a screening interview, focuses on reviewing your resumé and making certain that you can speak to everything listed there. If the interviewer asks you to tell him a little bit about yourself, don't immediately assume he hasn't read your resumé. He's really asking you to package for him the important things he needs to know about you. Don't ever say "as you can see on my resumé." Instead, use three sentences to describe yourself and your potential in a manner that will not only catch his attention but also give him a handle for the next set of questions. For example, say you are applying for a position in a nonprofit that does conflict resolution. Remember your theme, and say

> *My education in French and American universities has focused on the field of international relations, and I chose work experience in D.C. and in Africa that would complement my course work and increase my specific knowledge of refugee issues. My accounting class enabled me to prepare budgets as part of volunteer work for*

a small nonprofit, and my experience as assistant editor of our journal came in handy this summer when I wrote cables at our embassy in Togo. I have been following your organization's work in Rwanda and want an opportunity to contribute to and learn more about refugee assistance, as I hope to build a career in refugee relief.

Three sentences. What you've done is make yourself, your work, and your goals sound interesting and complementary. While linking your education and experience, you are simultaneously highlighting your skills and goals. By suggesting that you carefully chose, as opposed to drifted into, your internships and jobs, you've also hinted at decision-making skills. You've explained why you want to work for that organization and made it easy for the interviewer to imagine where you could be placed. Because you have the potential to do many things well, you're probably looking at a range of possibilities. You may not be perfectly clear about your goals, and your education and experience may not perfectly match the position. Don't worry.

The interviewer may ask about your accomplishments. If so, mention projects or experiences that highlight your abilities: a paper, a publication, an award. Some, more straightforward than others, will simply ask, "Why should we hire you?" This is not the time to rattle off a string of skills, but rather to *illustrate* them. This is when you make use of the examples you have prepared. And if you aren't asked, work them into the conversation anyway!

There are some old saws to avoid. Don't say you are a "people person." A sharp interviewer will ask you what you mean. In fact, don't say anything about yourself (i.e., I'm honest and hardworking, etc.). Instead, describe a situation that demonstrates a certain attribute. What have you done that makes you think you are a people person? Tell the interviewer that.

At the same time, you should be prepared to discuss one or two failures (everyone has them) and place a positive spin on them. Failures often come from taking risks. Perhaps you attempted too much, too soon. Remember that a risk taker can be valuable in a company, particularly if he or she learns from mistakes. Review your experience of not succeeding. Work out a satisfactory description of the event in question and provide insights to demonstrate not only what you did and why but also how you incorporated that into who you are today. No matter how you explain a disaster, your explanation must reveal that you learned from the experience.

It is a given that you always highlight your best in each answer. If you are asked whether your grades are an indication of your achievements, you have several options. If you are a straight-A student, you will want to say "yes," of course, but don't stop there. Mention that you worked hard to earn the high grades and briefly go on to say what it was that excited you enough to work so hard. If you are a B+ student, mention that you felt you learned how to balance study and work because you complemented your course work with an internship each semester. If some of your marks were less than ideal, emphasize that your best ones came when you developed a focus and moved away from general courses into your concentration. If there is one question you dread—about the year you failed all your classes, or something equally catastrophic—face it head-on *before* the interview.

> Remember, the interviewer wants to form favorable judgments about whether you can do the job, get along with the staff, manage people, and be realistic about your own skills and the requirements of the job. Do your best to help him come to such conclusions.

In the midst of all this preparation, it is easy to forget that you will be in the interview room with another human being, not just The Interviewer. You must be aware of the interviewer as a person, not just as an observer of your performance. He is prepared to like you, in fact, wants to like you, just as he wants to be impressed by your achievements and abilities so that he can hire you. Therefore, your aim should be to create good chemistry between yourself and the interviewer. Sometimes that's possible, sometimes it's not. If, for example, he comes unprepared, contribute to the success of the interview by jumping in with additional information or insights about yourself and your experience. Remember, he wants to form favorable judgments about whether you can do the job, get along with the staff, manage people, and be realistic about your own skills and the requirements of the job. Do your best to help him come to such conclusions.

Most interviewers are professionals who know the rules and who are familiar with the law, written and unwritten, governing what is permissible and what is not in an interview. Because it is their job to represent their agency well and to attract new hires, they are not likely to do or say anything that is inappropriate or, worse, illegal. You, too, should be aware of what is illegal—such as questions regarding age, race, religion, and so on. Still, there is always the possibility that an unfortunate question will arise. You should not allow it to throw you off stride. There are several ways to respond: Keep in mind that you don't have to answer if you don't want to, but if you do, you can do it in a civil manner: *"Perhaps I have misunderstood your question, but I don't believe it is appropriate for me to respond to it here."* Or, you can simply turn the question aside; that is, if they ask if you're planning a family, you can reply, *"I assure you that I make every effort to keep my personal and professional life separate, so you needn't have any concern about my private life."* Of course, there is a third alternative: you can leap up and threaten to sue! We would, however, recommend the first or the second alternative.

You might also consider volunteering some information. The choice is yours. For example, if it's clear you have the job and you are talking comfortably about benefits, and the interviewer mentions day care or health care for spouses, you can certainly say, "Marvelous, I have a three-year-old." Or, "My husband will be pleased to hear about the health care benefits." But remember, you decide whether to share this information. If you are anxious about such questions, there are many publications available to help you determine what is or is not legal in an interview setting.

Ordinarily, salary as an issue doesn't come up in a screening interview, but it might when you are asked to fill out an application. If the application form has a space for salary, don't agonize about it. Instead of a figure, just write "open." As a general rule, it's better not to discuss salary until you have convinced the interviewer that you are a good fit for the position or until he and his colleagues decide they want you to fill it.

If the interviewer asks for a salary figure once you have advanced beyond the screening interview, you might say that you would expect a salary that would enable you to live comfortably in that particular city, and you might also mention—if necessary—your need to pay off education loans. Then ask what the range is for the position. Whether or not he provides a range, he will probably press you for a ballpark figure, so you must be prepared to respond. You can research benchmark salaries in the field *(The American Almanac of Jobs and Salaries).* Be realistic. Presumably, you are applying for an interesting, exciting job along with a number of other excellent candidates. Most organizations are able to give a 10 percent increase over their original offer. But keep in mind that if you ask for more than their budget allows, they won't hire you because they will fear that you'll be unhappy with the salary they can afford. They may want to establish your salary history, so you should indicate your previous salary and current expectations. If there is a significant difference between the two, you will need to defend that difference. In short, you want to ask for a good amount—the Goldilocks salary!—not too high, not too low.

Ideally, you will have decided beforehand what you want and what you will settle for happily, and what is unacceptable. You might say you are flexible (if, in fact, you are!) and give yourself room to yield gracefully if they don't meet your demands, and you still want the job. Always preface any comments about a position by stressing how interested in and enthusiastic about it you are. Then, if you have to accept less than you had hoped for, you still have room to say that you are eager for the experience and thus willing to accept the lower figure.

But don't stop there. This is a negotiation. Ask if there is a possibility for a review and a bonus or a raise at the end of six months if you have proven yourself. And always remember, although salary is at the heart of the matter, benefits can be critical to your decision making. Benefits can amount to as much as an additional one-third of your salary. Consider health benefits—dental and optical plans. If the company can't give you the salary you want, but you want the job, see if the organization is willing to give you something else that is valuable. Inquire about parking and flexible hours, and remember that day care! Ask if they fund further education or relevant training. And don't forget vacation time—perhaps you could negotiate an extra week. Once you start to think about it, you may realize there are other things that are important to you.

All interviews have a beginning, a middle, and an end. At a certain point in the process, the interviewer will probably ask if you have any questions. You should have some prepared because they make you appear engaged and interested, but you should also interpret this to mean that the interview is drawing to a close. The last question you ask should be about the next step in the process. When might you hear from them? After hearing the answer, it is time for you to leave. Shake hands with and thank the interviewer. Tell him you are interested and you want the job and, if you are in early stages of the interview (before negotiations), you can truthfully say that if they offer it you will accept! Don't be shy about doing this, if you really want the job. Occasionally, people feel that expressing interest and offering a commitment puts them in a vulnerable position. That's not the case. You are affirming the interest that brought you to the interview and sending a message the interviewer can factor in to the decision. This does not mean that at a later date you can't change your mind. After all, they may not make an offer, or the offer may come in a package you find unacceptable. But until that happens, you've not only demonstrated in the interview that you are qualified, you've reinforced the notion that you are ready and willing.

When the organization actually makes an offer, ask for time to think the offer over. Both you and the interviewer may have deadlines to meet. Just as you can ask for time to consider, they can set a deadline for your answer. The time frame may be a flexible one; it may not be. If you want the job, but you are considering other offers (and want them to know that they have competition), you might mention that you have a deadline as well. It might speed up their response; it might not. You have to judge the situation.

Thank the receptionist on the way out. Remember, she's already been hired and is no doubt a valued staff member. If she has anything to say about you, her boss will listen carefully. You want to always make a positive impression on the staff you hope to work with because they, too, want to know if you are collegial, and they may have a say in who gets the job. Immediately after leaving, you should take a moment to jot down the main points discussed or any material you promised to send as a follow-up.

Follow up the interview with a written thank-you, again expressing enthusiasm about the job. In the note you might include additional information as well as a recap of a certain skill or experience of yours that is particularly applicable to the job. But keep it short! This can be done by e-mail, with a handwritten note (plain white card or paper and legible handwriting!) or a typed business letter. Do it immediately.

If you have not heard from them in two weeks, or within the time period mentioned if that is sooner, then you may telephone to discover if a decision has been made. In the meantime, evaluate your performance—note what was easy or difficult for you, and what you did well or where you might improve. Keep your perspective and keep looking. In the end, you will have developed a sharper image of who you are, what you want to do, and where you want to go—and be able to articulate it.

Three final pieces of advice:
- Forward movement often requires taking risks. You can afford calculated risks—don't only apply for the jobs you know you can do without effort. Interview for the job that will make you stretch.

- Every conversation has two sides: one is the ability to speak, the other is the ability to listen. Don't forget to listen.
- Prepare well and practice until you are practically perfect!

Finding and Working with a Mentor

MARIA PINTO CARLAND

We have all been involved in a mentoring relationship with family, friends, or colleagues at one time in our lives. Mentoring can be part of a formal program, a situational connection, a friendship, or a casual relationship without any formal structure. When we speak of mentoring here, however, we are discussing a professional relationship. Although you may find this essay simply confirms what you already know, it is also written to provide a framework for your ideas and future actions as you form and establish mentoring relationships.

In ancient times, young men and women were sent to other families to learn through observation and imitation how to behave and succeed in society. To be sure, sometimes they were hostages, but the old Irish word for such situations sounds more like what we have in mind: "fostering." In modern times, this concept—in schools, businesses, and the public sector—has become known as mentoring.

Mentoring is almost invariably a mutually beneficial relationship. It provides a sounding board for plans and strategies, it initiates a mental or physical move to another point in life, and it establishes a ritual of seeking and finding advice and support. Typically, mentoring is a relationship in which information and insights are shared by a more experienced person with a less experienced one. By listening to and observing the more experienced person, the less experienced individual receives personal attention and learns through precept and example. The more senior partner gains prestige and satisfaction from the junior partner's progress and success. Interestingly, the experience also lends itself to introspection and self-awareness. That is, the mentor must have a clear image of who she is, what she is good at, and what she has learned from life before she can know what she has to share.

When seeking a mentor, a distinction should be made between a mentor and a confidant. A mentor is usually someone on the inside—at school, at work, in a volunteer group, at a church—who can influence events. A confidant is someone on the outside, who may listen sympathetically without either involvement or the ability to influence. As a matter of prudence, it might be unwise or unfair to discuss some issues with an individual within your organization. For example, in the wake of a difficult experience, you might wish to share your immediate feelings with a confidant who could listen sympathetically. Later on, you might go to your mentor for advice and suggestions about the experience. However, whether it is one with a mentor or a confidant, your relationship must be one of trust and confidence.

You should keep in mind that your role model may not always be an appropriate choice for a mentor. For instance, you might identify an individual in your field whose career path impresses you and whose skills you wish to emulate. At the same time, you also realize that you will probably never get to know that person, and that he would never have the time or energy to provide you with the kind of one-on-one guidance you would expect from a mentor. Therefore, this isn't the person you should approach to be your mentor. You should select as a mentor someone with whom you are comfortable, probably not a direct supervisor but someone more senior, who knows you (or is willing to get to know you), understands your situation, and is in a position to be of assistance. Your mentor needn't be the same sex or race, but you should always stay within your comfort zone. And of course, remember that there is no rule that limits you to only one mentor!

Look for the following in your mentor and yourself (the mentee).
Mentor:
> Good powers of observation and a willingness to listen.
> The talent *and* time to guide and educate.
> A sense of tact, generosity, and understanding.
> Knowledge of the playing field and the players.

Mentee:
> The ability to initiate and cultivate.
> Clear goals and skill in articulating them.
> The ability to offer something/make a request/give back.
> The knowledge that most people enjoy helping and are flattered by requests, but also appreciate those who return favors

When Mentoring Goes Well—What's Going On?

In a good mentoring relationship, partners must establish the basics about each others' background, especially regarding education and experience, on the path to a solid relationship. The junior partner must know what she wants. At the least, she should be able to identify a career goal, and perhaps outline the route she might take to get there, so that her mentor can indicate alternate paths and suggest important sites to see and things to do along the way. The senior partner should be thoughtful, capable, and articulate. She should also be able to provide perspective and insight into the field, describe her career path, share examples of her successes and failures, demonstrate what she has learned and show how she has integrated that knowledge, and discuss what she reads to expand her expertise in the field. The mentor should be able to offer advice about her field tailored to the mentee. For example:

- Does the mentee's resumé appear appropriate for her field of interest?
- What skills should the mentee obtain and emphasize?
- How should the mentee view the field and position herself in it?
- What are the hot issues, organizations, and people, and what are future trends?

Both partners in a mentoring relationship should listen to and observe one another and be willing to give feedback on what they see and hear. Both also must be aware of what they have to offer each other: One partner may provide advice and insights; the other may bring a fresh eye and a youthful perspective. One may offer contacts, invitations, and opportunities; the other, university contacts—faculty, lectures, conferences, articles, and books.

Remember, mentoring is a process, and a dynamic one at that. In order to work, this relationship must be a two-way street.

What Can You Expect?
A successful mentoring relationship demands that you know what you want from the relationship. Is it advice? A good listener? Assistance? A professional friend? All of the above? Be clear about what you are willing to contribute to the relationship. Some of what you should offer should include openness to criticism, willingness to share information, a sense of humor, and, always, behavior worthy of your mentor. Be sure that your expectations are in line with your capabilities and your mentor's. Be realistic and be professional. Use your time with a mentor wisely: it's a precious commodity for each of you. Be a promise-keeper—if you promise to be somewhere or do something, be there and do it.

In any relationship, you can create a comfort zone by negotiating a set of guidelines. You should reach an agreement on these points:

- How will you get in touch? E-mail or phone? Day or night? At work or home?
- Where will you meet? At the university or office? At home or in public? For coffee, drinks, a meal?
- When will you meet? Once a month? Four times a year? What suits both partners' needs and schedules?
- Why will you meet? Always have a purpose, a goal, or an agenda for discussion or activity.

Make use of a variety of learning styles: discussion, observation, shared experience. Conversation is the most obvious and common style. However, observation of a mentor in action, by visiting his office or attending his staff or client meetings, can be equally rewarding. Shared experiences might include attending together a professional conference or a university class, or joining the audience when your mentor gives a speech, or attending a reception and obtaining introductions to his colleagues.

But remember, this is not an action adventure—doing things together is not the objective, doing something constructive while together is. There should be time for reflection and feedback for both partners. Each of you should make time for discussion of what you have observed in and heard from one another, so that it will be a learning and growing experience. After all, mentors don't just provide advice and support; they provide inspiration, too. And if you are fortunate enough to have such a mentor—someone who not only meets your expectations but also inspires you—remember that those who are mentored today are obliged to mentor tomorrow.

Chapter 3

THE INTERNET JOB AND CAREER SEARCH

Internet Job Searches

RITA JUPE

A stranger phoned. The caller announced the he was an employment consultant. "Would you be interested in a technical writer-slash-editor position at an environmental and engineering consulting company that works primarily on federal government contracts?" he asked, or something like that. "A what? Do you have the right number?" I replied. He did. So we began to talk.

The recruiter, who apparently trawls Internet-based job sites looking for environmental specialists, had seen my resumé. His search criteria must have found the words "writer" and "editor" in my employment history. I can only guess that the year I spent dredging the environmental record of George W. Bush for a television documentary also slipped into the recruiter's net without scrutiny. Long story short: that phone call led to an interview and a much broader job as a media consultant at the same company.

As you see, the Internet can be a useful yet haphazard tool for job and career searchers. A resumé posted on the Internet will be viewed by all manner of recruiters, and employers will see it. You may receive a phone call that leads your career in a surprising direction. Or an employment consultant, hungry for his finder's fee, may waste your time trying to wedge you into a business manager's position when you are looking to land a job as a business reporter. Put the Internet to work for you, explore possibilities, and stay in control of your search.

Rita Jupe, a 1998 graduate of the Master of Science in Foreign Service program at Georgetown University, is currently a Senior Counselor at Nichols Dezenhall. Prior to that, her career in media included working in Great Britain as a reporter for The Evening Echo *and* The Western Mail. *In the United States, she has served as edition editor for* The Jersey Journal; *news researcher for New Jersey Network-Public Television; news producer for Reuters television; and writer, associate, and package producer at CNN.*

Getting Started

Pick up the telephone or send out e-mails. Friends and colleagues will be able to recommend sites for their reliability, ease of use, and quality. Relevance is just as important; the preferred site of a friend who is interested in conflict resolution may not be the best stop for someone who is trying to break into management consulting. Although books about the Internet and employment research can be helpful, in this ever-changing area word of mouth is a powerful source.

Prepare a plain-text version of your resumé and cover letter. Bullets, italics, and indents do not show up when you copy and paste a formatted document into the crude online shells that are common to sites related to career searches. This shortcut will also remove the inconvenience of cleaning up a resumé online.

Decide what type of Internet site to visit. It may be helpful to think about seven categories:
- Career advice and research
- Job search
- Specific employers
- Professional associations
- Governments
- Online publications
- General search engines

The first-time job hunter to the career changer can find valuable information at these sites. Before we look at what each category has to offer, note that job sites can disappear quickly. During the research for this chapter, a first-rate resource for quality media, public affairs, and Capitol Hill job postings shut down citing a cooling economy, demonstrating that sites come and go, even the best ones.

Career Advice and Research

The best locations in this category provide profiles of industries and sectors; job descriptions (what does a public relations account manager do, anyway?); career ladders; market rates of pay and benefits; interview techniques; tips on writing cover letters; and information about job fairs, including dates, locations, and employers. At the micro level, profiles of individual companies also appear, although be aware that the businesses write their own answers to the site's questions, which can cover areas such as management philosophy or workplace atmosphere. Guides that reveal what to expect from the interview process at a particular firm are also available on these sites. Many are quite thorough and free of charge, and you can download or purchase more detailed guides online. If you like chat rooms, you'll find plenty in this category, although the quality of discussion may be patchy. From the general to the specific, career advice and research sites offer a great starting point.

Job Search

Think of job search sites as giant data banks packed with positions from internships to part-time jobs to mid-career posts. As a general rule, the more specific the information that a job seeker puts into the search categories, the better the results. Resist the temptation to search "All Types" of positions in a city; some sites will spit back scores of hits that you may feel compelled to scroll through. With time it is easy to determine which places offer the most employment opportunities in your chosen field. At that point, it is a good idea to sign up for free services. For example, it takes less than five minutes to set up online search agents that scour the Internet for listings that contain your key words, for example, *consultant, French,* and *DC-Metro.* Results or alerts can be delivered to an e-mail inbox; however, if you are already employed, consider who may be walking by while you open your mail in the morning. Many sites offer free accounts that allow job hunters to save and manage their searches.

Another useful feature is the online resumé. Some services allow for cut-and-paste documents, whereas others require line-by-line entries. The second method can take as long as forty-five minutes, depending on an individual's length of experience. Sites allow users to create and post several resumés that are tailored to different types of positions. At least one site indicates the number of times that employers or recruiters have looked at a resumé. But online resumés are not the be-all and end-all of job hunting. Keep using the self-directed search features of these sites because it may take months for a recruiter to call.

Specific Employers

Companies and organizations frequently post employment opportunities on their Web pages. Once you have identified target employers, bookmark their sites and check frequently for updates. Applying online with a cover letter and resumé can take up to forty-five minutes, depending on the format and length of work experience. Recruiters are increasingly using the Internet to find candidates. Nonetheless, the rules for differentiating yourself from the rest of the pack still apply. Call for an informational interview and use your collegiate and professional network to gain access. If you receive a postcard or e-mail acknowledging receipt of your application, try to follow up with an individual in the company or organization. Lastly, these particular Internet sites often describe career paths, job descriptions, and interview procedures in an organization.

Professional Associations

Every major profession, trade, or discipline has a presence on the Internet. Again, word of mouth and an eye on print publications will lead job hunters to the most effective and respected organizations. Sites in this category present information on recruitment fairs, pay and benefits, company rankings (e.g., the top revenue-earning public relations firms in the DC-Metro area), professional development advice, employment tips for those looking to work outside of the United States, and much more. Sites may require membership for access to their most comprehensive job bank features. But if you have moved beyond the career research stage into the active job hunt, it may be worth joining the association at what is usually a much reduced student rate in order to take advantage of networking events.

Governments

Governmental departments can provide abundant online resources for careers. For example, the U.S. Department of State site supplies links to recruitment areas of the United Nations, the World Trade Organization, the World Bank, and the North Atlantic Treaty Organization (NATO) to name a few. Embassy Internet pages contain information about work visas, professional associations, and academic and professional programs. At the employment sections of specific governments or international organizations, you can research career paths and compensation in the same way as on a private company page.

Online Publications

Newspapers, general-interest magazines, and trade journals (publications geared toward professionals in a certain sector such as finance or journalism) can all be found on the Internet, along with their employment sections. Geographical borders and cash constraints fall away thanks to these resources. Want a banking job in Britain? Check out the classifieds in British online newspapers. Want a visa to work in Britain? Well, that may be a little harder.

General Search Engines

Everyone has a favorite generic search engine for everyday research. Use this tool to find the home pages of professional associations, chambers of commerce, nongovernmental organizations (NGOs), firms, and career advice centers. Research the interests and professional backgrounds of interviewers or principals at your target company or organization. Search engines may be blunt tools, but the best ones produce solid results.

Pitfalls

Internet-assisted employment and career searches offer speed, convenience, and geographic reach at little cost. But there are some drawbacks.

- *Privacy*. There is no reason to think that a well-respected Internet employment site should be any less secure than an online bank. However, there are privacy concerns. Read the privacy statements carefully to understand whether a site plans to sell any part of your profile. A more immediate threat to privacy lies in the area of online resumés. Job hunters who do not want their current employers to know they are looking for new work can post resumés anonymously on job search sites.
- *Quality*. It is worth repeating: Not all sites are created equal. If the graphics, links, and language do not look entirely professional, chances are the site does not contain extensive or sophisticated resources.
- *Fees*. Advertising and other sources of commercial revenue power most employment specialty pages. Occasionally, job search sites offer to enhance the visibility of online resumés. Services range in price, depending on the intensity of the "push" to recruiters. I paid approximately $10 at one location for the lowest level of enhancement and received two telephone inquiries. Marketing pitches may exclaim the success of these fee-based services, but only an individual job seeker can determine whether the time is right to start paying.
- *Time management*. It is easy to fritter away hours on the Internet without having found a single want ad that fits your needs. Distractions, false leads, extinct URLs, and inferior sources abound. Keep your eye on the goal: finding realistic job leads in your target sectors.

Putting It All Together

The seven categories of employment-related Internet sites discussed in this chapter offer something for all levels of professional and educational experience. As the Internet continues to evolve, new sites and services will appear and further expand these categories. Good old-fashioned word of mouth and the news media are excellent ways to hear about the best innovations for your Internet career research. It is also important to include other methods in your search, such as on-campus recruitment fairs and informational interviews. The Internet is a powerful tool, especially when combined with the best off-line job hunting techniques.

> For a list of the top Internet sites and other job-searching guides and resources, see the "Resources" chapter at the end of this book.

Chapter 4

UNITED STATES GOVERNMENT

Careers in the U.S. Government

JOSEPH A. FERRARA

Before September 11, 2001, some observers worried that the concept of public service as a higher calling seemed in danger of becoming a quaint notion—a gauzy, nostalgic image of an American way of life that simply no longer existed in an age of Internet startups, a booming private sector economy, and government downsizing. But in the wake of the worst terrorist attacks ever on American soil, public service is staging an impressive comeback. Human resource specialists at numerous agencies—including the Central Intelligence Agency; the Departments of Defense, State, and Health and Human Services; and the Homeland Security office, among many others— are overwhelmed by the sheer numbers of job applicants hoping to come aboard and serve their country.

This is a natural, even stirring, response to the horrific events of September 11, and yet the truth is that public service never really went away. Public service—the sense of a commitment to larger things, a desire to influence public policy and the course of world events, a strong motivation to serve one's fellow citizens—has always been at the core of American life. And there have always been people interested in pursuing the sometimes challenging paths of government service. Certainly, September 11 has reminded people of the vitality and relevance of public service—who, after all, will

Dr. Joseph A. Ferrara directs the Executive Master's program in Public Policy Management at Georgetown University. Dr. Ferrara has previously worked as a legislative assistant on Capitol Hill, a budget analyst at the Office of Management and Budget, and in various senior executive service positions at the Department of Defense. He was a presidential management intern in the 1984 class. During his government career, Dr. Ferrara received numerous awards and honors, including the Secretary of Defense Medal for Civilian Service (three times) and the Vice President's Hammer Award for Reinventing Government (two times).

soon forget the searing images of public safety, fire, and rescue personnel risking death to help the victims at the World Trade Center and the Pentagon? The problem of public service in the United States, in short, was not that it had somehow lost its relevance and meaning; rather, it was that we had forgotten how important it truly is.

In this essay, I hope to portray a U.S. public service that, although clearly in transition, offers many opportunities for personal and professional growth, and, perhaps most importantly, a chance to make a real difference in your life and the lives of your fellow citizens. Specifically, I will focus on employment and career development within the federal government.

Why Choose Government Service?

The first answer is simple—government is where the action is. Where else can you defend your country? Negotiate international treaties with nations around the world? Work with Congress to draft legislation? Work with the White House to develop executive orders on key policy issues? Make presentations to the heads of Cabinet departments and members of Congress? Enforce the law? Influence the flow of billions of dollars in research grants? Provide economic assistance to developing countries?

Government in the United States has evolved from rather humble beginnings as a "night watchman" state that provided only the most basic services, such as military defense and law enforcement, into what one scholar calls "an immense network of organizations and institutions affecting the daily lives of all citizens in countless ways" (B. Guy Peters, *American Public Policy: Promise and Performance*, 5th ed. [New York: Chatham House, 1999], 3). Over the past 200 years, we have witnessed the slow but steady evolution from limited to positive government in the United States. This evolution has been largely the result of major military, social, and economic developments during the course of U.S. history, including wars, the struggle for civil rights for all citizens, and various economic dislocations, depressions, and recessions.

Over time, as each new shock to the system has occurred, citizens have demanded that government perform new and sometimes unprecedented functions—and Congress has responded. Today, the federal government has assumed responsibility for protecting the environment; regulating worker health and safety; ensuring the safety of the nation's food supply; overseeing air traffic control operations; curing AIDS; forging international partnerships in an era of globalization;

fighting ongoing battles against poverty, homelessness, and illegal drug use; and, most recently, conducting a global war against terrorism, among many other functions (Kenneth Meier, *Politics and the Bureaucracy*, 4th ed. [New York: Harcourt Brace, 2000], 2). Each of these functions requires a professional career bureaucracy with the expertise to write policy; oversee compliance; make recommendations to the president, Congress, and members of the Cabinet; and develop effective programs that ensure the highest level of citizen service.

Working within the U.S. government means working on the key issues of the day and being a direct participant in the policy debates central to the nation's idea of itself and its future direction. Although it is true that government today has devolved and outsourced a number of functions to private firms and nonprofit service delivery organizations, the public sector remains the sector most directly involved in policy making and national strategy. Recent surveys bear this out. For example, a major study of public policy graduates conducted in 1999 by the Brookings Institution's Center for Public Service found that graduates who went to work in the public sector were deeply impressed by the government's ability to have a major impact on society. As one survey respondent said: "It was motivating to get up every day and go to work and think that what I was doing was for the benefit of the common good. That was very motivating and made me feel good and that's what it was about. My friends who worked in the private sector didn't have that feeling or that experience or that reality. That was something lacking for them" (Paul Light, *The New Public Service*, chap. 3 [Washington, DC: Brookings Institution, 1999], 67).

> Working within the U.S. government means working on the key issues of the day and being a direct participant in the policy debates central to the nation's idea of itself and its future direction.

And the opportunity for policy impact in government service is closely related to another key reason for considering government service: the chance for rapid advancement to senior levels of responsibility. In today's public service, it is not uncommon for junior policy analysts to be given wide-ranging portfolios that connect them to senior decision makers throughout government.

One story from a former colleague at the Department of Defense (I'll call her Jane) illustrates this point. Within a few months of taking on a new assignment with the Under Secretary of Defense for Policy, Jane found herself on a military charter flight taking the Secretary of Defense (at the time, William Cohen) and other senior officials from Defense, State, and the National Security Council to a series of NATO defense meetings in various European cities. Civil unrest had flared up in Albania, one of the countries included in Jane's new portfolio, and it was likely that this issue would be discussed at the upcoming NATO meetings. Moreover, for security reasons, a decision was made to cancel Secretary Cohen's planned visit to Albania. Instead, the Secretary would do a one-hour live satellite interview with the Albanian media; the interview would be done from a Budapest television station shortly after the Secretary's plane had landed in Hungary. Secretary Cohen asked his military aide if a policy analyst familiar with the Albanian situation was on the plane and the answer came back: Yes, there was. A few minutes later, Jane, a twenty-eight-year-old junior analyst, was briefing the Secretary of Defense on the Albanian situation.

Such opportunities are likely to expand in the near future as the federal government confronts a potential mass exodus of senior talent. According to recent studies by the General Accounting Office and the Office of Personnel Management, more than 60 percent of the federal government's senior executives will be eligible to retire by 2005. Although this represents a real crisis in human capital for the government, it also represents a real opportunity for young men and women considering public service as a career (General Accounting Office, *Major Management Challenges and Program Risks: A Governmentwide Perspective* [Washington, D.C.: Government Printing Office, 2001]).

Federal Employment Demographics

The federal workforce is one of the most diverse in the United States. And where it is not diverse, the government is taking proactive steps to enhance the representation of historically underrepresented minority groups in the workforce. The Federal Equal Opportunity Recruitment Program provides for the Office of Personnel Management to conduct an ongoing program to help federal agencies eliminate the underrepresentation of women and minorities in the federal workforce (U.S. Code. 5 U.S.C. 7201. *Federal Equal Opportunity Recruitment Program*). As the following table shows, the federal government is striving to be a progressive employer that ensures diversity and representation in its workforce.

Table 4.1. Diversity in the Federal Workforce

Minority Group	Representation in the Federal Workforce %	Representation in the U.S. Civilian Labor Force %
Total Minority	30.4	27.6
Asian/Pacific Islanders	4.3	3.8
Blacks	17.6	11.2
Persons with Disabilities	7.2	*
Hispanics	6.6	11.8
Native Americans	2.0	0.9
Veterans	26.7	11.6
Women	43.8	46.6

Source: *Office of Personnel Management Diversity Profiles*
As of September 30, 2000
Data not compiled by OPM.

Total employment in the permanent General Schedule and Blue-Collar pay plans declined by 1.6 percent from 1,528,683 as of September 30, 1999, to 1,504,893 as of September 30, 2000. Despite the employment decline, the percentage representation of minorities in the federal workforce increased from 30 percent in 1999 to 30.4 percent in 2000. The federal workforce continued to exceed the civilian labor force in the representation of most minorities. Unfortunately, Hispanics and women continue to be underrepresented in the federal bureaucracy. To address this, the federal government has launched a series of outreach and recruitment programs. One such program is the Hispanic Initiative (Executive Order 13171, October 12, 2000. *Hispanic Employment in the Federal Government*). This initiative, established in 2000, provides for a plan for more actively recruiting Hispanics and to assess and eliminate any systemic barriers to the full consideration of Hispanics for federal positions.

Although these numbers are reassuring, it must be noted that serious problems still exist. Two areas in particular are troubling. Very recent research has shown that women and people of color (defined in this research as African Americans, Latinos, Asian Pacific Islanders, and Native Americans) still find themselves at a disadvantage with respect to promotion opportunities and are much more likely than the majority "Euro-American" group to be subject to disciplinary action or be fired from their federal jobs (Katherine Naff, *To Look Like America: Dismantling Barriers for Women and Minorities in Government*

[Boulder, Colo.: Westview Press, 2001]). Over the last several decades, a series of formal laws and regulations have been issued barring discrimination in hiring, firing, promotion, and other personnel practices. But despite this formal antidiscrimination regime, there is evidence to suggest that some managers rely on more subtle and informal methods, including stereotyping, that have a depressing effect on advancement opportunities for women and people of color. This is obviously bad news, but the good news is that federal agencies have come under sharp public criticism on these issues and are taking steps to address them. Many agencies—including the U.S. Postal Service, the U.S. Coast Guard, the National Institutes of Health, the National Oceanic and Atmospheric Administration, and others—are working to more fully integrate diversity objectives into their basic operating structure (Naff 2001).

One other aspect of employee diversity that should be noted is the geographical distribution of the federal workforce. U.S. government workers are found all over America and, indeed, all over the world. Table 4.2 provides a brief snapshot of the major geographical concentrations of federal employees within the United States. Finally, according to recent statistics, about half of the federal workforce is employed in just three agencies—the Department of Defense, the Department of Veterans Affairs, and the U.S. Postal Service—with the other half being distributed throughout the remainder of the federal agencies and departments.

Pay and Compensation

There is a persistent myth in American culture that government work is severely under-compensated. The truth is far more complicated, and, on balance, more positive than the mythology.

In fact, pay and compensation for federal employees is one of the best-kept secrets in U.S. professional circles. Most people leaving college with an undergraduate degree are eligible for entry-level jobs with the U.S. government at the GS-7 level on the pay scale, which ranges from approximately $28,000 to $36,000 a year. Graduate students with master's degrees (or Ph.D.s or J.D.s) are typically eligible for GS-9 and higher starting jobs, ranging from about $34,000 to $45,000 a year (based on the 2002 General Schedule table).

Although these starting salaries are sometimes lower than graduates would find in private sector organizations, the advantage in government is that quite often young professionals have the opportunity to enter what personnel managers call "career ladders"—a

Table 4.2. Major Geographical Concentrations of Federal Employees*

State (and D.C.)	% of all Federal Employees
California	9.3
District of Columbia	6.3
Texas	6.1
Virginia	5.1
New York	4.9
Maryland	4.6
Florida	4.0
Pennsylvania	3.9
Illinois	3.4
Ohio	3.0

Source: Office of Personnel Management Federal Data Charts as of December 31, 1998.
Does not include intelligence agency or seasonal employment figures.

series of promotions that occur over a period of time, and sometimes as rapidly as one every year—that move a person from the entry-level grade to a so-called journeyman grade at the top of the ladder, based on outstanding performance. The speed with which one can advance up this career ladder is often a function of both micro- and macro-environmental factors. At the micro level, for example, some agencies prefer to "season" their junior employees through a series of rotational assignments and special projects while gradually moving them up the General Schedule career ladder. At the macro level, presidents sometimes impose special initiatives that affect promotion rates. For example, presidential downsizing efforts in the early 1980s and again in the mid-1990s affected the total number of promotions in the federal workforce. In addition, there are other factors, some of which are under the employee's direct control, such as the level of performance exhibited in a series of demanding assignments, and some of which are not, such as whether the agency leadership happens to be emphasizing the policy area in which an employee works. While it is not unprecedented for a young professional to enter at the GS-9 level and be promoted to a GS-14 or GS-15 level within five to seven years (this would translate into an annual salary range starting at about $34,000 and culminating at approximately $83,000 within as little as five years), it is more likely to take on the average of ten to eleven years to progress to the GS-15 level.

It should also be noted that these figures are the base salary figures; federal agencies offer locality pay adjustments to reflect the general cost of living in major metropolitan areas around the country. So, if you are a GS-13 federal employee working in Los Angeles, California, your base salary will be $59,409, but your locality-pay-adjusted annual salary will be $68,944. In addition, Congress has authorized the establishment of special salary rates for specific disciplines, including medical officers, scientists, and engineers.

And beyond direct salaries, the federal government offers a comprehensive package of benefits, including the Federal Employees Health Benefits Program (FEHBP) that serves more than 9 million federal employees and their dependents and includes numerous outstanding health insurance policies administered by many of the top-rated insurance and health maintenance organizations in the United States. Participating employees can choose from a menu of fee-for-service plans, health maintenance organizations, and plans offering point-of-service products. What distinguishes the FEHBP from its private-sector counterparts is the wide range of participating health insurance programs and the relatively low premiums available to federal employees. In addition, there is a generous program of vacation time and sick leave.

In 1987, the U.S. government established a new retirement program called the Federal Employees Retirement System (FERS). Almost all new federal civilian employees hired after 1983 are automatically covered by this new retirement system. FERS is a response to the changing times and federal workforce needs. Many of its features are "portable" so that employees who leave federal employment may still qualify for the benefits. The new retirement system is flexible. Covered employees are able to choose what is best for their individual situation.

The three key components of FERS are Social Security, a Basic Benefit Plan, and a Thrift Savings Plan. Social Security provides monthly benefits for retired workers who have reached at least age sixty-two. The Basic Benefit Plan portion is financed by a very small contribution from the employee and from the government. Basic Plan benefits are a monthly payment depending on the employee's pay and length of service. As in most retirement plans, a formula is used to compute the payments under the Basic Benefit Plan. The government averages the highest three consecutive years of basic pay. This "high-3" average pay calculation, together with the employee's length of service, are used in the benefit formula. Employees who meet the criteria also receive a

"Special Retirement Supplement," which is paid as a monthly benefit until the employee reaches age sixty-two. This supplement approximates the Social Security benefit earned by the employee while they were employed by the federal government. The final element of FERS is the Thrift Savings Plan, which is a tax-deferred retirement savings and investment plan that offers the same type of savings and tax benefits that many private corporations offer their employees under 401(k) plans.

In sum, FERS is a flexible plan for a flexible workforce—a workforce that is more likely to work for several different employers during the course of a career. It allows for the fact that many employees may not retire from the federal government. It also builds on the Social Security credits that employees already have or may earn in the future from nonfederal work.

Continuous Learning

Many federal agencies have instituted programs of continuous learning to ensure that the workforce stays on the cutting edge of the knowledge and skill base. Continuous learning and training is also essential to ensuring a highly motivated workforce and to recruiting new employees. This concern is not new—indeed, the Government Employees Training Act (GETA) of 1958 still remains one of the key statutes in the policy area—but as the job market has become more competitive and the information technology revolution has continued to advance, the federal government has recognized that continuous learning must become part of the organizational culture within the public sector. Over the years, presidents have issued a series of executive orders that address various pieces of the training agenda. Executive Order 11348, for example, states that it is U.S. policy to develop its employees through the establishment and operation of progressive and efficient training programs. Executive Order 11491 mandates training in the critical area of labor-management relations. And since the passage of GETA in 1958, Congress has passed new laws to advance training issues. The Equal Employment Opportunity Act and the Civil Service Reform Act are two key examples.

Today, many federal agencies are not only implementing this guidance but moving beyond it by establishing their own career-development programs and mandating a minimum number of hours of continuous learning over specified periods. At the Department of Defense (DoD), for example, the Secretary has established the Defense

Leadership and Management Program (DLAMP). DLAMP consists of three elements: professional military education, civilian graduate education, and rotational assignments within the DoD. Other federal agencies, including the Departments of Transportation and Commerce, have established similar career development programs.

In addition to agency programs, the Office of Personnel Management (OPM) operates a series of training centers, including the Eastern Management Development Center (located in Shepherdstown, West Virginia) and its western counterpart (located in Denver, Colorado). These centers offer a wide range of professional-development training, including leadership and executive courses, public policy management seminars, and customized skills development seminars. In addition, OPM operates the Federal Executive Institute, located in Charlottesville, Virginia. Established in the 1960s by President Lyndon Johnson, FEI has served as the federal government's development center for senior executives. FEI brings members of the Senior Executive Service and other high-performing managers together for courses that help executives develop broad, corporate perspectives, understand the role of the bureaucracy in the constitutional design, and enhance essential management skills. More information about all of the OPM centers can be found at www.leadership.opm.gov.

Finally, many federal agencies have gotten serious about professionalization of the workforce. One indicator of this trend is the continuous learning emphasis discussed earlier. In addition, many agencies are creating specific career ladders and paths for professional disciplines, including financial and resource management, procurement and acquisition, science and engineering, and project management. The objective is to establish specific requirements for education, experience, and training that define progress along the career path and ensure that employees are working to the full extent of their abilities. This is good news for new workers because it means that agencies are taking an active role in ensuring a healthy program of career development and fulfillment.

What Is the Government Looking For?

In recent years, the federal government has become increasingly more flexible and innovative in searching for new talent. As one former director of the Office of Personnel Management has said, "As in the private sector, the future success of government requires finding creative ways to attract, manage, and retain talented employees, and to anticipate and plan for the workforce needs of the future. This is the real challenge" (Stephen Cohen, *Remarks before the Federal Executive Institute Alumni Association Executive Forum* [Reston, Virginia, March 30, 2000]). Although they have not always done so, federal government agencies today take human capital planning and workforce development very seriously. In part, this is in reaction to the potentially sizable retirement cohorts looming in the next few years, but agency leaders are also pushing workforce planning because it makes good business sense, whatever the environment. That is because the most important resource government has is its people. It takes people to make programs and policies come to life and actually work. The federal government has recognized that it must manage its people well and provide them challenging, fulfilling career opportunities.

As government has grown and public policy has become more complex, federal agencies have realized that one of the most important skills they need is leadership. Again, the government's top human resource agency, the Office of Personnel Management, seems to understand the challenge: "No matter what programs exist, or the size or composition of our workforce, the real key to a government that works is leadership. Without exceptional leaders who have the ability to design and implement strategies that maximize employee potential and foster high ethical standards, the government will not be able to serve the American people effectively" (Cohen 2000).

The terrorist attacks of September 11, 2001, and the government response to them, have made these employment needs even more critical. The current director of the Office of Personnel Management addressed this issue in a recent speech on government careers:

> It is clear, for example, that the FAA needs more air marshals. The FBI needs investigators. The CIA needs intelligence officers. The DoD needs more military recruits and civilian managers. There are pressing needs at Treasury, at Justice, and the list goes on. At the Federal Reserve Board, administrators and systems analysts keep the banking system and money supply stable. Along America's 7,600-mile land border and 12,000 miles of coastline, the U.S. Border Patrol and the U.S. Coast Guard keep watch. The agents of the U.S. Customs Service make sure shipments entering the country are safe. The people at the FDA ensure a quality blood supply while the Centers for Disease Control watch for signs of any new epidemic. The EPA monitors our air and water and is assisting in the ongoing cleanup operation in New York City. Are you getting the picture? We need doctors. We need lawyers. We need researchers.

We need analysts. We need teachers. We need people who will rise to the occasion and respond to the need for public service now (Kay Cole James, Remarks at the National Career Services Conference [University of Maryland, College Park, Maryland, September 25, 2001]).

In short, the federal government is committed to selecting and developing exceptional people who know how to lead and motivate people; are able to achieve results through developing partnerships and building coalitions; and are able to maximize their resources, especially human resources, to get the best results for American taxpayers.

Working with Political Appointees

An exciting—and sometimes very challenging—part of federal service, particularly in the Washington, D.C., area, is working with senior political appointees. Each president appoints (subject to confirmation by the U.S. Senate) hundreds of men and women to political executive positions throughout the government to help him achieve his policy agenda and manage the bureaucracy. Typically these political appointees come from distinguished careers in the private sector and academia. And quite often, they have substantial prior government service. The current team of political appointees running the government, for example, includes former members of Congress, cabinet secretaries, state governors, ambassadors and foreign service officers, chief executive officers, and state education superintendents. The opportunity to work alongside these officials is one of the key— and unique—benefits of government service.

The challenge, of course, is that many political executives do not stay in office for very long. Moreover, the Senate confirmation process can often be very cumbersome and time-consuming. This means that career federal employees, particularly those working in close proximity to political appointees, must be flexible and able to adapt to new leadership on a regular basis. But it also means that there are unparalleled opportunities for federal managers to be involved in policy making at the highest levels. In addition, particularly during times of transition from one administration to the next, career managers are often called to serve in top leadership roles, running the agency and maintaining forward progress as the new administration takes office.

The Responsive Work Environment

Like other employers, the federal government is working to adapt to the changing work environments of the twenty-first century. Clearly, today's employees want a challenging professional career, but they also want an active personal life and they expect employers to recognize and facilitate this balancing act. And the federal government is responding with an array of work–life initiatives designed to foster a more responsive federal work environment. Recent and ongoing initiatives include child- and elder-care programs, child-care subsidies for lower-income employees, flexible work schedules, and telecommuting programs. Congress has been strongly supportive of these programs, in some cases mandating action above and beyond current efforts. For example, in the fiscal year 2001 Transportation Appropriations bill, Congress required federal agencies to develop telecommuting policies that will cover the entire federal workforce by 2003. Another example is the Family and Medical Leave Act of 1993.

Under the guidance of the Office of Personnel Management, federal agencies have established "family-friendly" programs to help facilitate a healthy balance between work and life. Typically administered by the human resources or personnel office, such programs are designed to educate employees about work–life programs for which they may be eligible. Such programs also advocate for employees seeking alternative work arrangements (Janice Lachance, *New Tools for Parents and Families in the New Economy* [Memorandum for Heads of Executive Departments and Agencies, Washington, D.C.: Office of Personnel Management, 1999]).

International Affairs Positions

International affairs positions in government do not just exist in agencies such as the Department of State and the Agency for International Development. Indeed, just about every federal department and agency maintains an international affairs division. The United States is committed to a policy of engagement with many countries around the world and works through many international forums to influence the global debate and protect American interests.

Getting the Job

For most of this chapter we have discussed various dimensions of government careers. But of course such careers cannot even begin until one finds his or her first job with the government. There are a variety of entry paths into federal employment.

- *Case Examination.* Many jobs are filled through the so-called case examination process, which begins with the posting of a vacancy announcement. Many of these announcements are posted online on the World Wide Web (see www.usajobs.opm.gov, often referred to as "USAJOBS"). One can apply for the job online as well (see www.usajobs.opm.gov). The first step is to review the open positions at the USAJOBS site noted earlier. Typically, the vacancy announcement will provide either a "control number" or a "Vacancy Identification Number"; the applicant will need to enter this number at the beginning of the online application process.

The USAJOBS site is the federal government's worldwide employment information system. It provides job openings, employment fact sheets, online application forms, resumé development, and electronic transmission capabilities. The USAJOBS site is updated every business day and, on any given day, may contain upwards of 12,000 job openings worldwide. The key elements of the USAJOBS site include a comprehensive listing of job vacancies, an online resumé builder feature that allows job seekers to create online resumés specifically tailored to the federal application process, and links to agency online information kiosks that provide additional announcements and an automated, interactive voice response telephone system.

- *Changes in the Process.* Many federal agencies fill their jobs like private industry by allowing applicants to contact the agency directly for job information and application processing. Previously the OPM maintained large standing registers of eligibles and required applicants to take standardized written tests. In addition, applicants completed a standard application form, the SF-171, to apply for all jobs. Today, however, OPM no longer maintains registers of eligibles, and only a few positions require a written test. The SF-171 is obsolete and no longer accepted by most federal agencies. The new federal application form is the Optional Application for Federal Employment, OF-612. But applicants usually do not even need to submit this form; a standard resumé is acceptable. Another change in the job-seeking process is that applicants for nonclerical positions no longer need a rating from OPM to enable them to apply for jobs.
- *Competitive and Excepted Service.* There are two broad classes of jobs in the federal government: competitive civil service positions and excepted service positions. Competitive service jobs are under OPM's jurisdiction and subject to the civil service laws passed by Congress to ensure that applicants and employees receive fair and equal treatment in the hiring process. These laws give selecting officials broad authority to review more than one applicant source

before determining the best-qualified candidate based on job-related criteria. A basic principle of federal employment is that all candidates must meet the qualification requirements for the position for which they receive an appointment.

Excepted service agencies set their *own* qualification requirements and are not subject to the appointment, pay, and classification rules in Title 5, United States Code (although they are still subject to veterans' preference). Some federal agencies, such as the Federal Bureau of Investigation and the Central Intelligence Agency, have *only* excepted service positions. In other instances, certain organizations within an agency or even specific jobs may be excepted from civil service procedures. For example, certain jobs within the Department of Defense and Department of Transportation are excepted service positions.

- *Veterans' Preference.* The federal government has recognized the economic loss suffered by citizens who have served their country in the military by establishing a "veterans' preference" rating. This system ensures that veterans are in a favorable competitive position when applying for federal positions. In particular, Congress has historically reserved the highest preference for those veterans who have served in combat situations during certain periods of time or been disabled by their military service. It is important to note that although veterans' preference is a reasonable form of assistance, it does not guarantee a veteran a job.

- *Internships.* Many men and women who have gone on to build long, successful careers in the government—including individuals who have risen to Cabinet rank and elected office—started out as interns. Completing internships with federal agencies during undergraduate and graduate school is an excellent way to accomplish several key objectives, including learning about what the agency does and whether the work environment is interesting and challenging, building essential job skills, and developing contacts with key management officials who can serve as references for later job applications or who might be interested in hiring you once you graduate.

Many agencies offer part-time and full-time internships. One example is participation in the Federal Career Intern Program. Created by Executive Order 13162, this program is designed to help agencies recruit and attract exceptional individuals into various positions within the federal government. Typically, this intern program establishes positions at the GS-5, 7, or 9 levels, and the internship runs for a two-year period. Upon successful completion of the internships, individuals may be eligible for permanent placement with the agency. A key internship for graduate students is the Presidential Management Internship Program, discussed later in this chapter.

Many agencies also participate in the summer employment program. Typically, the fastest way to discover these opportunities is to go online at the USAJOBS site. Summer jobs usually offer a salary (depending on education and qualifications), and many agencies have reemployment programs that permit individuals who have held summer jobs with the agency to be reemployed without further competition.

- *Outstanding Scholars Program*. Another path to federal employment is the Outstanding Scholars Program. The program is a special hiring authority to be used as a supplement to competitive examining for some entry-level positions and is restricted to grade levels GS-5 and GS-7. Applicants for this program must be college graduates who have maintained a grade point average of 3.5 or better on a 4.0 scale.

- *Cooperative Education Programs*. The Cooperative Education program (or "co-op") is a key recruitment source for federal agencies. This initiative is part of the Federal Student Educational Employment Program. The co-op experience provides for work-study partnerships between students, their educational institutions, and the federal agencies. The program is available to students in high school through graduate school. The value of the co-op program is that it augments the educational process by providing students with relevant job experience and provides federal agencies with an opportunity to shape their future workforces. The co-op program is an excellent way to get a head start on a public service career by doing important (and paid) work while still in school. And once school is finished, co-op participants will be eligible for permanent employment.

- *Federal Jobs by Major*. The OPM provides a useful breakdown of the types of federal positions often filled by certain academic majors. This information can be found at the USAJOBS website. For example, people with accounting degrees usually fill contract specialist, financial manager, and auditor positions. Graduates with degrees in international relations, on the other hand, typically land jobs with titles such as foreign affairs specialist, language specialist, and intelligence specialist. Liberal arts and humanities graduates often move into management analyst and program analyst positions.

I have provided the following list of selected Web resources for students:

Table 4.3. World Wide Web Resources for Students

Name	Description	Address
USAJOBS	OPM's central federal employment resource, providing links to thousands of job openings worldwide	www.usajobs.opm.gov
Students.gov	A collaborative effort between the U.S. government and the higher education community to provide students with comprehensive information on jobs, careers, military service, and financial assistance programs	www.students.gov
StudentJobs.gov	A sub-site within Students.gov that provides detailed information on jobs available to students	www.studentjobs.gov
FirstGov	The central, one-stop portal to the U.S. federal government online	www.firstgov.gov
America's Job Bank	The nation's largest online employment exchange, sponsored by the U.S. Department of Labor	www.ajb.dni.gov

Some Rules of the Road

The federal government can be an exciting place to work. But it is also a very complex environment, with numerous internal and external forces operating on it on a daily basis and affecting the pace and content of the work agenda. These forces include new political appointees, congressional committees, new laws and regulations, new presidential administrations, elections, the media, and public opinion. To negotiate this complex terrain successfully, employees usually need some good old-fashioned "street smarts" to go along with their technical expertise.

What are some good rules of the road for surviving and thriving in the federal establishment?

- *Develop a good network.* A large network of friends and colleagues, inside and outside your agency, is invaluable and can serve as a good information source about new policies, trends, what jobs (and managers!) to avoid, what new positions might be coming open, and so on. One way to start building a network is to join one or more professional associations, such as the American Society for Public Administration.

- *Find a senior mentor (or mentors).* Some agencies have formal mentoring programs wherein new employees are assigned mentors (usually people who are longtime members of the Senior Executive Service). This is a very positive development, but employees should also look for other mentors—supervisors from your current or previous assignments, senior colleagues in other offices or agencies, academicians with good government contacts, and so on. Mentors can be an important source of support and counseling.

- *Take on new assignments.* One way of burnishing your resumé and making yourself more competitive for promotions is to take on new assignments when the opportunity presents itself. These assignments can take several different forms, including details to special interagency task forces and commissions, fellowships with Congress or research organizations, or simply a rotational assignment within your home agency. Selection boards for senior positions are looking for candidates with a wide diversity of job assignments. Another practical benefit of such a career strategy is that it keeps your work fresh and interesting and enables you to see old problems from new perspectives.

- *Make a splash, but show respect.* This is an important balancing act. On the one hand, one way junior employees get noticed and put on the fast track is by making a splash with a bold recommendation or a policy analysis that incorporates new data and fresh ways of looking at persistent problems. On the other hand, making a splash in a manner that seems to mock prior agency policies or ridicule senior managers who have advocated these policies can do more damage than benefit to a budding career. Do not be afraid to make your arguments, but ensure they are backed up by your analysis, and make your points in a way that shows respect.

- *Continuous learning.* Even though federal agencies are requiring a certain amount of professional development every year, there is always going to be pressure to put off such training in favor of working on agency initiatives with pressing deadlines. Be careful not to fall into the trap of constantly putting off such training. It is important for you and for your career development. Probably the best strategy is to schedule an appointment with your direct supervisor at the beginning of the year to chart out what professional development opportunities you would like to take advantage of so you both can define a mutually acceptable schedule that balances your individual development needs with the needs of the office.

Conclusion

Public service is an important calling, particularly in a democracy. The federal government—now more than ever—needs smart, motivated women and men to take on challenging positions of leadership and trust. If you are interested in serving your country, having an impact on public policy, making a positive difference in the lives of your fellow citizens or all of the above, then you should seriously consider a career with the U.S. government.

Not only will you get the opportunity to achieve these important goals, but you will find yourself working in a government committed to its employees. As this chapter has shown, the federal government has taken significant steps to improve the working environment of the average federal employee and continues to maintain an active effort to ensure meaningful work, competitive pay and benefits, substantial career development programs, a diverse workforce, and a responsive human resources system that balances work and personal life. And although the impending retirements are posing challenges for policymakers, they also present opportunities for young men and women interested in federal service and rapid advancement. In short, there has probably never been a better time to consider building a career in the U.S. government.

Resource Listings

Agriculture, U.S. Department of

The **United States Department of Agriculture** (USDA) has a wide variety of international functions. USDA's international work includes negotiating on farm products, running major export market development programs, and administering import regulations.

The **Foreign Agricultural Service** (FAS) has primary responsibility for administering export promotion programs and some agricultural import regulations. Through a global network of agricultural counselors and attachés, FAS helps build markets overseas, gathers and assesses information on world agricultural production and trade, and provides that information to U.S. farmers and traders. FAS manages USDA's export credit program and the food for peace program. FAS also maintains overseas trade offices that draw together the resources of private-sector agricultural trade promotion groups to ease access for foreign buyers and provide services to U.S. exporters. FAS coordinates and directs USDA's responsibilities in international trade agreement programs and negotiations.

As a career field, international agriculture has good employment prospects for applicants with strong backgrounds in economics, agriculture, and trade. With a current staff of about 300 professionals based in the United States and 100 overseas, the FAS hires about 15 professionals a year. Most career opportunities are in the field of agricultural economics and require a graduate degree (or equivalent experience) with substantial economics course work and work experience in agricultural economics. FAS has both a competitive career civil service and an excepted foreign service, thereby offering a broad range of activities and opportunities for promotion.

A number of other USDA offices also are concerned with international affairs. The **Federal Grain Inspection Service** performs grain export inspections, and the **Food Safety and Inspection Service** monitors import grades. The **Animal and Plant Health Inspection Service** checks imports for disease and examines plants, meat, and poultry at ports of entry. Technical assistance for overseas forestry programs, research on international forests, and arrangements for the training of foreign forestry experts are provided by the **International Forestry Staff** of the **Forest Service**. The **Office of Transportation** identifies transportation problems in areas of export and foreign trade and initiates remedial action. The **Agricultural Research Service** engages in cooperative research with foreign nations, and the **Extension Service** works on extension programs with foreign nations. The economists and meteorologists of the **World Food and Agricultural Outlook Board** compile all agricultural and food data used to develop USDA outlook and situation material.

U.S. Department of Agriculture
Fourteenth Street & Independence Avenue, SW
Washington, DC 20250
Tel.: (202) 720-2791
www.usda.gov

Commerce, U.S. Department of

The U.S. Department of Commerce encourages, serves, and promotes American international trade, economic growth, and technological advancement. In order to fulfill its task, the department provides a great variety of programs.

The **International Trade Administration** (ITA) carries out the U.S. Government's nonagricultural foreign trade activities. It encourages and promotes U.S. exports of manufactured goods, administers U.S.

statutes and agreements dealing with foreign trade, and prepares advice on U.S. international trade and commercial policy. The agency is divided into four main offices: International Economic Policy, Trade Administration, Trade Development, and the Foreign Commercial Service. The **Office of International Economic Policy** has specialists for each country and region of the world, as well as a multilateral affairs office. It devises and implements trade and investment policies and agreements of bilateral and multilateral nature. The **Office of Trade Administration** is concerned with the development of export policies for sensitive commodities and products with emphasis on the prevention of the illegal transfer of high technology to other nations. It administers programs to protect U.S. products from unfair competition and it enforces antiboycott provisions. The **Office of Trade Development** handles most departmental efforts to promote world trade and to strengthen the international trade and investment position of the United States.

The ITA is headquartered in Washington, D.C., and operates forty-seven district offices. The agency employs about 250 people in various positions. International trade specialists should have a strong academic background in marketing, business administration, political science, sales promotion, economics, or related fields. Applicants for international economist positions should have completed a full four-year course with substantial attention to economics and statistics, accounting, or calculus. Other professional positions at ITA include specialists in trade, industries, import and export administration, compliance officers, electronic engineers, trade assistants, and criminal investigators. All these positions require a degree in political science, economics, finance, history, electronic engineering, business or commercial law, business administration, international trade, or international relations. A bachelor's degree is accepted; however, a master's degree is preferred. In some instances, appropriate work experience (such as market research, sales promotion, advertising, industrial production operations, commercial law, administrative law enforcement, or application of investigative skills) can qualify a person for certain positions.

An important part of the ITA with independent personnel procedures is the overseas component of the U.S. and Foreign Commercial Service (US & FCS) known as the **Foreign Commercial Service** (FCS), which is part of the foreign service of the United States. The FCS is a career foreign service and has officers stationed in more than eighty foreign nations in addition to the United States. The mission of the FCS is to support and represent American trade and investment interests abroad, particularly in export expansion. FCS pursues these goals in three primary ways: promoting trade and facilitating investment; developing market and commercial intelligence; and representing the rights and concerns of U.S. commercial and investment interests abroad. The FCS professional profile emphasizes three elements: experience; commercial, policy, and linguistic skills; and behavioral characteristics. Junior officer entry is through the foreign service written examination. Competition for positions in FCS is extremely intense and many officers come from within the ITA or the Department of State.

The Commerce Department's **Bureau of the Census** is the world's largest statistical organization and generates a considerable quantity of international demographic and foreign trade statistics. Approximately 105 professionals in the **Foreign Trade Division** compile current statistics on U.S. foreign trade, including data on imports, exports, and shipping. The **Center for International Research** has a staff of sixty-two people and gathers in-depth current data on a broad range of socioeconomic and demographic indicators for individual nations as well as particular world regions. Employment with the census bureau requires a background in statistics, demography, mathematics, economics, or area studies combined with a reading knowledge of a foreign language.

The **National Oceanographic and Atmospheric Administration** (NOAA) is involved in a number of international activities in connection with its responsibilities for the weather service, civilian satellites, ocean fisheries, charting and mapping, and oceanic and atmospheric research. Each of these activities has an office specializing in international affairs. The **National Marine Fisheries Service** collects extensive data on foreign fishing and acts as staff in connection with negotiation of bilateral fisheries agreements. A small **Office of International Affairs** coordinates the work of the line organization, represents NOAA in certain international negotiations, and acts as a point of contact on international matters. A few positions with NOAA overseas also are available at weather stations and observatories for scientists with meteorological, electronic, or geophysical backgrounds.

The **Bureau of Economic Analysis** (BEA) monitors the state of the U.S. economy, including international transactions. BEA's **International Investment Division** measures U.S. direct investments abroad and studies the economic impact of multinational corporations. Accountants and economists constitute the majority of the division's thirty-member professional staff. The bureau's **Balance of Payments Division** employs about forty-five professionals who prepare current statistics and analyses of the U.S. balance of international payments and international investment position.

International matters are dealt with by a number of other offices within the department. The **Maritime Administration** compiles statistics on U.S. seaborne trade, manages U.S. maritime relations with foreign countries, and administers the development and operation of the U.S. Merchant Marine. The **National Bureau of Standards** represents the United States in several international standards-setting organizations, maintains contacts with individual agencies in policy-making on international science and technology issues, and offers technical assistance to nations wishing to engage in standards research. The secretary is advised on policy for the U.S. telecommunications industry by the **National Telecommunications and Information Administration**. The **Patent and Trademark Office** processes international trademark laws and regulations and represents the United States in international efforts to cooperate on patent and trademark policy.

U.S. Department of Commerce
Personnel Division
14th Street & Constitution Avenue, NW
Washington, DC 20230
Tel.: (202) 482-2000
www.doc.com
www.ita.doc.gov

Bureau of the Census
Personnel Division
Room 1412-3
4700 Silverhill Road
Suitland, MD 20746
www.census.gov

National Oceanographic and Atmospheric Administration
Personnel Division
Silver Spring, MD 20910
Tel.: (301) 413-0900
Tel.: (301) 713-3050 (Personnel)
www.noaa.gov

Commission on Security and Cooperation in Europe

Also know as the Helsinki Commission, the commission is a U.S. government agency created in 1976 to monitor and encourage compliance with the Final Act of the Conference on Security and Cooperation in Europe, which was signed in Helsinki in 1975 by the leaders of thirty-three countries, including the United States, and Canada. The addition of Albania, the Baltic States, the newly independent states of the former Soviet Union, and several of the former Yugoslav republics has increased the number of participants to fifty-three.

The Commission consists of nine members each from the U.S. House of Representatives and the U.S. Senate, and one member each from the Departments of State, Defense, and Commerce. The posts of chairman and cochairman are shared by the House and Senate and rotate every two years when a new Congress convenes. A professional staff of approximately fifteen persons assists the commissioners in their work.

The Commission carries out its mandate in a variety of ways. It gathers and disseminates to the U.S. Congress, nongovernmental organizations, and the public information about Helsinki-related topics. Public hearings and briefings focusing on these topics are held frequently. The Commission also reports on the implementation of the Organization for Security and Cooperation in Europe (OSCE) Commitments by the countries of Central and Eastern Europe, the former Soviet Union, and the United States. Some meeting reports are published. The Commission plays a unique role in the planning and execution of U.S. policy in the OSCE, including member and staff participation on the U.S. delegations to OSCE meetings and in certain OSCE institutions. Finally, members of the Commission have regular contact with parliamentarians, government officials, and private individuals from OSCE-participating states.

> Commission on Security and Cooperation in Europe
> 234 Ford House Office Building
> Washington, DC 20515
> Tel.: (202) 225-1901
> Fax: (202) 226-4199
> www.csce.gov/helsinki.cfm

Congressional Research Service

The Congressional Research Service (CRS) is a legislative branch agency that conducts nonpartisan policy analysis and research exclusively for the U.S. Congress. The Service's Foreign Affairs, Defense, and Trade division, one of five subject area divisions, provides information and analysis on foreign, defense, and trade policy. The division employs approximately eighty staff members, including sixty-five policy analysts, in several regional and functional sections: Asia; Europe/Eurasia; Latin America, Middle East, and Africa; foreign policy management and global issues; international trade and finance; defense resources; and military forces and threat reduction. Foreign affairs analysts follow political and economic developments in every region of the world. They provide analysis and information on U.S. economic and political relations with particular countries, U.S. foreign aid programs, international organizations, international financial institutions, and transnational issues such as terrorism and refugees. Defense policy analysts cover national security policy, military strategy, the U.S. defense budget, the defense acquisition process, weapons systems, military compensation, civil rights within the military, military research and development, and U.S. military bases both domestic and overseas, among other issues. Trade analysts follow trade-related legislation, policies, and programs and provide analysis of U.S. trade performance and investment flows. They provide analysis and information on trade negotiations and reciprocal trade agreements, export promotion, import regulations, tariffs, and the organization of trade policy functions.

CRS employs a highly educated professional staff who are hired, retained, and promoted on the basis of merit and accomplishment. Positions are available periodically throughout the year.

> Congressional Research Service
> 101 Independence Avenue, SE
> Library of Congress Madison Building
> Washington, DC 20540
> Tel.: (202) 707-8823
> Fax: (202) 707-2615
> www.loc.gov/crsinfo

Council of Economic Advisers

The Council of Economic Advisers (CEA) is the president's key advisory panel on economic issues. The CEA has a staff of about twenty economists who retain their positions for an academic year and who analyze economic issues, provide economic advice, evaluate the federal government's economic programs and policies, and make recommendations concerning economic growth and stability.

CEA has one senior international finance economist and one senior international trade economist. The holders of these positions have Ph.D.s in economics and have published in peer-reviewed journals. CEA generally hires two junior economists in the international area, either doctoral candidates or recent economics graduates with bachelor's degrees.

> Council of Economic Advisers
> Old Executive Office Building, Room 314
> Washington, DC 20502
> Tel.: (202) 395-5084
> www.whitehouse.gov/cea

Defense, U.S. Department of

The Department of Defense (DoD) and related establishments offer a variety of opportunities to pursue careers in military, strategic, and intelligence activities. Although many positions are filled by military personnel, most of the offices and agencies related to the defense establishment also require civilian employees. For the sake of simplification, the related establishments will be treated as distinct from the main department.

The DoD is responsible for giving the United States the military forces it needs for its security. The department's organization and civilian recruitment procedures are extremely complex. For a better understanding of the structure of the department, consult the latest edition of the United States Government Manual (available from the U.S. Government Printing Office) for assistance.

The DoD and the military services (Army, Navy, Air Force, and Marine Corps) have their own separate personnel offices that independently recruit civilians for domestic positions. In general, all of the offices seek candidates with broad-based academic training. International affairs majors with a strong preparation in history and applied economics and an understanding of defense issues make attractive candidates.

The **Office of the Under Secretary of Defense for Policy** develops and coordinates U.S. national security and defense policies and conducts analysis and research in the fields of international political, military, and economic affairs. General issues include international security, force structure, counter-proliferation, special operations, stability operations, homeland security, and similar subjects. It administers overseas military assistance programs and arms sales to allied and friendly governments and provides policy guidance for U.S. military abroad and for U.S. representatives to international organizations and conferences. The office is also responsible for negotiating and monitoring agreements with foreign governments concerning proliferation, counter-proliferation, and transfers of equipments and service. The organization includes the **Offices of the Assistant Secretaries of Defense for International Security Affairs, International Security Policy,** and **Special Operations and Low-Intensity Conflict.**

The **Office of the Secretary of Defense** (OSD) itself has limited occasions for hiring master's graduates with previous work experience. Typically, foreign affairs specialists are hired at GS-13 or GS-14 levels. Positions filled at the entry level are done through the Presidential Management Intern Program.

There are also many other DoD offices with significant international responsibilities. The **Office of the Secretary of Defense for Acquisition and Technology** oversees DoD research and development activities and exercises export control responsibilities. The office is involved in export licensing decisions, technology transfer policy, review of foreign military sales proposals from a techno-military viewpoint, security assessments of proposed exports, munitions control cases and technology training, and sharing programs with allies. The **Office of the Secretary of Defense for Force Management Policy** develops policies, plans, and programs for employing foreign national employees with the DoD and participates in the negotiations of Status of Forces Agreements with foreign governments. The **Army Material Compound** operates an **Office of International Cooperative Programs.** Policy papers and estimates for the Joint Chiefs of Staff relating to U.S. security interests overseas are prepared by the **Director for Strategic Plans and Policy** of the Joint Chiefs of Staff.

Each of the military services has two offices where domestic employment opportunities in the international field are most numerous: intelligence and operations. Each service runs its own intelligence unit that gathers information on the activities of foreign elements as they relate to the interests of each organization. Each branch also has an office concerned with operating and planning. Within each of these offices are desk officers who follow political and military developments abroad and who prepare policy papers on issues confronting the particular service.

Applicants applying for positions serviced by the Human Resources Services Center (HRSC) are encouraged to apply in accordance with the instructions in the HRSC Civilian Job Kit. The job kit contains instructions on how to apply for a vacancy advertised by the HRSC and includes sample resumés. A resumé formatted in accordance with the HRSC procedures will improve an applicant's chances of employment within serviced organizations. Once an initial application has been submitted, applicants need only self-nominate in order to be considered for any advertised positions he or she feels would be commensurate with his or her skills and abilities.

General information about the Department of Defense is available at http://www.defenselink.mil/. This web page has links to other Department of Defense sites that contain additional information about employment opportunities in the DoD.

> Washington Headquarters Services
> Human Resource Services Center
> 5001 Eisenhower Avenue, Room 2E 22
> Alexandria, VA 22333-001
> http://persec.whs.mil/hrsc
>
> Personnel & Employment Service/Washington
> Department of the Army
> Room 1A881 – The Pentagon
> Washington, DC 20301
> Tel.: (703) 693-7911
> Tel.: (703) 693-6781
>
> Human Resources Center Naval Sea Systems Command
> Department of the Navy
> 2531 Jefferson Davis Highway
> Arlington, VA 22242-5161
> Tel.: (703) 607-1816
>
> Civilian Personnel Office
> Department of the Air Force
> Room 5E871 — The Pentagon
> Washington, DC 20330-1460
> Tel.: (202) 767-5449
>
> Human Resources Office
> United States Marine Corps
> Code ARCA, Room 1215
> 2 Navy Annex
> Washington, DC 20380-1775
> Tel.: (703) 614-1046

Department of Defense Education Activity
Defense Dependents Schools, U.S. Department of
More than half a century ago, the United States military established schools for the children of the occupying forces in Europe and the Pacific. Today, U.S. Department of Defense Dependents Schools (DoDDS) are located overseas in more than a dozen countries around the world. DoDDS has approximately 4,500 teachers serving in more than 150 schools with a student population that numbers approximately 75,000 children. Courses of study parallel those of the public schools in the United States.

Requirements for educators seeking placement in the DoDDS system are rigorous and match those for competitive U.S. public schools. Applicants must be U.S. citizens available for worldwide placement and must have a minimum of forty semester hours of work in general education in fields such as English, history, social studies, mathematics, fine arts, languages, science, philosophy, and psychology. In addition, at least eighteen semester hours of course work in the field of professional teacher education are required. All applicants must have student teaching or have served an internship as part of an approved teacher education program in an accredited institution. In addition to academic requirements, applicants must also be able to participate in extracurricular activities. A state teaching certificate or license is also desirable.

> Department of Defense Dependents Schools
> Personnel Center Professional Recruitment Office
> 4040 N. Fairfax Drive
> Arlington, VA 22203
> Tel.: (703) 696-3067 (Recruitment)
> Fax: (703) 696-2699
> www.odedodea.edu

Defense Security Cooperation Agency
Defense Security Cooperation Agency (DSCA) is at the forefront of America's National Security Strategy. The work done by DSCA and the DSCA team advances America's interests all over the world and takes many forms—it can be seen in the modern equipment fielded by U.S. allies, in the ranks of technically armed forces of allied nations, or even in the provision of emergency relief supplies in the wake of a natural disaster. The activities of DSCA span the spectrum of security cooperation even as our global reach spans the globe.

The agency's professional staff comprises more than 130 security staff assistants, program analysts, country program directors, comptrollers, budget analysts, and data analysts. Academic preparation in international relations, national security studies, or area studies provides good training for positions as security staff assistants and country program directors. Expertise or experience in defense issues, military sales programs, or weapons systems is an asset for any potential recruit.

Defense Security Cooperation Agency
Suite 303
1111 Jefferson Davis Highway
Arlington, VA 22202
Tel.: (703) 601-3731
www.dsca.osd.mil

Defense Threat Reduction Agency
The Defense Threat Reduction Agency (DTRA) protects the United States and its allies from weapons of mass destruction (WMD). The agency's work is wide-ranging, from preventing the spread of WMD to deterrence to preparing for future WMD threats.

Under DTRA, the resources of the Defense Department are used to ensure that the United States is ready and able to address present and future WMD threats through combat support, threat control, threat reduction, and technology development.

The DTRA employs about 2,100 military and civilian personnel. Although headquarters are in Fort Belvoir, Virginia, most personnel work in the Washington, D.C., area. Some personnel also hold international posts. DTRA employees include policy analysts, nuclear physicists, linguists, and engineers, among others.

Defense Threat Reduction Agency
8725 John J. Kingman Road
MSC 6201
Fort Belvoir, VA 22060-6201
Tel.: (703) 767-5870
Fax: (703) 676-4450
www.dtra.mil

Drug Enforcement Administration
The Drug Enforcement Administration (DEA) enforces the controlled substances laws and regulations and investigates and prepares for prosecution those individuals suspected of violating federal drug-

trafficking laws. The DEA regulates the manufacture, distribution, and dispensing of licit pharmaceuticals. On an international level, the DEA attempts to reduce the supply of illicit drugs entering the United States from abroad, conducts investigations of major drug traffickers, exchanges intelligence information with foreign governments, stimulates international awareness of the illicit drug problem, and assists foreign nations with the development of institutional capabilities to suppress drug trafficking.

In addition to the DEA's domestic field officers, the agency has special agents, diversion investigators, intelligence analysts, and support personnel stationed in offices around the world. About half of the agency's 9,000 employees are special agents. Minimum qualifications for these positions are a combination of work experience and a four-year college degree.

Students of international affairs may be particularly interested in the Intelligence Division and the Operations Division. The Intelligence Division is responsible for constructing a complete picture of the international drug-trafficking situation and operations focusing on enforcing the drug laws; the Operations Division is responsible for conducting enforcement operations. Many of the employees in these offices have investigative, computer, financial, foreign affairs, and intelligence backgrounds.

> Drug Enforcement Administration
> Personnel Division
> 700 Army Navy Drive
> Arlington, VA 22202
> Tel.: 1-800-DEA-4288
> www.dea.gov

Education, U.S. Department of

The Department of Education's international activities are primarily the concern of two offices. The **Office of Postsecondary Education's Center for International Education** administers programs supported under the Fulbright-Hays and the Higher Education Acts. These programs serve to develop and maintain high levels of expertise in foreign languages and area studies and increase the general understanding of other languages and world areas. Less commonly taught languages and related cultural and area studies are emphasized. The **Office of Intergovernmental and Interagency Affairs** provides overall leadership in establishing and directing effective intergovernmental and interagency affairs for the department through communication with intergovernmental, interagency, and public advocacy groups and constituencies.

Department of Education
400 Maryland Avenue, SW
Washington, DC 20202
Tel.: (202) 205-3885 (Employment Information)
www.ed.gov

Energy, U.S. Department of

The Department of Energy (DOE) coordinates and develops national energy policy and administers the federal government's energy research and development functions. DOE also prepares long- and short-range national energy estimates and plans concerning supply and utilization of energy resources of all types.

International energy policy development and implementation are the principal responsibilities of the **Office of the Assistant Secretary for Policy and International Affairs.** Additionally, the office has responsibility for international energy activities, including international emergency management, national security, and international cooperation in science and technology.

Professionals assigned to the office generally are trained as economists, analysts, and engineers. Individual backgrounds range from international relations and international economics to foreign area studies and contingency planning and business administration. A significant number of the staff have earned master's and/or doctoral degrees.

Personnel Division
Department of Energy
Forrestal Building
1000 Independence Avenue, SW
Washington, DC 20585
Tel.: (202) 586-5000
www.energy.gov

Environmental Protection Agency

The Environmental Protection Agency (EPA) is responsible for executing federal laws for the protection of the environment. The EPA's mandate covers water quality, air quality, waste, pesticides, toxic substances, and radiation. Within these broad areas of responsibility, EPA program efforts include research and development and the development, implementation, and enforcement of regulations. The EPA is involved in many policy and technical aspects of transboundary, regional, and global environmental and health-related issues. These international activities also include information sharing within many international organizations and directly with other countries on common issues, problems, and solutions.

EPA involvement in international efforts is coordinated by the **Office of International Activities**. Qualifications for employment with the office preferably should include education and experience in one or a combination of the following areas: international affairs, environmental issues, or management with a demonstrated ability to work on policy and technical issues that are responsibilities of the EPA.

> Environmental Protection Agency
> Office of International Affairs (2610R)
> 1200 Pennsylvania Avenue, NW
> Washington, DC 20460
> Tel.: (202) 564-6613
> Fax: (202) 565-2411
> www.epa.gov

Export-Import Bank of the United States

The Export-Import Bank of the United States (Ex-Im Bank) is an independent agency of the U.S. government that facilitates the export financing of U.S. goods and services. It supplements and encourages, but does not compete with, commercial financing. By neutralizing the effect of export credit subsidies from other governments and by absorbing risks that the private sector will not accept, Ex-Im Bank enables U.S. exporters to compete effectively in overseas markets on the basis of price, performance, delivery, and service. Ex-Im Bank's programs include the Working Capital Guarantee Program, the Export Credit Insurance Program, and several finance and loan guarantee programs.

Ex-Im Bank is a small but dynamic agency with about 360 employees working in Washington, D.C. It offers many career opportunities in the fields of accounting, computer science, economics, financial analysis, law, marketing, and public affairs. Competition for jobs is keen. Staff vacancies generally are filled through individual vacancy announcements that outline specific job duties, salary, and qualification requirements. The announcements are widely distributed to colleges and universities, federal job information centers, professional organizations and newspapers. About twenty-five professional positions are filled annually. Most jobs at Ex-Im Bank require Office of Personnel Management competitive eligibility. They are filled from a federal listing of qualified candidates, which is open to those with undergraduate degrees or significant work experience. For interested applicants with graduate degrees or relevant experience, there are some trainee positions open to those with majors in finance, accounting, or economics. The bank also employs a small number of students during the year under various intern programs.

> Export-Import Bank of the United States
> Office of Human Resources
> 811 Vermont Avenue, NW
> Washington, DC 20571
> Tel.: (202) 565-3300
> www.exim.gov

Federal Bureau of Investigation

The responsibility for investigating violations of most federal laws and civil matters of interest to the U.S. government rests with the Federal Bureau of Investigation (FBI). In addition to these duties, the FBI provides the executive branch with information relating to national security and interacts with cooperating foreign police and security services.

The principal professional position within the FBI is that of special agent. Applicants for this position must be U.S. citizens who have reached their twenty-third but not their thirty-seventh birthday and qualify under one of four entrance programs: The Law Program, for those with a law degree; the Accounting Program, for those with an accounting degree; the Language Program, for those with at least a bachelor's degree and fluency in a foreign language for which the FBI has a current need; and the Diversified Program, which covers any academic program. Applicants must possess a four-year college degree and three years of full-time work experience. There are currently more than 10,000 special agents within the FBI. All special agent applicants must pass a battery of written tests (Phase 1) and a structured interview and written exercise (Phase II) of the special agent selection system. Applicants must also undergo a drug test, polygraph examination, and physical examination. Besides special agents, the FBI employs language specialists who possess the ability to translate foreign languages.

Those interested in a position with the FBI should contact the applicant coordinator at the nearest FBI field office, listed under U.S.

government in the telephone directory, or visit the FBI's website at www.fbi.gov.

Federal Communications Commission

The Federal Communications Commission (FCC) is responsible for U.S. telecommunications policy. The core functions of the FCC's **International Bureau** are to develop, recommend, and administer policies, standards, procedures, and programs for the regulation of international telecommunications facilities and services and the licensing of satellite facilities under its jurisdiction. The bureau also assumes the principal representational role for commission activities in international organizations.

The International Bureau currently consists of three divisions. The Policy Division has responsibility for the following key areas: (1) petitions for reconsideration addressed to the bureau; (2) international spectrum rulemakings; (3) international telecommunications policy development; and (4) service to the commission as experts on Section 310 foreign business and foreign government ownership issues in merger proceedings. The Satellite Division is responsible for (1) satellite policy development and rulemakings; (2) satellite licensing activities; and (3) service to the commission as consultants on satellite and satellite-related spectrum issues. The Strategic Analysis and Negotiations Division is charged with (1) economic and industry analysis of trends in international communications markets and services; (2) the bureau's consolidated intergovernmental and regional leadership, negotiation, and planning functions; and (3) research and studies concerning international regulatory trends, as well as their implications for U.S. policy.

> International Bureau
> Federal Communications Commission
> 445 12th Street, SW
> Washington, DC 20554
> Tel.: (202) 418-0500
> www.fcc.gov

Federal Maritime Commission

The Federal Maritime Commission regulates the ocean-borne foreign commerce of the United States, assures that U.S. international trade is open to all nations on a reciprocal basis, and protects against unauthorized activities in U.S. ocean-borne commerce. The commission's work includes accepting or rejecting tariff filings, attempting to eliminate the discriminatory practices of foreign governments against United States shipping, and trying to achieve comity between the United States and its trading partners.

The commission employs about 135 people in its headquarters and field offices. Most of the professionals have backgrounds in law, transportation, business administration, and economics.

> Federal Maritime Commission
> 800 North Capitol Street, NW
> Washington, DC 20573
> Tel.: (202) 523-5725 (Public Information)
> Tel.: (202) 523-5773 (Personnel)
> www.fmc.gov

Federal Reserve Bank of New York

The Federal Reserve Bank of New York (FRBNY) is one of twelve regional Federal Reserve banks that, along with the Federal Reserve Board in Washington, D.C., and the Federal Open Market Committee (FOMC), comprise the Federal Reserve System, the nation's central bank. The role of the FRBNY is unique within the system. At the direction of the FOMC, the top policymaking unit of the system, the FRBNY conducts open-market operations on behalf of the entire Federal Reserve system. Open-market operations—the purchase and sale of U.S. government securities—are the means through which the system conducts monetary policy, by influencing the cost and availability of credit. The FRBNY is responsible within the Federal Reserve System for relationships with foreign central banks as well as all intervention within the foreign exchange market that is conducted on behalf of the Federal Reserve and the U.S. Treasury. The presence in the New York region of many of the nation's largest banks as well as the majority of foreign banks that operate in the United States ensures the FRBNY an active and important role in bank supervision and regulation matters.

Many career opportunities exist at the FRBNY with a significant international component. Candidates for positions with the FRBNY should have a master's degree in business administration, economics, finance, or public policy and possess highly developed qualitative and quantitative skills. Strong financial analysis, writing, and research abilities, and a background in finance, accounting, and economics are desirable.

Federal Reserve Bank of New York
33 Liberty Street
New York, NY 10045
Tel.: (212) 720-6310
www.newyorkfed.org

Federal Reserve Board

The primary function of the Federal Reserve Board is the setting of monetary policy to foster stable economic conditions and long-term economic growth. International career opportunities exist with the **Division of International Finance.** The division analyzes the international policies and operations of the Federal Reserve System; major economic and financial developments abroad that affect the U.S. economy and U.S. international transactions; and a wide range of issues connected with the working of the international monetary system and the balance of payments adjustment process. The staff produces both analysis and interpretation of recent developments and research projects of a longer-run nature. Staff members regularly serve on U.S. delegations to international financial conferences and maintain liaison with central banks of foreign countries.

The division has a continuing need for economists who already have achieved or are working toward their doctorates and for exceptionally qualified economists holding a master's degree. In addition, many opportunities exist for applicants with a bachelor's degree in economics, strong quantitative skills, and knowledge of computer programming to work closely with the economists and assist in basic research projects.

Supervision and regulation of foreign banks operating in the United States and of foreign branches of state member banks are provided by the **Division of Banking Supervision and Regulation.** The division also analyzes specific issues of monetary and international financial policies that have a bearing on regulatory policy. Individuals interested in pursuing employment opportunities as a financial analyst in Banking Supervision and Regulation should possess an M.A. or M.B.A. in a related field or an undergraduate degree with one to three years of relevant work experience.

The Federal Reserve Board, located in Washington, D.C., has a staff of more than 1,500 employees. Most professional positions require formal education or specialized equivalent experience in such fields as economics, finance, law, and data processing.

Board of Governors of the Federal Reserve System
20th Street and Constitution Avenue, NW
Mail Stop 129 (Human Resources)
Washington, DC 20551
Tel.: (202) 452-3000 (Information)
Tel.: (202) 452-3880 (Personnel)
Fax: (202) 452-3863
www.federalreserve.gov

General Accounting Office

The General Accounting Office (GAO), an independent, nonpartisan agency in the legislative branch of the government, assists Congress in its legislative and oversight responsibilities. The GAO examines virtually every program or activity funded by the federal government and provides a variety of services, the most prominent of which are audits and evaluations of federal programs and activities. GAO's reports and recommendations frequently result in agency actions to improve their operations or legislation to improve program objectives and management. Its issue areas cover a wide range of topics, including international activities such as foreign aid, trade, energy, defense, environment, agriculture, transportation, and financial systems.

Of particular interest to those searching for an internationally oriented career is the GAO's **International Affairs and Trade** office, which analyzes the effectiveness of U.S. foreign aid programs and assesses how trade agreements further U.S. interests, among other issues. Its oversight responsibilities include the State Department, the U.S. Agency for International Development, the Office of the U.S. Trade Representative, the International Monetary Fund, the United Nations, the World Bank, and some Department of Defense functions. Work in other GAO divisions such as **Defense Capabilities and Management** or **Information Technology** frequently involves international issues. In addition, GAO's regional offices are increasingly involved in carrying out work in an international environment.

The GAO employs more than 3,200 people. GAO's professionals come from a variety of educational backgrounds, including public administration, computer science, business, political science, international affairs, and accounting. GAO also employs specialists in the social sciences, economics, computer science, mathematics, and other specialties. Approximately 200 new professionals are hired each year to work in the GAO Washington headquarters or in regional offices. GAO maintains a personnel system separate from the executive branch.

Employment at GAO requires a bachelor's degree or equivalent work experience. Increasingly, candidates for positions with GAO who have master's degrees and doctorates are preferred.

Office of Recruitment
General Accounting Office
441 G Street, NW
Washington, DC 20548
Tel.: (202) 512-3000
Tel.: (202) 512-4500 (Personnel)
www.gao.gov

General Services Administration

The General Services Administration (GSA) manages the federal government's real and personal property. Its responsibilities include construction and management of federal buildings, procurement and management of supplies and services for the government (including automated data processing and telecommunications services), and promulgation of federal policy concerning acquisition and management of property and services. It employs about 14,000 people nationwide. Most of GSA's international work involves the administration of a small amount of U.S. property located overseas and some overseas engineering projects.

The majority of the professionals with GSA have academic backgrounds in business, finance, economics, engineering, and computer sciences.

General Services Administration
1800 F Street, NW
Washington, DC 20405
Tel.: (202) 501-0370 (Personnel)
Fax: (202) 219-0149
www.gsa.gov

Health and Human Services, U.S. Department of

The Department of Health and Human Services (HHS) is the U.S. government's principal agency for protecting the health of all Americans and providing essential human services, especially for those who are least able to help themselves.

With more than 65,000 employees and a budget of $460 billion in fiscal year 2002, HHS administers more grant dollars than all other federal agencies combined. The department administers more than 300 programs, which are managed by eleven operating divisions, including eight agencies of the U.S. Public Health Service and three human service agencies. The eleven operating divisions are the **National Institutes of Health** (NIH), the **Food and Drug Administration**, the **Centers for Disease Control and Prevention**, the **Agency for Toxic Substances and Disease Registry**, the **Indian Health Service**, the **Health Resources and Services Administration**, the **Substance Abuse and Mental Health Services Administration**, the **Agency for Healthcare Research and Quality**, the **Centers for Medicare and Medicaid Services**, the **Administration for Children and Families**, and the **Administration on Aging**.

Within HHS, the **Office of Global Health Affairs** (OGHA) is responsible for:

- Representing the department to other governments, other federal departments, and agencies, international organizations, and the private sector on international and refugee health issues.
- Developing U.S. policy and strategy positions related to health issues and facilitating involvement of the Public Health Service in support of these positions and in collaboration with other agencies and organizations.
- Providing leadership and coordination for bilateral programs with selected countries, such as the U.S.-Russian and U.S.-South Africa Health Committee, in support of presidential and vice presidential initiatives.
- Facilitating cooperation by Public Health Service Operating Divisions with the Agency for International Development.
- Providing policy guidance and coordination on refugee health policy issues, in collaboration with Public Health Service Operating Divisions, the Office of Refugee Resettlement, the Department of State, and others.

Additionally, the mission of NIH's **Fogarty International Center** is to promote and support scientific research and training internationally to reduce disparities in global health.

U.S. Department of Health and Human Services
200 Independence Avenue, SW
Washington, DC 20201
Tel.: (202) 619-0257
www.hhs.gov

Office of Global Health Affairs
Office of the Director
5600 Fishers Lane
Room 18-105
Rockville, MD 20957
Tel.: (301) 443-1774
Fax: (301) 443-6288

Housing and Urban Development, U.S. Department of

The U.S. Department of Housing and Urban Development (HUD) has a small international staff in the **Office of Policy Development and Research** responsible for coordinating HUD's participation in international activities. Its major aims are to facilitate exchanges between senior officials responsible for large-scale housing and urban development programs by maintaining regular channels of communication with foreign governments and to share American research and experience in housing and urban development with other countries. Employment opportunities are limited.

U.S. Department of Housing and Urban Development
451 Seventh Street, SW
Washington, DC 20410
Tel.: (202) 708-1112
www.hud.gov

Immigration and Naturalization Service

The Immigration and Naturalization Service (INS), a component of the U.S. Department of Justice, administers federal laws covering the admission, exclusion, deportation, and naturalization of aliens in the United States. Working with the Department of State, the INS adjudicates refugee applicants referred to the United States from the United Nations High Commissioner for Refugees for entry into the United States. Additionally, the service investigates aliens to ascertain their admissibility into the country; adjudicates aliens' requests for benefits under the law; guards against illegal entry into the United States; investigates, arrests, and removes aliens residing in the nation illegally; and examines aliens wishing to become citizens. The service maintains liaison with federal, state, local, and foreign offices (in consulates and embassies at forty locations around the world).

More than 90 percent of the service's employees are located outside the Washington, D.C., metropolitan area. The service primarily employs officers in the following key categories: border patrol, investigations, detention and deportation, adjudications, asylum, inspections, and intelligence. Officers are trained at the Federal Law Enforcement Training Center at Glynco, Georgia. Because of the complexity of U.S. immigration law, former officers hold most management positions. Administrative positions generally are filled from open recruitment sources for the headquarters and the three regional offices at Burlington, Vermont; Dallas, Texas; and Laguna Nigel, California.

> Immigration and Naturalization Service
> Office of International Affairs
> 425 I Street, NW
> Washington, DC 20536
> Tel.: (202) 514-2530 (Headquarters Personnel)
> Tel.: (612) 725-3496 (National Hiring Center)
> www.ins.gov

Inter-American Foundation

The Inter-American Foundation was established to promote social change and development in Latin America and the Caribbean. It provides support through grants and the financing of projects for private, community-level, self-help efforts in solving basic social and economic problems. This approach springs from the belief that only the recipients themselves can define their communities' problems and needs. The wide variety of projects funded by the foundation has included workers' self-managed enterprises, peasant associations, informal education, credit and production cooperatives, cultural awareness programs, self-help housing, legal aid clinics, and worker-run bank and agricultural extension services.

The foundation has an average turnover of one or two positions per year. There is a tendency to hire generalists rather than people with specific, technically oriented backgrounds. The skills needed by the foundation are defined by its wide array of activities. Employees have backgrounds in such diverse fields as economics, rural and urban development, finance, agriculture, housing, banking, law, labor relations, nutrition, education, statistics, and industrial management. Although not a prerequisite for employment, virtually all professionals on the staff have at least a master's degree.

> Inter-American Foundation
> 901 N. Stuart Street, 10th Floor
> Arlington, VA 22203
> Tel.: (703) 306-4301 Fax: (703) 306-4365
> www.iaf.gov

Interior, U.S. Department of the

As the nation's principal conservation agency, the U.S. Department of the Interior (DOI) has responsibility for most of our nationally owned public lands and natural resources. From its establishment in 1849, the department has managed many varied programs including Indian Affairs, administering land grants, improving historic Western emigrant routes, marking boundaries, and conducting research on geological resources. DOI's bureaus include the National Park Service, the U.S. Fish and Wildlife Service, the U.S. Geological Survey, the Bureau of Land Management, the Bureau of Reclamation, the Bureau of Indian Affairs, the Minerals Management Service, and the Office of Surface Mining Reclamation and Enforcement.

The department's mission is (1) to encourage and provide for the appropriate management, preservation, and operation of the nation's public lands and natural resources for use and enjoyment both now and in the future; (2) to carry out related scientific research and investigations in support of these objectives; (3) to develop and use resources in an environmentally sound manner and provide an equitable return on these resources to the American taxpayer; and (4) to carry out trust responsibilities of the U.S. government with respect to American Indians and Alaska natives.

The department's International Affairs staff, located in the Office of Policy Analysis, provides oversight and coordination of bureau international activities. For nearly 100 years, the DOI has conducted international activities that (1) facilitate DOI's domestic responsibilities, including managing protected areas adjacent to international borders; sharing scientific findings, technology, and other information beneficial to domestic programs; protecting migratory wildlife; and fighting cross border fires; (2) meet DOI's congressionally mandated international activities such as elephant, rhino, and tiger protection and migratory bird preservation; (3) support U.S. foreign policy objectives at the request of the White House or State Department, such as providing technical and scientific advice on wildlife, water and other natural resources (e.g., water issues in the Middle East peace talks), and park management, and addressing environmental hazards (e.g., monitoring volcanoes and earthquakes); and (4) meet U.S. Treaty obligations such as the Convention on International Trade in Endangered Species (CITES), the Convention to Combat Desertification, Convention on Nature Protection and Wildlife Preservation in the Western Hemisphere, Convention Concerning Protection of the World Cultural and Natural Heritage (World Heritage

Convention), the 1909 U.S.-Canada Boundary Waters Treaty, the 1944 U.S.-Mexico Water Treaty, Convention on Wetlands of International Importance (Ramsar), 1996 U.S.-Canada Migratory Bird Convention, Migratory Bird and Game Mammal Treaty with Mexico, and the Convention on the Prevention of Marine Pollution by Dumping of Wastes and Other Matter (London Convention 1972).

Of DOI's 65,740 employees, only 125, or 0.2 percent, work almost exclusively on international programs. Almost all of these employees are located within the DOI technical Bureaus. (The U.S. Fish and Wildlife Service and the U.S. Geological Survey have the largest staff.) Despite the many offices within the department with some form of international responsibility, employment opportunities for graduates in international affairs are extremely limited. Perhaps no more than four or five of these positions were vacant last year. In most cases, the professionals are trained in the particular discipline of the office involved rather than in international studies. For more information on the Bureaus' international programs, please see the following websites:

- Bureau of Land Management, Office of Fire and Aviation, International Program, www.fire.blm.gov/WhatWeDo/intntl.htm
- Bureau of Reclamation: International Affairs, www.usbr.gov/international/
- Minerals Management Service, International Activities, and Marine Minerals Division, www.mms.gov/intermar/intover.htm
- U.S. Fish and Wildlife Service, International Affairs, http://international.fws.gov/
- U.S. Geological Survey: Middle East Regional Water Data Banks Plan, http://water.usgs.gov/international/Hague/wwf.pdf
- U.S. Geological Survey, National Mapping Program, http://mapping.usgs.gov
- U.S. Geological Survey, Biological Resources, International, http://biology.usgs.gov/
- International Technical Assistance Program, www.doi.gov/intl/itap/index.html

Information on general employment opportunities with the department can be found online at www.doi.gov/hrm/doijobs.html.

U.S. Department of the Interior
1849 C Street, NW
Washington, DC 20240
Tel.: (202) 208-3100
www.doi.gov

International Trade Commission

The U.S. International Trade Commission (ITC) studies and makes recommendations on international trade and tariffs to the president, Congress, and government agencies. The major thrust of the commission's work is the analysis of all possible effects of imported products on U.S. industries. Special emphasis is placed on the effects of imports from countries with nonmarket economic systems. The commission also conducts studies on a broad range of topics relating to international trade and publishes summaries of trade and tariff information. In order to carry out its responsibilities, the commission must engage in extensive research and maintain a high degree of expertise in all matters relating to the commercial and international trade policies of the United States.

The staff of the ITC, which numbers about 240 professionals, provides six commissioners with the expertise required to carry out the responsibilities of the organization. International economists form one of the primary groups of employees on the staff. They must have a minimum of twenty-one credit hours in economics and three credit hours in statistics earned at the bachelor's and/or master's level. Of particular importance are courses in microeconomics, industrial and labor economics, and international economics and trade. Other prevalent staff positions include international trade analysts, investigatory economists (both frequently require course work in accounting and international economics), and attorneys (especially patent, antitrust, and customs-related). Additional academic specializations of special interest to the commission are marketing, international law, international trade, business administration, and regional studies.

> U.S. International Trade Commission
> 500 E Street, SW
> Washington, DC 20436
> Tel.: (202) 205-2000
> Tel.: (202) 205-2651 (Personnel)
> www.usitc.gov

Justice, U.S. Department of

Within the Department of Justice, most international issues are handled by four of the six department divisions: Antitrust, Civil, Criminal, and Environment and Natural Resources. The **Antitrust Division** is responsible for the enforcement of federal antitrust laws. The **Foreign Commerce Section** of the division is responsible for the implementation of division policy on issues of trade and international antitrust enforcement. The section is active in the interagency process of administering trade laws and assessing the competitive aspects of U.S. trade policy. The Foreign Commerce Section is the division's liaison with international organizations, including antitrust enforcement agencies of the European communities, Canada, and other countries. In conjunction with the State Department, the section exchanges information with foreign governments concerning investigations and cases that the division initiates involving foreign corporations and nationals.

The **Civil Division** represents the United States in virtually all types of civil proceedings. Litigation based on international maritime agreements is handled by the division's **Torts Branch. Commercial Litigation Branch** attorneys within the Civil Division represent the United States in virtually all cases initiated in the Court of International Trade. These cases include challenges brought by domestic and foreign producers contesting antidumping and countervailing duty investigations, as well as actions commenced by the government to enforce civil penalties for customs fraud. Attorneys in the Civil Division's **Office of Foreign Litigation** pursue claims on behalf of the United States and defend the government's interests in foreign courts. Foreign litigation attorneys frequently become involved in "white-collar" crime cases and recovery of offshore assets. Decisions in this area often have significant foreign policy implications. The Civil Division's **Federal Programs Branch** handles the defense of challenged government activity ranging from domestic welfare programs to international agreements. The Federal Programs Branch's responsibilities include matters as diverse as litigation involving federal banking statutes and regulations to suits raising national security and foreign policy issues.

In enforcing most of the nation's criminal laws, the **Criminal Division** participates in criminal justice activities involving foreign parties where a centralized national approach is desired. The **Internal Security Section** supervises the investigation and prosecution of cases affecting national security, foreign relations, and the export of military and strategic commodities and technology. The Criminal Division's **Office of International Affairs** supports the department's legal divisions, the U.S. attorneys, and state and local prosecutors regarding questions of foreign and international law, including issues related to extradition and mutual legal assistance treaties. The office also coordinates all international evidence gathering. In concert with the State Department, the office engages in the negotiation of new extradition and mutual legal assistance treaties and executive agreements throughout the world. Office attorneys also participate on a number of committees established under the auspices of the United Nations and other international organizations that are directed at resolving a variety of international law enforcement problems such as narcotics trafficking and money laundering.

The **Environment and Natural Resources Division** is the nation's environmental lawyer. The **Policy, Legislation and Special Litigation Section** of the division coordinates and directs the division's legislative program, including representing the department on interagency groups that develop the administration's position on legislation and at meetings with congressional staff. The section's attorneys coordinate both the division's international environmental activities and environmental justice activities.

The **Foreign Claims Settlement Commission** is an independent, quasi-judicial agency within the department, responsible for adjudicating claims of United States nationals against foreign governments that have nationalized, expropriated, or otherwise taken property of those nationals without paying compensation as required under international law.

The bulk of the professionals employed by these offices and divisions are attorneys assisted by paralegals and other support staff. Attorneys and law students interested in employment with any department organization may contact the Office of Attorney Personnel Management at the address and telephone number indicated below. The current Legal Activities Book (LAB) is also available on the Internet at the addresses noted above. The LAB describes the department's legal employment programs and the legal responsibilities of each organization in the department.

U.S. Department of Justice
Office of Attorney Recruitment and Management
Room 7254, Main Building
950 Pennsylvania Avenue, NW
Washington, DC 20530-0001
Tel.: (202) 514-3396

General Employment:
Justice Management Division
Personnel Staff
Suite 1175
1331 Pennsylvania Avenue NW
Washington, DC 20530
Tel.: (202) 514-6818
www.usdoj.gov

Labor, U.S. Department of

The Department of Labor's international activities are concentrated in the **Bureau of International Labor Affairs**. The bureau's major duties include helping formulate international economic and trade policies; carrying out overseas technical assistance projects; administration of the North American Agreement on Labor Cooperation (NAALC), the labor supplemental agreement to NAFTA; preparation of reports on international child labor issues and management of international programs to eliminate child labor exploitation; arranging trade union exchanges and other programs for foreign visitors to the United States; furnishing directions to U.S. labor attachés at embassies abroad; assisting with the representation of the United States in bilateral and multilateral trade negotiations and in various international organizations; evaluating U.S. immigration policy; representing the United States in the International Labor Organization and in the Manpower Committee of the Organization for Economic Cooperation and Development; and reporting on and analyzing the activities of foreign trade unions. To handle these responsibilities, the bureau is divided into three offices: foreign relations, international economic affairs, and international organizations.

The majority of professional positions with the bureau require a strong economics background (especially microeconomics) combined with some knowledge of statistics, international trade, and/or labor relations. In addition, some hiring may be done of those with backgrounds in area studies, international organizations, and comparative politics. Employment opportunities are limited.

The only other office dealing with international issues is the **Bureau of Labor Statistics**. The bureau's small Division of Foreign Labor Statistics and Trends collects data and conducts research on topics such as foreign employment and wage levels, labor forces, costs, benefits, and productivity.

Department of Labor
200 Constitution Avenue, NW
Washington, DC 20210
Tel.: (202) 523-7316
www.dol.gov

Bureau of International Labor Affairs
Office of Operating Personnel Services
Room C-5512
U.S. Department of Labor

Washington, DC 20210
Tel.: (202) 523-6717
www.dol.gov/ilab

Management and Budget, U.S. Office of

The Office of Management and Budget (OMB) performs a wide variety of functions. The OMB prepares and administers the federal budget; analyzes proposed legislation and executive orders; reviews all major administration testimony and all legislation enacted by Congress; assesses federal program objectives, performance and efficiency; and tracks the progress of government agencies with respect to work proposed, work actually initiated, and work completed.

The Associate Director for National Security Programs holds paramount responsibility for OMB's review of international programs. The director's staff is partitioned into two divisions: international affairs and national security.

The **International Affairs Division** is concerned with trade, monetary, and investment policy and deals with such specific issues as international energy policy and commodity agreements. The division reviews all foreign aid, trade financing, grant military assistance, and foreign military credit and cash sales programs as well as the budgets of the agencies primarily responsible for international economic activities and the conduct of foreign affairs. Reviewing and advising on the Defense Department budget and national security policy is the task of the **National Security Division**.

The OMB employs approximately 400 professionals. Candidates for entry-level positions are expected to have graduate training in economics, business administration, public policy, law, or (to a lesser extent) science and mathematics. Previous experience in budget analysis or management is considered helpful but not essential. Applicants should possess an ability to analyze problems and communicate effectively both orally and in writing. All potential recruits must meet Office of Personnel Management eligibility requirements. Paid summer internships are available for graduate students with the same qualifications.

Office of Management and Budget
Executive Office Building
Room 9026
Washington, DC 20503
Tel.: (202) 395-7250 Fax: (202) 395-3504
www.whitehouse.gov/omb

National Aeronautics and Space Administration

The National Aeronautics and Space Administration (NASA) ensures that activities in space are devoted to peaceful purposes for the benefit of all humankind. In addition, the act that created NASA in 1958 charged the agency to conduct its activities "so as to contribute materially to . . . cooperation by the United States with other nations and groups of nations." In fulfillment of this mandate, NASA has entered into more than 3,000 agreements with more than 150 countries and international organizations. These relationships have covered a broad spectrum of collaborative endeavors, ranging from the development of major space hardware to the sharing of space data among scientists around the globe.

The External Relations Office (OER) is responsible for all international activities of the agency. This includes liaison with foreign entities, international agreements, export control, and foreign visitor and foreign travel policies. The staff consists of about thirty-five professionals with backgrounds in international relations, political science, science, engineering, or related fields. A graduate degree is preferred and communications skills are emphasized. The ability to speak a foreign language is helpful in many of the positions. The staff assignments include responsibility for relations with particular countries and/or space projects or functional areas, such as export control.

> National Aeronautics and Space Administration
> 300 E Street, SW
> Washington, DC 20546
> Tel.: (202) 358-0000 (Public Information)
> Tel.: (202) 358-0450 (Office of External Relations)
> www.nasa.gov

National Science Foundation

The National Science Foundation (NSF) was established in 1950 to promote and advance scientific progress in the United States. The foundation does this primarily by sponsoring scientific and engineering research and by supporting selected activities in science and engineering education. The NSF does not itself conduct research.

The NSF Office of International Science and Engineering complements other foundation activities in support of scientific research. The programs are designed to support the work of U.S. scientists cooperating with scientists in other countries in research and related activities. Four types of activities may receive support:

cooperative research projects designed and conducted jointly by principal investigators from the United States and the foreign country; international research fellowships; research-oriented joint seminars or workshops; and scientific visits for planning cooperative activities or for research.

The office has a staff of about twenty-five professionals and fills approximately two vacancies a year. Scientists with Ph.D.-level training and with six to eight years of postdoctoral research experience, as well as an international background, are sought by the division to fill these senior-level positions. Whenever vacancies at the entry or middle level do occur, they are normally handled through the Office of Human Resources Management. The booklet *NSF Guide to Programs* contains helpful information on the division's operations.

National Science Foundation
4201 Wilson Boulevard
Arlington, VA 22230
Tel.: (703) 292-8070 (Public Affairs)
Tel.: (703) 292-8180 (Human Resources Management)
Tel.: (703) 292-8710 (International Programs)
www.nsf.gov

Nuclear Regulatory Commission
International activities at the U.S. Nuclear Regulatory Commission (NRC) are directed at contributing to the safe operation of licensed reactors and fuel cycle facilities and the safe use of nuclear materials; improving worldwide cooperation in nuclear safety and radiation protection; assisting U.S. efforts to restrict U.S. nuclear exports to peaceful use only; and supporting U.S. foreign policy and national security objectives.

The **Office of International Programs** is the commission's primary organization for coordinating international activities and policies, as well as licensing U.S. exports and imports of nuclear materials and equipment. The U.S. NRC's international bilateral cooperation efforts traditionally have focused on power reactor safety, but increased attention is also being given to broader radiation protection matters, waste management activities, and other areas of materials safety. International Programs also works with the **International Atomic Energy Agency** (IAEA) in Vienna, Austria, in promoting effective international safeguards and cooperation on nuclear safety.

The Office of International programs helps recruit qualified Americans for IAEA positions by listing the positions in the NRC's weekly vacancy announcements.

The Office of International Programs mostly is staffed by twenty-two professionals, most of whom have backgrounds in public administration or international relations. A technical background combined with international relations is highly desirable. A language ability in French, Spanish, Russian, German, or in the languages of the Pacific rim is useful. Very few openings are expected in the future.

U.S. Nuclear Regulatory Commission
Office of Personnel
Washington, DC 20555
Tel.: (301) 415-1534
www.nrc.gov

Overseas Private Investment Corporation

The Overseas Private Investment Corporation (OPIC) provides political risk insurance, financing, and a variety of investor services to encourage U.S. private investment in more than 140 developing nations and emerging markets around the world. Although wholly owned by the U.S. government, OPIC is organized along the lines of a private corporation.

OPIC's mission is "to mobilize and facilitate the participation of United States private capital and skills in the economic and social development of less developed countries and areas, and countries in transition from nonmarket to market economies, thereby complementing the development assistance objectives of the United States."

To achieve this mission, OPIC focuses on four principle activities:
• Insuring overseas investments against political risks.
• Financing businesses overseas through loans and loan guarantees.
• Financing private investment funds to provide equity to businesses.
• Advocating for the interests of U.S. businesses abroad.

OPIC employs approximately 200 employees, of whom about 60 percent are professionals. OPIC's requirements for professional personnel generally include training in law, finance, business, economics, or international affairs. Based on the job requirements, foreign language skills may be required. Computer skills are often important. OPIC has only occasional vacancies, but welcomes applications for employment from qualified U.S. citizens.

Office of Human Resources Management
Overseas Private Investment Corporation
1100 New York Avenue, NW
Washington, DC 20527
Tel.: (202) 336-8799
www.opic.gov

Peace Corps

The Peace Corps seeks to promote world peace and friendship, to help the peoples of other countries meet their needs for trained manpower, and to promote mutual understanding and cooperation between Americans and other peoples. To meet these goals, the Peace Corps trains volunteers in the appropriate local languages, the technical skills necessary for the particular task they will be performing, and cross-cultural skills needed to work with peoples of a different culture. Following successful completion of the two- to three-month training, volunteers are sent to various sites within a country where they spend a period of two years aiding in the country's economic and social development.

There are more than 7,000 Peace Corps volunteers in seventy developing countries. Assignments vary according to volunteers' qualifications and host-country needs. Volunteers work primarily in the fields of agriculture, forestry, fisheries, education, health, engineering, business, the skilled trades, and community development-related activities. In greatest demand are those with degrees and/or backgrounds in forestry, fisheries, mathematics, science, and agriculture. It is important to remember that education is not the only avenue to acquiring the background necessary for these positions; such backgrounds can be obtained through a variety of experiences.

Although host countries have asked for volunteers with practical training, the Peace Corps still recruits volunteers with no specific skilled experience. Many of these volunteers work on forestry and fisheries projects, teach handicrafts, establish cooperatives, or teach community nutrition and maternal child care. Foreign language proficiency, especially in Spanish or French, past experience living or working abroad, or extensive volunteer or community service work would greatly increase a generalist's chances of acceptance.

Applicants to the Peace Corps must be U.S. citizens, have no dependents under the age of eighteen, and be at least eighteen years of age. In view of specific requests, however, it is extremely rare that anyone under twenty has the skills or experience to qualify.

Although specific skills or work experience and foreign language proficiency are highly desired in potential volunteers, the Peace Corps also looks highly upon those who demonstrate a desire to serve others, a sense of dedication, emotional maturity, and a great deal of flexibility and adaptability. The Peace Corps covers round-trip transportation from the United States to the country of assignment and provides medical care. It also provides each volunteer with a living allowance to cover basic necessities such as housing and food, including a modest amount of spending money. Upon completion of service, each volunteer receives a $225 readjustment allowance for every month he or she has served. The Peace Corps recruits approximately 3,000 volunteers per year.

Additionally, the Peace Corps has employees stationed in Washington, D.C., in eleven regional recruiting offices around the United States, and in Peace Corps offices abroad. These employees are involved in such fields as volunteer recruitment, program development, support, and personnel. The Peace Corps has exhibited a tendency to hire former volunteers for many of these positions. The Peace Corps prefers delivery of applications through e-mail or fax.

Peace Corps
The Paul D. Coverdell Peace Corps Headquarters
1111 20th Street, NW
Washington, DC 20526
Tel.: 1-800-424-8580

Peace Corps
Office of Human Resource Management (HRM)
1111 20th Street, NW, Room 2300
Washington, DC 20526
Tel.: (202) 692-1200
Fax: (202) 692-1201
www.peacecorps.gov

Postal Service, United States
The United States Postal Service (USPS) furnishes mail processing and delivery services to U.S. and foreign individual and business mailers. The USPS operates an **International Postal Affairs** (IPA) function that is responsible for coordinating relations and activities with foreign postal administrations, international postal organizations (such as the Universal Postal Union) and with U.S. government agencies concerning international postal issues. IPA supervises the

exchange of mail with other countries based on multilateral and bilateral treaties.

IPA has fifteen professional positions for the following functions: developing overall USPS international mail policies, conducting bilateral and multilateral postal business negotiations, representing the USPS at international postal organization meetings, and coordinating technical cooperation and postal development activities with other postal administrations and international development institutions such as the UN Development Program and the World Bank.

Graduate degrees in international relations constitute the most relevant background for a career in IPA. Fluency in foreign languages, particularly French and Spanish, is extremely useful.

> International Postal Affairs
> Room 4400-E
> 475 L'Enfant Plaza
> Washington, DC 20260-6500
> Tel.: (202) 268-2444
> Fax: (202) 268-4871
> www.usps.gov

Science and Technology Policy, U.S. Office of

The office of Science and Technology Policy (OSTP) serves as a source of input for the president on issues of science and technology policy. The office advises the president of scientific and technological considerations involved in areas of national concern, including the economy, national security, and foreign policy. In executing its mandate, OSTP frequently deals with such issues as export controls, arms control, information technology, technology transfer, foreign aid, energy, space cooperations, transborder data flows, and ocean policies.

From a total staff of about forty, about one-quarter deal directly with international affairs. Candidates must have strong technical backgrounds combined with relevant experience. Employment opportunities are limited.

> Office of Science and Technology Policy
> Room 360, Old Executive Office Building
> Washington, DC 20506
> Tel.: (202) 456-7116
> www.ostp.gov

Securities and Exchange Commission

The Security and Exchange Commission's (SEC) Office of International Affairs has primary responsibility for the SEC's international initiatives. These include international enforcement cooperation and the negotiation of memoranda of understanding with the SEC's foreign counterparts, international regulatory initiatives, and the promotion of high regulatory standards worldwide, and technical assistance and international training.

> Securities and Exchange Commission
> 450 Fifth Street
> Washington, DC 20549
> Tel.: (202) 942-0020 (Public Information)
> Tel.: (202) 942-4140 (Personnel)
> www.sec.gov/asec/secjobs.htm

Smithsonian Institution

The Smithsonian Institution is the world's largest museum and research complex, a trust instrumentality of the federal government and repository of the U.S. national collections. It was established in 1845 with funds left to the people of the United States by English natural scientist James Smithson. Today the Smithsonian consists of sixteen museums and galleries, the National Zoo and various program divisions, research institutes, and support offices in the United States and abroad. Smithsonian researchers have ranged the globe, assembling unique collections, forming a worldwide network of "friends and correspondents" and organizing research or participating in cooperative museum projects in almost every country of the world.

Given the nature of the Smithsonian's activities, there are a number of its divisions that are significantly international in scope. Research, exhibition, and program staff conduct their work in many countries, and foreign colleagues regularly come to Smithsonian facilities to work with its staff and members. The **Office of International Relations (OIR)** serves as the point of contact for the Smithsonian with foreign institutions or individuals, with international organizations and with government agencies. The OIR has a staff of fewer than a dozen people, with infrequent turnover, though other parts of the Smithsonian do appoint support, research, and program staff involved with international operations. Required training or experience varies: the majority of curatorial, research, and exhibitions positions require specialized training or experience, whereas candidates for liaison officer positions generally have practical experience in international exchanges and advanced training in a relevant academic discipline. About 70 percent of staff positions are federal civil service, and hiring for them involves adherence to U.S. Office of Personnel Management guidelines.

Smithsonian Institution
Main Office of Human Resources
750 Ninth Street, NW, Suite 6100
Washington, DC 20560-0912
Tel.: (202) 275-1102
www.si.edu

Trade and Development Agency, U.S.

The Trade and Development Agency (TDA), an independent U.S. government agency, has two objectives: to assist in the economic development of friendly developing and middle-income countries and to promote the export of U.S. goods and services to those countries.

The TDA accomplishes these objectives by providing grants for feasibility studies, training programs, and other project planning services for public-sector development projects. The TDA assists U.S. firms by identifying major development projects that offer large export potential and by funding U.S. private sector involvement in project planning. TDA activities serve as a catalyst to encourage U.S. private sector involvement in fewer infrastructure projects. This approach helps position U.S. firms for follow-on contracts when these projects are implemented. TDA grants are not tied to follow-on procurement, yet TDA-funded feasibility studies have led to more than $6.5 billion in direct exports for the United States.

TDA activities cover a wide range of sectors of high priority to host governments and international development efforts. U.S. technological expertise can help accelerate the development process in all these sectors.

A small staff runs the program. Virtually all entry-level positions are at the higher grade levels and are usually filled by candidates with an advanced degree and previous experience.

U.S. Trade and Development Agency
1621 N. Kent Street, Suite 200
Arlington, VA 22209-2131
Tel.: (703) 875-4357
Fax: (703) 875-4009
www.tda.gov

Trade Representative, Office of the U.S.
Working out of offices in Washington, D.C., and Geneva, Switzerland, the employees of the United States Trade Representative (USTR) are responsible for setting and administering overall U.S. trade policy. This objective includes multilateral trade negotiations implementation, import remedies, East-West trade, international investment, energy trade, international commodity, and export expansion policies. Furthermore, USTR plays the lead American role in bilateral and multilateral trade, commodity, and direct investment negotiations involving the World Trade Organization (WTO), the Organization for Economic Cooperation and Development (OECD) and the U.N. Conference on Trade and Development (UNCTAD).

Employment opportunities are limited and highly competitive. Notable skill in economics with expertise in negotiations and trade is required of all applicants. A doctorate in economics or trade is preferred. A nonremunerated, yearlong University Intern Program exists for graduates and undergraduates with concentrations in economics, international relations, law, political science, business, and finance. Typically, 40 to 50 students are selected from a pool of 275–325 applicants.

Director, Office of Management
Office of the U.S. Trade Representative
600 17th Street, NW
Washington, DC 20506
Tel.: (202) 395-7360, (202) 395-3350
www.ustr.gov

Transportation, U.S. Department of
The Department of Transportation (DOT) is responsible for planning and administering the nation's overall transportation policy. The **Office of Policy and International Affairs** provides departmental leadership for international transportation policy issues and assesses economic, financial, technological, and institutional implications. The office coordinates international transportation cooperative research; organizes technical assistance programs for developing nations; formulates and presents the U.S. position on transportation matters before international conferences; develops, coordinates, and evaluates international air and marine transportation policy in concert with various elements from government, industry, and labor; and negotiates and implements multilateral and bilateral aviation agreements.

The educational experiences of the staff professionals vary widely. Most common backgrounds are law, international relations, and public administration. Many of the professionals have joined the staff with previous work experience in areas such as bilateral negotiations, aviation and maritime policy, cooperative technical exchange programs, and technical assistance programs.

The **Federal Aviation Administration** (FAA) has an **Office of International Aviation** that promotes aviation safety and civil aviation abroad by managing the FAA's foreign technical assistance programs, providing training for foreign nationals in areas of the agency's expertise, developing and coordinating the FAA's international policies, and exchanging information with foreign governments. In addition, the office provides technical representation to international organizations and conferences and participates in cooperative efforts with other U.S. government agencies and the U.S. aviation industry in order to promote aviation safety abroad. The office's professionals stationed in the United States fall into two broad categories: international specialists and those with technical backgrounds. The international specialists have degrees or backgrounds in economics, international relations, or international marketing. For the people with technical aviation backgrounds, the emphasis is on experience. The majority are former pilots, air traffic controllers, flight safety inspectors, and so on. Some have engineering degrees, but many others have nontechnical degrees in areas such as the liberal arts.

There are three other major offices within the department involved in international issues. The **Federal Highway Administration** (FHWA) employs highway design, construction, maintenance, and bridge engineers and specialists to provide assistance and advice to foreign governments in various phases of highway engineering and administration. It also is active in a number of international organizations interested in road-related affairs. FHWA's **National Highway Institute** trains foreign highway officials interested in American highway practices. The **Saint Lawrence Seaway Development Corporation** operates that portion of the seaway within the territorial limits of the United States and coordinates its activities with those of its Canadian counterpart. International maritime and related U.N. matters are dealt with by the **U.S. Coast Guard**, which falls under DOT's jurisdiction during peacetime. The Coast Guard maintains an Office of Public and International Affairs. Additional Coast Guard offices are concerned with the enforcement of international laws and treaties, the international impact of environmental questions, and the operation of deep-water ports.

U.S. Department of Transportation
Departmental Office of Human Resource Management
400 Seventh Street, SW, Room 7411
Washington, DC 20590
Tel.: (202) 366-4088
Fax: (202) 366-6806
www.dot.gov

Federal Aviation Administration
Human Resource Management Division
Attn: AHR-19
800 Independence Avenue, SW
Washington, DC 20590
Tel.: (202) 267-8007
www.faa.gov

Treasury, U.S. Department of the

The Department of the Treasury develops and recommends economic, financial, tax, and fiscal policies; serves as the federal government's financial agent; performs many law enforcement activities; and manufactures coins and currency.

The **Office of the Assistant Secretary for International Affairs** (OASIA) offers the most attractive international career opportunities. OASIA is concerned with the development and implementation of international monetary, financial, and economic policy and programs. The functions of OASIA include conducting financial diplomacy, attempting to improve the structure and operations of the international monetary system, monitoring international gold and foreign exchange markets, coordinating U.S. participation in bilateral and multilateral development lending programs and institutions, monitoring and formulating policy concerning international indebtedness, formulating policy concerning financing of trade, coordinating policies toward foreign investments in the United States and U.S. investments abroad, analyzing balance of payments information, and monitoring energy developments.

OASIA has about 140 professionals on its staff, including those stationed overseas. The vast majority of these employees have advanced degrees. A strong background in economics, finance, statistics, or trade is the single most important requirement for any position with OASIA. Although these are the predominant academic specializations, M.B.A.s and foreign affairs specialists are represented on the staff.

The Department of the Treasury serves as the focal point for international tax policy questions. Under the Assistant Secretary for Tax Policy is the small **Office of International Tax Affairs,** composed of economists and lawyers who study and formulate international tax legislation and regulation, negotiate tax treaties, and perform economic analyses of international tax matters.

The **Office of the Comptroller of the Currency** (OCC) has two offices with responsibilities in the international area. The **Office of the Deputy Comptroller for Multinational Banking** is responsible for the direct supervision of the nation's largest national banks, foreign banks and federal licenses, and international examination activities. The other office, headed by the **Deputy Comptroller for International Relations and Financial Evaluations,** focuses on the assessment of the international financial situations to determine the impact of global economic problems on OCC's regulatory functions in international banking institutions. There are more than 2,000 professional positions within the OCC; about 100 positions are filled annually. Candidates must have either three years of experience in positions requiring a thorough knowledge and application of commercial accounting or auditing principles and practices or a college or university degree with a minimum of twenty-four semester hours in accounting, banking, business administration, commercial or business law, economics, finance, or in a directly related field.

U.S. Department of the Treasury
15th Street & Pennsylvania Avenue, NW
Washington, DC 20220
Tel.: (202) 622-1260 (Switchboard)
www.ustreas.gov

Office of the Assistant Secretary for International Affairs
U.S. Department of the Treasury
Room 3430, Main Treasury
Washington, DC 20220
www.treas.gov/offices/international-affairs/index.html

Office of the Comptroller of the Currency
490 L'Enfant Plaza, SW
Washington, DC 20219
Tel.: (202) 874-4700 (General Information)
www.occ.treas.gov/index.htm

United States Agency for International Development
The United States Agency for International Development (USAID) was created by Congress in 1961 to administer the foreign economic and humanitarian assistance programs of the U.S. government. It operates from headquarters in Washington, D.C., through field missions and representatives in developing countries in Africa, Asia, the Near East, Europe and Eurasia, Latin America, and the Caribbean.

USAID's purpose is to help people in the developing world acquire the knowledge and resources to build the economic, political, and social institutions needed to promote and maintain national development. USAID works in concert with the Department of State, Peace Corps, and other federal and private voluntary organizations.

The assistance covers many diverse sectors, including but not limited to, environment, agriculture, economic growth, strengthening democracy, health and family planning, education, disaster preparedness, and humanitarian assistance.

The new entry professional (NEP) program is the agency's program for bringing well-qualified applicants into the agency's Foreign Service. USAID's Foreign Service provides successful applicants with a career-long system of rotational assignments overseas. Like the U.S. Department of State and other agencies employing Foreign Service personnel, successful applicants are offered a clear path for planning their career from the intake level through the most senior executive positions.

Candidates for employment with USAID should have background in one or more of the following areas: political science, economics, government, public administration, international development, business administration, law, banking, international transportation, procurement, contracting, finance, agriculture, anthropology, biology, fisheries, food science, forestry, geography, natural resource management, resource economics, rural sociology, agricultural economics, administration of justice, international affairs, comparative government, public policy, agribusiness, public health/nutrition, trade, management, environmental engineering, urban planning, public health, medicine, nursing, midwifery, demography, social/behavioral science, material management, or marketing.

The Office of Human Resources advertises approximately 100 international job openings per year.

USAID
320 21st Street, NW
Washington, DC 20523-0056
Tel.: (202) 647-1850
www.usaid.gov

It should be noted that as this chapter goes to press, the Bush administration has delivered a proposal to Congress to establish a new cabinet department, the Department of Homeland Security. The primary missions of the new department are to prevent terrorist attacks in the United States, reduce U.S. vulnerability, minimize damage, and assist in the recovery from such attacks. The new department will perform several major functions, including information analysis and infrastructure protection; countermeasures against chemical, biological, or nuclear attacks; border and transportation security; and emergency preparedness and response. Several existing functions and organizations will be transferred, either in whole or in part, to the new department, including the Coast Guard, the Immigration and Naturalization Service, the Transportation Security Administration, and the Federal Emergency Management Agency.

Careers in the Foreign Service

Ambassador Ruth A. Davis

Not long ago, someone asked me this question: "If you could live your life all over again, would you have joined the Foreign Service?" It was a serious and perceptive question, and I'm glad that I didn't have to pause for deep soul-searching in order to come up with an answer. It's an answer that I want to share with you as well. Because if I could do it all over again—if I could shed a few years, a few wrinkles, and maybe even a few pounds—I'd still join the Foreign Service of the United States. In a heartbeat. No further questions asked.

I was excited when I first joined as a junior officer in 1969, and I'm still excited today. I therefore don't just want to tell you about the Foreign Service; I want you to get a feel for why I feel this was a good choice, a fulfilling choice, and, for me, the right choice.

First and foremost, the Foreign Service gives you a unique opportunity to represent this great country and its people overseas. That means advancing U.S. security, promoting America's economic well-being, defending democracy and human rights, serving the needs of American citizens overseas, and contributing to the eradication of terrorism, drug trafficking, and environmental damage.

Let me give you a few examples. As a junior consular officer I helped American citizens who had lost passports overseas or who were adopting a child or who had run afoul of the local authorities. I visited jails, hospitals, ships, and more airports than I would care to count. Not only was there variety in the work, there was plenty of

Ambassador Ruth A. Davis is the director general of the Foreign Service and director of human resources at the U.S. Department of State. Ambassador Davis holds the rank of career minister in the Senior Foreign Service. She joined the Foreign Service in 1969 and has held jobs of increasing responsibility in Zaire, Kenya, Japan, Italy, Spain, and Benin, where she served as ambassador. Her most recent domestic assignment was as director of the Foreign Service Institute. Among her career highlights are that she is credited with playing a significant role in Atlanta's successful bid for the 1996 Olympics and was the driving force for the establishment of the School of Leadership and Management at the Foreign Service Institute. Ambassador Davis is the recipient of a Presidential Distinguished Service Award and the Department's Arnold L. Raphel Memorial Award for mentoring and developing people around her. She is also the recipient of several honorary degrees, including an Honorary Doctor of Laws Degree awarded in 1998 by her alma mater, Spelman College.

variety of scenery as well—from a safari park in Kenya to the Imperial Gardens in Tokyo. And if that wasn't enough, there were plenty of different languages to struggle with.

As a senior officer, I have helped develop a foreign-aid program that expanded educational opportunities for young girls in Benin, supervised our worldwide consular operations, and helped train scores of new ambassadors at the Foreign Service Institute. I also am very proud of the work I did to establish the School of Leadership and Management at our Foreign Service Institute.

From all this, I hope you can see that the Foreign Service isn't just any old job. It is a profession. It can take you all over the world. And it means doing the nation's business as part of "America's first line of defense" at some 240 embassies, consulates, and other diplomatic missions all over the world. It is truly the opportunity of a lifetime.

The challenges in today's Foreign Service are even more varied than when I joined. Here are just a few examples of new challenges that face U.S. diplomacy (and hence U.S. diplomats): international terrorism; democratization and human rights; the proliferation of weapons of mass destruction; international peacekeeping; environmental degradation; population, refugee, and migration issues; and ethnic and religious affairs. Members of the Foreign Service are making major contributions on all these issues. They are doing so with perceptiveness, dedication, and creativity.

Now let me take some time to talk about some nuts and bolts issues. And at the end, I'm going to attach a few briefing papers that I hope you will find useful.

The Foreign Service is set up along five career tracks (or "cones"): administrative affairs, consular affairs, economic affairs, political affairs, and public diplomacy. All five areas are vital to the success of a U.S. embassy. An officer chooses a particular career track early in his or her career, but the department expects that officers specializing in one area will also gain substantial experience in at least one other area, making true "generalists" of all officers.

There is no one Foreign Service career. No two officers are likely to follow the same career path or have the same experiences. Most new Foreign Service officers are assigned a first tour of duty overseas in a consular section. From there on, work assignments depend on area of specialization, interests of the officer, and needs of the service.

The State Department also employs hundreds of Foreign Service specialists (FS specialists). The opportunities that exist for FS specialists are as diverse as the countries in which they serve. FS specialists provide important technical, support, or administrative services in Washington, D.C., or at one of our missions worldwide. Their backgrounds can range from information technology professionals to security officers to office management specialists. Foreign Service specialist jobs are broken down into seven major categories: administration, construction engineering, information technology, international information and English language programs, medical and health, office management, and security. FS specialists typically serve only in their area of specialty.

Foreign Service officers and specialists are expected to be "worldwide available." This is often a real test of commitment to public service and many times requires personal sacrifice from both the officer and family members. Many overseas posts are in small or remote countries where harsh climates, health hazards, and other discomforts exist, and where American-style amenities frequently are unavailable. Therefore, success in the Foreign Service requires motivation and an ardent dedication to public service. A sense of humor often comes in handy as well.

> Many overseas posts are in small or remote countries where harsh climates, health hazards, and other discomforts exist, and where American-style amenities frequently are unavailable. Therefore, success in the Foreign Service requires motivation and an ardent dedication to public service. A sense of humor often comes in handy as well.

The selection process is rigorous. It takes time, energy, and strong skills to make it through. For Foreign Service officers, the process starts with a written exam, which is open to all U.S. citizens between the ages of twenty and fifty-nine. The passing grade for the exam is keyed to hiring requirements, and the percentage of people who pass has varied between 20 percent and 30 percent. Candidates who pass the written exam are invited to participate in a daylong oral assessment that tests a variety of skills essential to a career in the Foreign Service. Successful oral examination candidates, currently about 30 percent to 40 percent of those who take the orals, may then be invited to complete the selection process by undergoing security and medical clearances and a final review.

Candidates who have cleared all these hurdles will have their names entered on a ranked register. Your position on the register is a composite of your oral assessment score, plus a language bonus and veterans' bonus, if applicable. From this register, individuals are offered appointments as new "classes" of Foreign Service officers are formed. The entire process takes approximately ten months. Although FS specialists do not take the written exam, they do follow the other steps toward hiring.

I'm often asked, "What should I study?" My answer is, "Study what you're really interested in, and what you're good at." There is no set way to prepare yourself for a career as a Foreign Service officer (FSO), and no specific educational background is required. That said, most successful candidates have a broad knowledge of U.S. domestic and international affairs, U.S. and world history and government, as well as foreign policy and culture. But they have majored in subjects as diverse as management, history, government, international relations, geography, literature, economics, business, public administration, U.S. politics, political science, language, social sciences, and international trade.

Most FSO candidates have at least a bachelor's degree. In recent years, many candidates have also entered with advanced degrees in international relations, economics, business administration, law, journalism, or other areas. Many also had work experience in various fields before their appointment and have worked, attended school, or traveled overseas.

FS specialists generally have experience related to their specific areas. This includes subjects such as accounting; civil, electrical, or mechanical engineering; computer science; industrial arts; medicine, medical technology, or nursing; physics; science; and systems management.

If you are wondering whether this is a good time to join, the answer is an emphatic "yes." A substantial buildup of the Department of State is expected over the next three fiscal years. Between October 1, 2001, and September 30, 2004, the department plans to recruit and hire personnel for more than 1,000 new career positions, distributed fairly evenly among the categories of Foreign Service officer, Foreign Service specialist, and Civil Service employees. This includes an intense effort to attract and hire minority candidates. Because the Foreign Service represents the incredible, wonderful diversity of the United States and all of its people, we are doing everything we can to ensure that the Foreign Service looks like America as it goes about representing America.

Looking back over my career and trying to imagine what yours might look like, I am truly amazed at how much change I have experienced. When I joined, we were in the middle of the Cold War.

U. S. Department of State
Recruitment, Examination, and Employment
2401 E Street, NW
Room H518
Washington, DC 20522
Tel.: (202) 261-8888 (9 A.M. to 5 P.M. Eastern
Standard Time)
Fax: (202) 261-8841
www.careers.state.gov

Foreign Service Specialists

The Department of State offers career opportunities to professionals in specialized functions needed to meet Foreign Service responsibilities around the world. Foreign Service specialists provide important technical, support, or administrative services in Washington, D.C., or at one of more than 240 posts worldwide. Specialists are an integral part of a team of working professionals who are dedicated to representing America's interests in other countries.

The opportunities that exist for Foreign Service specialists are as diverse as the countries in which they serve.

Administration

- *Facilities Maintenance Specialists (FMSs)* are among highly skilled and trained facilities managers accountable for daily administration of maintenance and repair operations at overseas embassies and consulates. FMSs administer large holdings of U.S. government-owned and long-term leased properties and maintain them within accepted U.S. standards in a safe and operable condition.
- *Financial Management Officers (FMOs)* are responsible for the management of the financial activities of diplomatic and consular posts, including financial services to other U.S. government agencies.
- *General Services Officers (GSOs)* are responsible for a broad range of functions including the management of physical resources and logistical functions at diplomatic and consular posts.
- *Human Resources Officers (HROs)* are responsible for recruitment, employee training and development, performance management, employee relations, salary and benefits administration, employee policies and procedures, and position classification.

Construction Engineering

- *Construction engineers* monitor and report on contract work overseas to ensure that the construction of new properties and renovation of existing properties are completed properly, on time, and within budget.

Information Technology

- *Information Management Specialists* manage and operate worldwide information technology infrastructure, including PC local and wide-area networks, telecommunications systems, telephone and wireless programs, and diplomatic pouch and mail services.
- *Information Management Technical Specialists* survey, install, and maintain associated hardware and software of PC local and wide-area networks, of UHF/VHF land mobile wireless programs, and of office telephone PBX systems. Three separate technical divisions are PC LAN/WAN, wireless, and telephone.

International Information and English Language Programs

- *English Language Officers (ELOs)* are responsible for all Department of State-sponsored English teaching activities overseas. When assigned to Washington, D.C., ELOs provide general administrative support to overseas programs, work on research and development materials, and provide consultative services.
- *Information Resource Officers (IROs)* provide professional guidance and direction to 170 Information Resource Centers (IRCs) located at U.S. embassies abroad. Through extensive travel within an assigned region, IROs counsel Mission officials on effective information program resources and services, assess staff development needs and carry out regional training programs, demonstrate and promote U.S. electronic information resources, and establish contacts with host country information and library institutions.
- *Printing Specialists* are responsible for coordinating worldwide publishing, printing management programs, printing information technology, and related systems. The work is diverse and challenging. Printing specialists employ printing production technology ranging from state-of-the-art systems to older legacy systems. They manage production operations at overseas facilities and perform other duties such as consulting and researching new developments in printing information technology.

Medical and Health

- *Health Practitioners* are assigned to selected posts overseas and in the United States. Many of these posts have significant health risks, and local medical facilities are often inadequate to cope with them. Health practitioners assume the role of primary-care provider and are responsible for administering a full range of community health-care services.
- *Regional Medical Technologists (RMTs)* perform routine visitations to regional area health units to evaluate and monitor performance of local laboratory technologists and maintain laboratories and X-ray equipment at posts.

• *Regional Medical Officers (RMOs)* may work independently or in conjunction with other Foreign Service medical personnel. The RMO's duties include providing primary medical care and appropriate health information and disease-prevention programs.
• *Regional Medical Officer/Psychiatrists (RMO/Ps)* may work independently or in conjunction with other Foreign Service medical personnel. The RMO/P's duties include providing primary psychiatric care for each post in the supported geographical region as well as a host of other psychiatric and mental health-related responsibilities.

Office Management
• *Office Management Specialists (OMSs)* are called upon to perform a variety of duties at diplomatic and consular posts, including general office management, conference and visitor support, and administrative and secretarial support.

Security
• *Diplomatic Couriers* are entrusted with ensuring the inviolability of diplomatic pouches and their secure delivery throughout the world.
• *Security Engineering Officers* provide technical security support and engineering expertise to protect U.S. Foreign Service posts.
• *Security Technical Specialists* provide support and assist in worldwide technical security programs. These specialists give overall program management, maintenance, and support for programs that provide protection for Department of State facilities and personnel from technical espionage, acts of terrorism, and crime.
• *Special Agents* are specially trained Foreign Service security professionals; they are also sworn federal law enforcement officers. Overseas, Regional Security Officers (RSOs) advise ambassadors on all security matters and manage a complex range of security programs designed to protect personnel, facilities, and information. In the United States, special agents protect the secretary of state and visiting foreign dignitaries, investigate passport and visa fraud, and conduct personnel security investigations.

For more information on Foreign Service specialist career opportunities, please visit www.careers.state.gov or contact:

U. S. Department of State
Recruitment, Examination, and Employment
2401 E Street, NW
Room H518
Washington, DC 20522

Tel.: (202) 261-8888 (9 A.M. to 5 P.M. Eastern
Standard Time)
Fax: (202) 261-8841

Civil Service Personnel

The Civil Service "arm" of the State Department is not unlike the civilian component of the military services. While soldiers and sailors march off or sail away to foreign shores waging war or preserving peace, the civilian employees back home provide support and stability and offer many different services. And since they stay put while the military are constantly on the move, they sustain the corporate memory.

A similar situation exists in the Department of State. While Foreign Service officers travel far and frequently, advancing the nation's diplomatic interests, civilians at home provide a pool of stability in Washington and in a small number of field offices and passport agencies throughout the country. The department also provides career development opportunities that allow Civil Service employees to serve overseas. Like their military counterparts, Civil Service employees are cast in a variety of supporting roles—attorneys, information technology specialists, telecommunications specialists, office assistants, passport examiners, foreign affairs advisors, accountants, budget and intelligence experts, human resources specialists, and procurement and contract specialists. With nearly 7,000 permanent employees in the Civil Service workforce, the list of occupations could go on and on. The following is a list of typical job opportunities at the Department of State:

- *Accountant or Auditor* (GS-510/511).* Employees determine the accounting and financial requirements that must be met in the design, development, operation, analysis, or inspection of accounting systems, in order to meet the financial management needs of the worldwide operations of the bureaus, offices, and posts of the Department of State.
- *Architect/Engineer* (GS-800 Series).* This is an outstanding opportunity to apply practical skills and creative problem-solving skills worldwide. These employees help program, design, build, acquire, and maintain embassies, consulates, residences, office buildings, and compounds around the world.
- *Attorney* (GS-905).* Attorneys get involved in critical negotiations and legal issues. Attorneys provide advice on international and domestic legal questions; negotiate treaties, agreements, and contracts; draft and interpret legislation; and handle other matters in support of the department's work.

- *Budget Analyst (GS-560)*. Employees perform or supervise work related to the systems of budget administration currently in use by the Department of State. Such work requires knowledge and skill in the application of related laws, regulations, policies, and techniques of budgeting.
- *Contract Specialist* (GS-1102)*. Employees are involved in the procurement of a wide variety of supplies, services, and construction and in the negotiation of contract price proposals to establish agreements that are in the best interest of the government.
- *Criminal Investigator (GS-1811)*. Criminal investigators are armed and have arrest authority. They perform a variety of security functions, including background investigations on personnel, passport, and visa fraud investigations, counterintelligence, and other criminal investigations. They investigate alleged espionage incidents and conduct damage assessment of confirmed acts of espionage.
- *Economist* (GS-110)*. From the North American Free Trade Agreement (NAFTA) to the General Agreement on Tariffs and Trade (GATT) negotiations to environmental policy and its effect on worldwide economy, few positions offer such an array of challenging assignments. These assignments at the State Department keep economists on the leading edge of their career discipline.
- *Financial Management Specialist (GS-501)*. Employees perform financial management functions, including identifying and resolving financial and operational irregularities and problems, providing financial advice and analyses, and completing a variety of financial management improvement projects.
- *Foreign Affairs Officer* (GS-130)*. Foreign Affairs Officers research, analyze, and evaluate information on issues affecting U.S. policy. These employees also develop and manage programs and provide advice and policy analysis for specific geographic or functional areas.
- *Human Resources Specialist (GS-201)*. Employees perform work in various human resources areas, including recruitment, selection and placement, employee development, training, classification, employee/management relations, and performance evaluation. They ensure the right people with the right skills are in the right place at the right time.
- *Information Technology Specialist (GS-2210)*. As the world continues to move toward client/server technology and a global information highway, these employees are responsible for helping to keep the State Department a step ahead in information technology. More specifically, they design and implement systems and operating procedures to meet the department's daily goals for the rapid sharing and storing of information worldwide.

- *Intelligence Analyst (GS-130/132).* Intelligence analysts provide all-source intelligence analysis on specific functional areas or geographic regions. The analysts advise on and perform research and other professional work in support of the formulation and direction of U.S. foreign policy and bearing on U.S. relations with foreign governments and international organizations. Other analysts gather information on terrorist incidents and other criminal activities and analyze data to determine potential threats to department employees and facilities.
- *Passport Specialist (GS-967).* Passport specialists serve American citizens by processing applications for U.S. passports and providing related privileges and services. They determine applicants' claims to U.S. citizenship, issue passports, and correspond with applicants regarding their applications.
- *Public Affairs and Public Information Specialist (GS-1035).* These specialists perform work involved in disseminating information about government programs to the general public. Public information specialists work through newspapers, radio, and television stations, and general circulation magazines. Public affairs specialists coordinate speeches and briefings for a variety of audiences in Washington and around the world.
- *Security Specialists (GS-080).* Security specialists develop and implement comprehensive security programs and procedures designed to protect U.S. and overseas personnel, property, buildings, and information against terrorists, foreign intelligence agents, and criminals. They educate employees on counterintelligence and vulnerabilities that might be exploited by foreign intelligence.
- *Visa Specialist (GS-967).* Visa specialists adjudicate cases concerning foreign citizens who have applied at U.S. embassies and consulates for visas. These cases involve determination of the application's suitability for admission to the United States under the provisions of the Immigration and Nationality Act.

* Education Requirement

For general inquiries, www.careers.state.gov, or contact:

Office of Civil Service Personnel Management
Tel.: (202) 663-2176 (8:30 A.M. to 4:30 P.M. Eastern Standard Time)

International Organization Affairs, U.S. Department of State Bureau of

The Department of State's U.N. Employment Information and Assistance Unit in the Bureau of International Organization Affairs (IO/S/EA) and other federal agencies assist U.S. citizens interested in considering employment opportunities with international organizations. While pursuing a rewarding work experience, such international civil servants also impart to their chosen organizations their standards of integrity, competence, and dedication to the needs of the world community.

In addition to positions with the U.N. Secretariat in New York, IO/S/EA compiles and publishes vacancy information for the agricultural agencies in Rome (the Food and Agriculture Organization, International Fund for Agricultural Development, and World Population Fund); the agencies in Vienna (International Atomic Energy Agency and U.N. Drug Control Program); the health, labor, refugee, telecommunications, and other agencies in Geneva (International Labor Organization, International Telecommunications Union, U.N. High Commissioner on Refugees, World Intellectual Property Organization, and the World Health Organization); and the economics-oriented commissioxns throughout Europe and elsewhere (European Court of Auditors, Economic Commission for Latin America and the Caribbean, Economic and Social Commission for West Africa, the World Trade Organization, and the Organization for Economic Cooperation and Development). This vacancy list (published biweekly), along with relevant fact sheets and points of contact, is available on the State Department website at www.state.gov/p/io/empl/. Instructions are included on how to access specific announcements.

U.N. and other international organization positions range from entry to senior levels. At a minimum, candidates for entry-level positions must have advanced degrees, at least one foreign language (preferably Spanish, French, Chinese, Russian, or Arabic) and three years of relevant work/field experience. For other junior positions, as much as five years of experience is required. Senior positions require at least sixteen years of experience, including some international work. In most U.N. agencies there is a mandatory retirement age of sixty-two for most professional positions, and most agencies will not appoint persons who have reached or nearly reached that age.

Individuals who believe they meet the stated requirements for specific positions and are interested in competing for these positions should send a detailed resumé (or U.N. personal history form) directly to the organization, stating the specific vacancy for which they are applying. If a resumé is used, it should be detailed and include the applicant's date of birth and citizenship. The final selection of the candidate, of course, is always the prerogative of the international organization and often is based on a desire to maintain a geographical balance among member countries. As most agencies receive a very large number of applications from all over the world, competition is always keen. It should be understood that selection does not depend on U.S. government support, and sponsorship from the U.S. government is rarely required.

The respective U.S. government agencies responsible for liaison with international organizations constitute an important source of information and serve as contact points for interested candidates. A list of some of these organizations is included in some of the Fact Sheets noted earlier.

Reflections on Joining the Foreign Service
RICK WATERS

Four months after arriving at the U.S. Embassy in Beijing, I traveled twenty-four hours to Earth Mountain Village in central He-nan province to look into reports of a peasant demonstration. Soon surrounded by a ring of peasants, we learned that they had chased out a corrupt party secretary ten years before and recently elected a head and deputy of their local village council. When the Party-controlled county government imposed bizarre and illegal fees, their elected leaders led villagers to the county seat to protest. Authorities there allowed the villagers to leave, but the leaders were imprisoned. "They are our elected leaders! They have no right to do this!" one peasant insisted indignantly.

The path to this ringside seat at China's local democratic experiment began three years earlier, when I read a Foreign Service Exam application touting "the most interesting job in the world." The written exam marked the beginning of a nineteen-month application process (now shortened to a year). Nearly 12,000 applicants signed up for the standardized exam, administered once a year in several hundred locations in the United States and overseas. Approximately one-quarter passed, of whom almost 300 joined the Foreign Service. (The Department projects hiring 466 new officers in each of the next three years.)

The next step was a daylong oral assessment, starting with a group negotiating exercise. Watched by several examiners, my group of five assumed the role of embassy officials with projects (mine was a $60,000 environmental protection grant) in a fictitious country. Each of us was instructed to advocate for funding from a small embassy discretionary account. At the end of an hour, the group agreed to fully fund one project and partially fund another—my environmental grant was shelved.

In the individual exercise, each of us met with two examiners pretending to be foreign officials. This was followed by a series of hypothetical scenarios. "The local police call you, a duty officer at an overseas embassy, to say an American citizen was arrested for swimming naked in a fountain. What do you do?" Each answer produced complications: the swimmer's father is a well-connected politician; the theocratic host-country government pursues strict punishment, and so on. I came away with no idea how I had performed.

Today, the hypothetical questions are still used, but the meeting with foreign officials has been replaced by interviews—a change likely to benefit those with international experience and language ability. Successful candidates must then complete background investigations and medical clearances, time-consuming steps that delay employment by as much as twelve months.

Almost two years later, I arrived for orientation with sixty others—the eighty-seventh class of new Foreign Service Officers—at the Department of State's training center in the Washington, D.C., suburbs. The seven-week initiation featured visits to other agencies, training on procedures, simulation exercises, and a team-building retreat. Early on, we received "bid lists"—sixty open assignments—from which each of us could choose twenty where we were willing to serve. Cities such as Nouakchott and Abuja took on new meaning as we researched potential destinations. Most two-year posts were in consular sections, but some included one-year rotations to other Embassy sections.

On "Flag Day," the personnel director presented each of us with a small flag and announced our assignments—including mine to Beijing. Soon afterward, the class disbanded, and we started training in consular affairs, political or economic tradecraft, or languages.

The first year in Beijing, I worked in the Embassy's Economic Section covering rural stability. A typical day involved meetings in the morning and drafting reports in the afternoon. Trips to the countryside and support work for official visitors were a large part of my assignment. In my second year, I served in the consular section interviewing nonimmigrant visa applicants for several weeks before joining the front office as a staff assistant. The experience of junior officers in Beijing and at other posts varied greatly. Most worked in a consular section for two years. Some spent their entire tours interviewing visa applicants, or assisting American citizens. Facilities varied greatly—a 51 percent decline in the foreign affairs budget since the mid-1980s meant some worked in hastily erected facilities or even in a converted stable. At my embassy, Microsoft Windows-compatible computers arrived in the late 1990s; the main chancery lacked reliable Internet connections until 2001.

The Foreign Service is not for everyone. Spouses sacrifice careers because of multiple moves; not all families adapt well to frequent uprooting; not all officers have an impact on policy, especially during the early part of their careers. But overall, junior officers with reasonable expectations came away largely satisfied with the Foreign Service. Today, the future looks bright. Rising budgets mean increased recruitment and hiring, improved facilities, and better information technology. While fewer officers see it as a career, the Foreign Service is an attractive job.

But by any objective measure, it remains one of the most interesting and rewarding professions around.

Rick Waters graduated from the joint Bachelor of Science in Foreign Service/Master of Science in Foreign Service program at Georgetown in 1997. He has served in Beijing, China, and Quito, Ecuador. Prior to joining the Foreign Service, he served as a presidential management intern in the Bureau of Political-Military Affairs at the Department of State and as a program assistant at the Georgetown University Institute for the Study of Diplomacy. The views expressed in this article do not reflect the official position of the Department of State.

Capitol Hill Careers

Denis McDonough

The Constitution ensures that Capitol Hill can offer challenging career opportunities to those with expertise and background in foreign affairs and an interest in public service. Although the Constitution names the president as the Commander-in-Chief, it also ensures that Congress retains both the purse strings on the nation's treasury and an aggressive role on oversight of the president's conduct of all policy, including foreign and defense policy. From the League of Nations to Vietnam to Central America, history has demonstrated that a successful U.S. foreign policy demands an informed, involved, and expert Congress.

To fulfill this important constitutional duty, every House member and senator has at least one staff person who spends his or her time on foreign policy issues, including defense, homeland security, intelligence, and trade. Committees such as the Senate Foreign Relations Committee, the House International Relations Committee, the Senate and House Select Committees on Intelligence, the House and Senate Armed Services Committees, the House and Senate Government Affairs Committees, and Appropriations Committees have entire professional staffs devoted to foreign policy and defense issues. Other committees in both houses—Agriculture, Finance, and Budget, among others—also have staff who devote a bulk of their time to international issues.

Since September 11, 2001, the demand for qualified people to handle these issues and advise members of Congress on international affairs has drastically increased, making this a remarkably interesting and challenging time to work on Capitol Hill.

The pace is frenetic, the hours unpredictable, job security nonexistent, and issues change from day to day, even hour to hour.

Denis McDonough, a 1996 graduate of Georgetown University's Master of Science in Foreign Service program, is a legislative assistant in the office of Senator Tom Daschle, where he is responsible for U.S. foreign policy. Prior to joining the Daschle's staff in 2000, he worked as a Democratic professional staff member on the House International Relations Committee. He is a 1992 graduate of St. John's University in Collegeville, Minnesota.

However Hill staffers are compensated for these uncertainties: They draft legislation, have access to top policymakers both foreign and domestic, have opportunities for foreign travel, and influence the national agenda—often unencumbered by the layers of bureaucracy found in the executive branch. Staffers enter an arena with the potential to influence national policy while opening up an array of further career-development opportunities.

Hill Job-Seeking Strategies

Hiring practices vary from office to office, and there is no magic formula for landing a Capitol Hill job. Some staff—those still in or recent graduates from college or graduate school—start off as unpaid interns or as paid support staff or legislative correspondents and work their way up through the ranks.

All around the Hill and in both parties one will find examples of interns becoming top policy advisers. One key Senate staffer started years ago as a driver for a senator from New York. Another key Senate floor staffer worked in the Capitol parking lot as he earned his master's degree in Russian studies. In 1995, two members of my Georgetown class used unpaid internships to get to know the Hill and thus position themselves for permanent jobs—one in a committee and one as foreign policy staffer for a senior Republican senator from the Midwest—upon graduation a year later. Another graduate student, using her home state connection and foreign policy background, landed an entry-level job as a legislative correspondent with a committee after two years at the State Department. After several months, due to staff turnover, she was given increased responsibilities and, within a couple of years, also became a professional staff member.

Others at more mid or senior levels with no previous Hill experience may make a lateral move by bringing to their new job a great deal of substantive experience in a particular field such as arms control, trade policy, or foreign aid. Still others manage to land professional Hill jobs as a result of their campaign or political work for state or national parties or for individual campaigns. As with any job search, finding a job on the Hill often boils down to talking to the right person or being in the right place at the right time. But to suggest it is merely luck misses a key point—those who succeed in landing jobs, be they starting positions or mid-career assignments, know the substance of foreign policy and the workings of the House and Senate. Since there are a plethora of talented international policy experts in Washington, the successful job seeker may distinguish herself from other candidates by knowing parliamentary procedure, including, for example, how to file an amendment or draft a bill.

Equally important—as much for job satisfaction as for success in finding a job—is the politics of the Congress. Those seeking a job on Capitol Hill should have some sense of their own ideological persuasion—and on what core principles they will not compromise— before approaching members' offices. Several times individuals interested in jobs on the Hill have told me that they do not care if they work for a Democrat or a Republican. This is a mistake. If you do not share the bulk of your boss's convictions, your job will be very uncomfortable and unsatisfying. That may even be the case when you and a particular member are of the same party. There is such a diversity of views on foreign policy (e.g., multilateralists vs. unilateralists) and defense policy (e.g., hawks vs. doves) within parties that you may find yourself at odds with your boss about issues on which you have to spend many hours.

Identifying a potential boss's views is easy enough. Every vote cast and statement made on the floor of Congress is recorded in the *Congressional Record.* It is published daily and available online through any number of websites. Before applying for a job in a particular office, job seekers should spend some time reviewing the *Record* for insider information.

Everyone Need—or Should—Apply

Although individual senators and representatives do their own hiring, both houses of Congress operate placement offices to which individual offices may turn for resumés. More often than not, the placement office helps fill offices for support staff, but anyone interested in a Hill job should invest the few minutes it takes to drop off a resumé and take a typing test at the placement offices. When job hunting, leave no stone unturned.

The offices of the home state delegation should be one of the first stops of any job seeker, as many members prefer to hire natives of their home state. Even if members don't have an opening, they do want to be responsive to their constituents, so job seekers should take advantage of this resource, even if it is just for job tips. Constituents have an automatic "foot in the door" that is unavailable to others and should arrange a meeting with the administrative assistant, chief of staff, or legislative director as a first resort.

After approaching one's own senator and representative, job seekers should identify members serving on committees that have jurisdiction over foreign policy, defense, and intelligence or those who, although they might not serve on one of those committees, have a high profile on or particular interest in certain foreign policy issues. These committees receive hundreds of resumés a month, so before mailing resumés and knocking on doors, it is wise to learn something about the chairman or ranking member of the committee and even the individual professional staff members working for the committee.

Committee professional staffs are divided into majority and minority staffs, with the majority staff significantly larger than the minority. Some are further divided into full committee and subcommittee staffs, whereas others limit their staff to full committee. When targeting committees or members who serve on committees of jurisdiction, it is best to know their staffing policies. Although staff on some committees may serve all the members on the committee, staff on other committees may serve only the chairman or the ranking minority member. In the latter case, members who serve on the committee may hire staff to do committee work directly out of their personal offices.

> Several times individuals interested in jobs on the Hill have told me that they do not care if they work for a Democrat or a Republican. This is a mistake. If you do not share the bulk of your boss's convictions, your job will be very uncomfortable and unsatisfying.

Job seekers should talk to as many current and former staffers as possible for tips on job strategies and openings—find out which of your university's alumni are on the Hill and look them up. Vacancies are often not advertised, and offices that do advertise are usually flooded with resumés. Most candidates are recruited by word of mouth, so personal contacts are critical. Although job seekers may wish to drop off resumés by hand, making an appointment will guarantee being taken seriously. Congressional recess periods or days when there are no votes (often Monday mornings and Friday afternoons) are the most convenient times to talk to congressional staff about job opportunities.

Job Descriptions

The following are job descriptions for professional positions. They do not include administrative or support positions. Someone right out of school or with limited work experience seeking a non-administrative position may wish to focus on getting a job in one of the following categories:

- *Legislative Correspondent (LC).* Staff member who drafts responses to member's mail and deals with constituent requests. LC positions are not just limited to personal offices; some committees hire LCs to answer the chairman or ranking member's mail.
- *Legislative Aide/Research Assistant.* Staff person hired to do research for and provide support to legislative assistants. These slots are available in only a handful of Hill offices and fall somewhere between legislative assistant and legislative correspondent.
- *Press Assistant.* Staff person who provides backup and assistance to the press secretary. This position is more common in the Senate than in the House.

Someone seeking a more mid-level position might also wish to look for jobs in the following categories:

- *Legislative Assistant (LA).* Staff person who advises a member on various substantive issues. In the House, where staffs are generally smaller than in the Senate, an LA may juggle five or six separate substantive areas. In the Senate or in leadership offices, an LA is more apt to focus on one specific area, such as foreign policy.
- *Professional Staff Member.* Committee staff members who work for and are paid by the committee are referred to as professional staff. Their areas of responsibility are generally defined regionally (e.g., Asia, the Middle East) or topically (e.g., terrorism, arms control, budget). Until the early 1970s, professional staffs were nonpartisan and worked for all the Committee members, be they Republican or Democrat. Since then, staffs have become partisan, with the chairman hiring the majority staff and the ranking member hiring the minority staff.
- *Press Secretary.* Staff person who is the key link between the member and the media.
- *Counsel.* Lawyer who serves on a committee or personal staff and who deals with parliamentary and procedural matters.

As a rule, personal staff serve the member, and much of the agenda is driven by the member's personal interests, the member's committee assignments (members in both houses are assigned committees by a steering committee of members elected from each party's caucus), and election cycle. They draft legislation for the member, advise the member on what positions to take and how to vote on particular issues, write statements and speeches for the member, and assist the member during meetings with constituents, lobbyists, other members, and administration officials.

Committee staff conduct oversight of the administration's conduct of matters within the committee's jurisdiction (the Foreign Relations Committee, for example, oversees the State Department and the Agency for International Development). In addition to conducting the same types of activities described previously, committee staff also arrange for briefings and hearings with government officials and private sector witnesses. They draft legislation, write reports explaining the legislation, and provide staff support for committee members during committee markups and floor consideration of legislation. They may also conduct and report on international fact-finding missions.

What It Takes

Working on Capitol Hill requires a great deal of flexibility. Often, staff are called on to perform a juggling act, to work simultaneously on several different issues, and to perform a variety of different tasks well, from drafting legislation to meeting foreign dignitaries to representing the member to constituents.

A Hill staffer should also possess initiative, creativity, and motivation. Ever aware of the desires and interests of the residents of a member's state or congressional district, a good staffer will devise initiatives for the member to take, including introducing legislation, writing an op-ed, or initiating a letter-writing campaign. The goal is to advance the country and the member's constituents. Good staff work is done behind the scenes, often with little credit or glory for the staff members themselves.

Good written and oral communication skills are essential. Members of Congress do not have the time necessary to read lengthy memos. As such, staff who write clear and concise background papers and policy memos are a benefit to any office.

Similarly, since nearly every word a member says becomes a part of the permanent record—in the *Congressional Record,* hearing and markup transcripts, and press conferences—Hill staff must write accurate and pithy statements.

And because a staffer is often required to represent his or her boss in meetings with constituents, lobbyists, or administration officials, public speaking skills are a necessity.

Finally, the demands on members of Congress, from constituents at home and from events abroad, highlight the need for and the role of staff on Capitol Hill. One can always assume that job opportunities for newcomers looking for entry-level positions will be constantly created by staff leaving the Hill for new positions. The outlook for congressional staff careers focusing on international affairs is bright, and such jobs offer a challenge to young men and women seeking to contribute to the field of foreign relations.

House Committees
Committee on Agriculture
Committee on Appropriations
Committee on Armed Services
Committee on the Budget
Committee on Education and the Workforce
Committee on Energy and Commerce
Committee on Financial Services
Committee on Government Reform
Committee on House Administration
House Permanent Select Committee on Intelligence
Committee on International Relations
Committee on the Judiciary
Committee on Resources
Committee on Rules
Committee on Science
Committee on Small Business
Committee on Standards of Official Conduct
Committee on Transportation and Infrastructure
Committee on Veterans Affairs
Committee on Ways and Means
Joint Economic Committee
Joint Committee on Printing
Joint Committee on Taxation

Senate Committees
Standing
Agriculture, Nutrition, and Forestry Committee
Appropriations Committee
Armed Services Committee
Banking, Housing, and Urban Affairs
Budget Committee
Commerce, Science, and Transportation Committee
Energy and Natural Resources Committee
Environment and Public Works Committee
Finance Committee
Foreign Relations Committee

Governmental Affairs Committee
Judiciary Committee
Health, Education, Labor, and Pensions Committee
Rules and Administration Committee
Small Business Committee
Veterans' Affairs Committee

Special, Select, and Other

Senate Special Committee on Aging
Senate Select Committee on Ethics
Senate Select Committee on Indian Affairs
Senate Select Committee on Intelligence

With House

Joint Economic Committee
Joint Committee on Taxation

Placement Offices

Senate Placement Office
Room SH-142
Senate Hart Building

House Placement Office
Room H2-219
House Office Building Annex 2

Democratic Study Group "DSG Job Referral Service"
Room 1422
Longworth House Office Building

Presidential Management Intern Program

KATHLEEN A. KEENEY

The Presidential Management Intern (PMI) program was established by Executive Order in 1977. It is designed to attract to the federal service outstanding individuals from a wide variety of academic disciplines who have an interest in and commitment to a career in the analysis and management of public policies and programs. By drawing graduate students from diverse social and cultural backgrounds, the PMI program provides a continuing source of trained men and women to meet the future challenges of public service.

The federal government, as the nation's largest employer, looks for individuals who are academically prepared, motivated, and innovative. Assignments as a PMI may involve domestic or international issues, technological changes, criminal justice, health research, financial management, and many other fields in support of public service programs. Federal departments and agencies strive to provide interns with challenging and rewarding assignments. All cabinet departments and more than fifty federal agencies have hired Presidential Management Interns.

- *Eligibility.* Individuals eligible to be nominated for the PMI program are graduate students from a variety of academic disciplines completing or expecting to complete a master's or doctoral-level degree from an accredited college or university during the current academic year. These individuals must also have a clear interest in and a commitment to a career in the analysis and management of public policies and programs.
- *Nomination Process.* Students need to be nominated for the PMI program by the appropriate dean, director, or chairperson of their graduate program. Students participate in a competitive nomination process devised by their educational institution.

Kathleen A. Keeney has been the director of the Presidential Management Intern Program since 1998. Ms. Keeney has thirty-one years of federal service, all served with the Office of Personnel Management and its predecessor agency, the Civil Service Commission, where she has worked in a variety of program areas including staffing, recruitment, and college relations.

This competitive nomination process ensures fair and open competition among all interested and eligible students.

- *Selection Process.* Students will be invited to participate in a structured assessment center process. Selection as a PMI finalist is based on the student's participation and performance in the one-day assessment center process.
- *Appointment.* PMIs receive an initial two-year appointment at the GS-9 level. After successfully completing the two-year program, PMIs may be eligible for conversion to a permanent government position and further promotional opportunities.
- *Career Development.* The PMI program places a strong emphasis on career development. During the two-year internship, PMIs experience a myriad of challenging career opportunities. The Office of Personnel Management (OPM) facilitates and provides structured orientation and graduation training programs. Federal agencies arrange for seminars, briefings, and conferences, as well as on-the-job training and other developmental opportunities. Federal agencies also provide PMIs with rotational assignments. These assignments expose the PMIs to another area of their agency, another agency, or another branch of the federal government.

No matter what agency or type of position you choose, through selection and appointment as a PMI, you will be able to put your knowledge and experience to work in the service of your country.

Graduate students interested in applying to the PMI program should visit www.pmi.opm.gov for more information.

Four Years Later, a PMI Looks Back
NICOLE BIBBINS

Almost four years after entering the State Department as a 1997 PMI, I can say the program fulfilled my expectation as a challenging and dynamic path into international public service. Being at State—particularly given its expanding programs—was an excellent opportunity to contribute to policy making, understand foreign policy interplay, and travel. Three jobs and some twenty countries later, I am amazed at the experience the program has provided.

So how do you move from graduate student to PMI in international public service? Three key lessons are know your strengths and what you want; use your networks; and be determined, flexible, and creative.

Throughout the university screening, PMI central testing, and interviews, I was asked to identify my area of expertise and explain my interest in public service and my area of expertise, refugees and human rights. Given the stiff competition and the need for dedication to public service, it was imperative that I clearly articulate my commitment.

Georgetown's career counselors, former PMIs, and professors—many of whom had worked in federal government—were invaluable coaches during the interview and job search process. If you want a post suited to your skills and interests, don't be afraid to use such resources. Their knowledge and guidance are priceless.

The all-day PMI interview was a challenge. The best preparation is thinking about your motivations and skills, fine-tuning strong speaking and writing skills, and honing your role in group dynamics.

I was advised to begin contacting agencies before I was officially selected, so I targeted several offices at State while remaining open-minded about other offices and agencies. There are innumerable international opportunities in other departments; look at all of them. If done cautiously and modestly, this approach is useful in showing interest and demonstrating determination.

Even after selection, obtaining a PMI position in government is a highly competitive process, requiring creativity, determination, and patience. The PMI job fair is an excellent opportunity to educate yourself about the government and job availability there and to apply for jobs. However, many of us in the D.C. area did most of our searching directly with agencies.

After many interviews, I received an offer from the Bureau of Population, Refugees, and Migration for a newly created post that had not been advertised in the PMI network. Due to the coalescence of the Balkans crisis, my interest and experience in refugee affairs, strong support from the Georgetown network, and great people in my bureau, a match was made. I spent eighteen months working on Balkans refugee issues, including two rotations to State's Bureau of European Affairs and the Joint Chiefs of Staff Balkans Policy Division. I sat and listened to refugees in temporary shelters in Kosovo, the Krajina, and Eastern Slavonia and was able to offer U.S. assistance. I saw firsthand how the military planned and executed missions that helped end the violence in Kosovo in 1999.

Shortly afterward, I received an unexpected offer to serve as Special Assistant to the new Coordinator for Counterterrorism (an MSFS alum), whom I had worked with during the Kosovo crisis. I finished my PMI in that office, while traveling to fascinating places like North Korea, Yemen, Colombia, Pakistan, and Lebanon to help advance American counterterrorism policy.

At that point, I was offered my current position working for the Under Secretary of State for Global Affairs covering issues such as democracy promotion, human rights, and trafficking in persons. All the positions I held offered me incredible challenges, eye-opening experiences, and great learning. None were without trials, but that is part of professional development and learning in any job.

Before I close, a few more words of advice. Approach the PMI interviewing process with the same rigor as a private sector interview. Occasionally PMIs are not as scrupulous about preparing as they should be. Although you are a talented graduate, approach your interviews and jobs with humility, as you are a newcomer to a team that's been working on "your issues" for years. Some PMIs misstep by failing to realize that their contribution is a part of—not the focus of—our policy or programmatic efforts. Also, remember that PMIs' paths vary greatly:

some don't rotate; some fill in gaps as needed; some become the backbone of an office. Discuss your expectations and those of your office early on. Be open about your objectives, but flexible to their needs.

All in all, the PMI program and public service have been great experiences, ones that I wouldn't trade if I could.

Nicole Bibbins, a 1997 graduate of Georgetown University's Master of Science in Foreign Service, is a former PMI who worked for the Department of State and the Department of Defense. She is currently Special Assistant to the Under Secretary of State for Global Affairs. Previous positions included work with the Regional Center for Foreigners' Concerns in Berlin, the Fund for Peace in Washington, D.C., and internships with the UN High Commissioner for Refugees in Turkey, Search for Common Ground, and the US Committee for Refugees.

Chapter 5

INTERNATIONAL
ORGANIZATIONS

Careers in International Organizations

MICHAEL A. SHEEHAN

Several times a week I meet with people who want to work in the United Nations system. They come from all walks of life and from around the world—with experiences ranging from recent graduates of Georgetown's School of Foreign Service to former ambassadors. My message is usually a variation of the same theme: If you are willing to go to the field, work hard, and be a little patient, the United Nations offers very dynamic and rewarding career opportunities.

The United Nations and its affiliated agencies represent activities in virtually every professional field. The ones that most immediately come to mind are in the fields of diplomacy, human rights, and humanitarian affairs—and indeed there are many opportunities in these areas. In addition, the United Nations also seeks expertise in a wide range of functional areas, including logistics, personnel management, and information technology.

Getting Started at the United Nations

Most professional posts within the United Nations and its specialized agencies require an advanced degree and a significant amount of recent, relevant, and specialized work experience. For that reason, it is often very difficult to begin a career straight out of graduate school at headquarters in New York or other capitals for the specialized agen-

Michael A. Sheehan, a 1988 graduate of Georgetown University's Master of Science in Foreign Service program, was appointed Assistant Secretary-General in the Department of Peacekeeping Operations by Secretary-General Kofi Annan on January 2, 2001. His office has responsibility for providing executive direction and coordination of all management, administrative, and logistics support for UN peacekeeping missions. Mr. Sheehan also has served as Coordinator for Counterterrorism at the U.S. Department of State and as the Deputy Assistant Secretary of State in the Bureau of International Organization Affairs. Mr. Sheehan also holds degrees from the U.S. Military Academy at West Point and the U.S. Army Command and General Staff College.

cies. Vacancies at headquarters are very competitive from internal candidates and from field positions in the agency. In my particular area of peacekeeping, an average vacancy at headquarters usually has multiple qualified candidates from within the organization or from one of the many peacekeeping operations being conducted worldwide. Nevertheless, if a candidate has exceptional experience in a particular area of need, the United Nations does hire directly from outside the organization. The best opportunities, however, for new recruits to the UN system remain in the field.

> It is often very difficult to begin a career straight out of graduate school at headquarters in New York or other capitals for the specialized agencies. Nevertheless, if a candidate has exceptional experience in a particular area of need, the United Nations does hire directly from outside the organization. The best opportunities, however, for new recruits to the UN system remain in the field.

I began my UN career in the field on loan from the U.S. government. In 1992 and 1993, I worked on the National Security Council (NSC) staff in both the Bush and Clinton administrations as a staff officer handling policy issues regarding the United States-led intervention in Somalia and the subsequent transition to UN operation. In 1995, I had a similar experience during the UN peacekeeping operation in Haiti. In both cases, I was loaned to the United Nations and worked on the staff of the Special Representative to the Secretary General. Although I had a military background and was on loan from a government, my colleagues in the field came from a wide range of backgrounds, including academia, nongovernmental organizations (NGOs), other UN agencies, and the private sector. Many of these people who started in peacekeeping in the early 1990s are still with the organization today—both at headquarters and the field.

Working conditions in the field, especially at the beginning of an operation, can be arduous. In peacekeeping or other UN humanitarian interventions, the area is often torn by war, famine, and massive dislocation of the population. Local infrastructure is often limited to begin with and normally damaged by conflict. Working hours, especially during these initial periods, can be around the clock and seven days a week. As a mission matures, however, the hours do normalize somewhat—but most missions remain very busy throughout their life cycle. However, it is during the initial periods of intervention or expansion when there are the most opportunities for employment—and more importantly, the most opportunities to truly contribute to peace, security, or humanitarian relief. In the field you can see the product of your work on a daily basis. You see the organization in action—and the mandates that are decided in headquarters and world capitals implemented on the ground. It is invaluable experience for a career within the organization—or indeed in other related fields. For in the field, there are opportunities to manage programs and deliver services and to supervise local and international staff at a fairly junior level of experience. In addition to the career experience, many also enjoy the camaraderie and esprit that is often found in the field.

Geographical and Gender Representation
The United Nations' primary consideration in the selection of staff is excellence of job performance. Most organizations have intensified efforts to recruit qualified women for professional posts, especially at senior levels. In addition, they seek to maintain geographical balance across the membership of the organization. Although no quotas are used, most organizations track the numbers of staff from each country and try to keep within certain ranges based on the population of the country and its financial contribution to the organization.

Americans, for example, are relatively better represented in New York, at the UN Secretariat and the UN Development Program (UNDP), although there are still opportunities for Americans in New York. However, in other capitals such as Rome (Food and Agriculture Organization [FAO] and World Food Council [WFC]), Geneva (World Health Organization [WHO], UN High Commission for Refugees [UNHCR], International Labor Organization [ILO]), Vienna, and Nairobi, the United States often is very underrepresented. In most cases, English language proficiency is sufficient, but fluency in one or more languages greatly enhances your opportunities for many jobs.

Conclusion
The United Nations was created out of the ashes of World War II, led primarily by Franklin Roosevelt and the wartime alliance of the United Kingdom and the Soviet Union. It was built on the Wilsonian idealism of the League of Nations and tempered by the bitter experience of its failure in the 1930s. Since its conception in San Francisco in 1945, the United Nations has evolved in its size, structure, and roles in

international diplomacy. It often comes up short in achieving the lofty goals of its charter to "save succeeding generations from the scourge of war" and to "reaffirm the dignity and worth of the human person," but it remains committed to these ideals every day and around the world.

The future of the United Nations in peacekeeping, human rights, humanitarian relief, and many other functions remains bright. It is not the panacea for all of the world's problems, but a vital instrument in helping to alleviate the suffering of many and to bring hope to all. As it has been since its inception, the United Nations will only be as effective as the commitment of its member states, particularly the United States—and, of course, the ability and dedication of its international staff. For those interested in a career in international affairs, the United Nations and its affiliated organizations offer many rewarding opportunities.

Resource Listings

African Development Bank

The African Development Bank is the premier financial development institution of Africa, dedicated to combating poverty and improving the lives of people of the continent and engaged in the task of mobilizing resources toward the economic and social progress of its regional member countries. The African Development Bank Group is a multinational development bank supported by seventy-seven nations (member countries) from Africa, North and South America, Europe and Asia. Headquartered in Abidjan, Côte d'Ivoire, with field offices in Ethiopia, Egypt, Gabon, Mozambique, and Nigeria, the Bank Group consists of three institutions: The African Development Bank (ADB), The African Development Fund (ADF), and The Nigerian Trust Fund (NTF).

African Development Bank: The ADB's principal functions are (1) to make loans and equity investments for the economic and social advancement of the regional member countries, (2) to provide technical assistance for the preparation and execution of development projects and programs, (3) to promote investment of public and private capital for development purposes, and (4) to respond to requests for assistance in coordinating development policies and plans of regional member countries. In its operations, the ADB is also required to give special attention to national and multinational projects and programs that promote regional integration.

The ADB's operations cover the major sectors, with particular emphasis on agriculture, public utilities, transport, industry, the social sectors of health and education, and concerns cutting across sectors, such as poverty reduction, environmental management, gender mainstreaming, and population activities. Most ADB financing is designed to support specific projects. However, the ADB also provides program, sector, and policy-based loans to enhance national economic management. The ADB also finances nonpublicly guaranteed private sector operations. The ADB actively pursues cofinancing activities with bilateral and multilateral institutions.

The African Development Fund: The ADF provides development finance on concessional terms to low-income regional member countries that are unable to borrow on the nonconcessional terms of the ADB. In accordance with its lending policy, poverty reduction is the main aim of ADF development activities in borrowing countries.

Its sources of funds are mainly contributions and periodic replenishments by state participants. The ADF is normally replenished on a three-year basis, unless state participants decide otherwise. The total subscriptions, at the end of 1996, amounted to U.S.$12.58 billion.

The Nigerian Trust Fund: The NTF was established by the Government of Nigeria in 1976, with an initial capital of U.S.$80 million that was subsequently replenished with U.S.$71 million in 1981. The purpose of the NTF is to assist in the development efforts of the poorer ADB members.

The NTF is required by its Agreement to use its resources to provide financing for projects of national or regional importance that further the economic and social development of the low-income regional member countries whose economic and social conditions and prospects require financing on nonconventional terms.

In addition to the applications sought for specific vacancies, which can be found on the website at www.afdb.org, the African Development Bank is presently seeking qualified applicants mainly in the following fields of specialization: agronomy specialists, audit specialists, legal officers, economists, engineering specialists, financial analysts, gender specialists, human resources management specialists, information technology officers, investment officers, private sector investment officers, procurement specialists, and treasury officers.

Interested applicants are requested to download and complete the Personal History Form (PHF) after due consideration of the position descriptions provided herewith and send the PHF by e-mail to recruit@afdb.org. Applicants, however, have the option to mail a comprehensive curriculum vitae along with a cover letter to the following address:

> Division Manager
> Recruitment & Staff Development Division
> Human Resources Management Department
> African Development Bank
> 01 BP 1387 Abidjan 01
> Côte d'Ivoire
> Tel.: (225) 20-20-43-03
> Fax: (225) 20-20-49-43
> www.afdb.org

Asian Development Bank

The Asian Development Bank (ADB), headquartered in Manila, Philippines, is an international financial organization created in 1966 to help in the planning and financing of high-priority projects in the developing countries of Asia and the South Pacific. Its stockholders are the governments of fifty-nine countries of North America, Western Europe, and the Asian Pacific region. The bank is not an organization within the UN system.

The Asian Development Bank extends loans and equity investments to its developing member countries for their economic and social development, provides technical assistance for the planning and execution of development projects and programs and for advisory services, promotes and facilitates investment of public and private capital for development, and responds to requests for assistance in coordinating development policies and plans of its developing member countries.

ADB's Young Professionals program was established in 1983 to recruit and assimilate annually into ADB a small number of exceptionally well-qualified younger personnel. Candidates should have a superior academic record and, preferably, work experience in areas related to ADB's activities. Candidates must be less than thirty years old; a citizen of a member country; hold at least a master's degree (or equivalent professional training), with advanced training in economics, finance, business administration, or in other fields relevant to ADB's work; and preferably have work experience in areas related to the activities of ADB.

> Headquarters:
> 6 ADB Avenue, Mandaluyong City
> 0401 Metro Manila, Philippines
> Tel.: (632) 632-4444 Fax: (632) 636-2444

Mailing Address:
P.O. Box 789
0980 Manila, Philippines
www.adb.org

Caribbean Development Bank

The Caribbean Development Bank (CDB) serves to contribute to the harmonious economic growth and development of its member countries and promote economic cooperation and integration among them. Its mandate also includes paying "special and urgent regard to the needs of the less developed members of the region." CDB promotes the orderly expansion of international trade; provides technical assistance to members; promotes public and private investment in development projects; and assists efforts to promote financial institutions and regional markets for capital, credit, and savings.

CDB has twenty regional members and five nonregional member states.

CDB's recruitment policy is to attract and retain staff of the highest calibre and gives due regard to recruiting staff on as equitable a geographic basis as is possible from among its member countries. The bank employs people with a wide range of skills, including environmental science, engineering, banking, finance, human resource management and development, information technology, macroeconomics, law, general management, public administration, and project management. CDB offers indefinite, fixed-term, and temporary appointments. The bank does not have a junior professional program.

Deputy Director
Human Resource and Administration
Caribbean Development Bank
P.O. Box 408
Wildey, St. Michael
Barbados
www.caribank.org

Consultative Group on International Agricultural Research

The World Bank, Food and Agricultural Organization and the UN Development Program cosponsor the Consultative Group on International Agricultural Research (CGIAR). CGIAR's mission is to contribute to food security and poverty eradication in developing countries through research, partnerships, capacity building, and policy support, promoting sustainable agricultural development based on the environmentally sound management of natural resources. CGIAR provides and coordinates funding for a network of sixteen research centers. The United States traditionally has contributed about one-fifth of the group's annual budget.

Each of the agricultural research centers acts independently within the group, recruiting its own staff. Centers primarily employ persons with a Ph.D. or equivalent advanced academic degree, several years of experience in the field, and fluency in at least two languages. Any person interested in employment should write directly to the institution or institutions that are of specific interest and relevance to them.

> Centro Internacional de Agricultura Tropical (CIAT)
> Apartado Aereo 6713
> Cali, Columbia
> www.ciat.cgiar.org
> *Focus:* sustainable development, crop improvement, agro-biodiversity, pests and diseases, soil and systems, and land management
>
> Centro Internacional de Mejoramiento de Maiz y Trigo
> Apdo. Postal 6-641
> Mexico 06600, D.F. Mexico
> www.cimmyt.org
> *Focus:* sustainable crops, improving productivity of maize, wheat, and barley
>
> Centro Internacional de la Papa (CIP)
> Avenida La Universidad 795, La Molina
> P.O. Box 1558
> Lima 12, Peru
> Tel.: (51-1) 349-6017-5783-5777
> Fax: (51-1) 317-5326
> www.cipotato.org
> *Focus:* potato, sweet potato, other Andean root and tuber crops, and natural resource management
>
> International Center for Agricultural Research in Dry Areas
> P.O. Box 5466, Aleppo,
> Syrian Arab Republic
> www.icarda.cgiar.org
> *Focus:* improve and integrate the management of soil,

water, nutrients, plants, and animals to optimize
sustainable agricultural production in North Africa and
West Asia

International Center for Living Aquatic Resource
Management (ICLARM)
P.O. Box 500
GPO 10670 Penang, Malaysia
www.iclarm.org
Focus: promote sustainable development and use of
living aquatic resources based on environmentally
sound management

International Center for Research in Agroforestry
P.O. Box 30677
Nairobi, Kenya
www.icraf.cgiar.org
Focus: alleviating poverty, improving food and nutritional security, and enhancing environmental resilience
in the tropics

International Crops Research Institute for the Semi-Arid
Tropics
Patancheru 502 324
Andhra Pradesh, India
www.icrisat.org
Focus: to reduce poverty, hunger, and environmental
degradation across the semi-arid tropics of the world

International Food Policy Research Institute
2033 K Street, NW
Washington, DC 20006-1002
www.ifpri.org
Focus: poverty alleviation and sound management of the
natural resource base that supports agriculture

International Institute of Tropical Agriculture
IITA c/o Lambourn (UK) Limited
Carolyn House
26 Dingwall Road
Croydon CR9 3EE, UK
www.iita.org
Focus: improving food production in the humid tropics
and to develop sustainable production systems

International Livestock Research Institute
P.O. Box 30709
Nairobi, Kenya
www.cgiar.org/ilri/
Focus: enhancing the diverse and essential contributions
livestock make to smallholder farming

International Plant Genetic Resources Institute
Via dei Tre Denari 472/a
00057 Maccarese (Fiumicino) Rome, Italy
www.ipgri.cgiar.org
Focus: conserving gene pools of current and potential
crops and forages

International Rice Research Institute
DAPO Box 7777
Metro Manila, Philippines
www.irri.org
Focus: help farmers in developing countries produce
more food on limited land using less water, less labor,
and fewer chemical inputs, without harming the
environment

International Service for National Agricultural Research
P.O. Box 93375
2509 AJ The Hague, The Netherlands
www.isnar.cgiar.org/
Focus: to help bring about innovation in agricultural
research institutions

International Water Management Institute
141 Cresswell Street
0184 Silverton, Pretoria, South Africa
www.cgiar.org/iwmi/
Focus: sustainable use of water and land resources in
agriculture and the water needs of developing countries

West Africa Rice Development Association
01 B.P. 2551
Bouake 01, Côte d'Ivoire
www.warda.cgiar.org
Focus: the sustainable productivity of rice-based crop-
ping systems while conserving the natural resource
base

European Bank for Reconstruction and Development

The European Bank for Reconstruction and Development (EBRD) was established in 1991. It exists to foster the transition toward open market-oriented economies and to promote private and entrepreneurial initiative in the countries of Central and Eastern Europe and the Commonwealth of Independent States (CIS) committed to and applying the principles of multiparty democracy, pluralism, and market economics.

The EBRD seeks to help its twenty-seven countries of operations to implement structural and sectoral economic reforms, promoting competition, privatization, and entrepreneurship, taking into account the particular needs of countries at different stages of transition. Through its investments it promotes private sector activity, the strengthening of financial institutions and legal systems, and the development of the infrastructure needed to support the private sector. The EBRD applies sound banking and investment principles in all of its operations.

In fulfilling its role as a catalyst of change, EBRD encourages cofinancing and foreign direct investment from the private and public sectors, helps to mobilize domestic capital, and provides technical cooperation in relevant areas. It works in close cooperation with international financial institutions and other international and national organizations. In all of its activities, the bank promotes environmentally sound and sustainable development.

> Personnel Department
> European Bank for Reconstruction and Development
> One Exchange Square
> London EC2A 2EH
> United Kingdom

European Free Trade Association

The European Free Trade Association (EFTA) is a group of small European countries (Iceland, Liechtenstein, Norway, and Switzerland) working for the removal of import duties, quotas, and other obstacles to trade in Europe and the upholding of liberal, nondiscriminatory practices in world trade. The EFTA, headquartered in Geneva, keeps watch on developments that could restrict or distort trade flows and ensures the observance of EFTA's rules for fair competition in matters such as the use of subsidies. Within Europe, EFTA works to strengthen and develop its special relationship with the European Union. In world trade, EFTA works with larger organizations such as the Organization for Economic Cooperation and Development (OECD) and the World Trade Organization (WTO).

The EFTA Secretariat in Brussels employs a staff of fewer than 100 professionals. It offers preparation and servicing of all EFTA and EFTA-EU meetings. The staff provides appropriate research and analysis of all questions dealt with by the association. The working language of the secretariat is English.

> Headquarters:
> (Third Country Relations)
> 9-11 rue de Varembé, CH-1211
> Geneva 20, Switzerland
> Tel.: (41) 22-749-11-11
> Fax: (41) 22-733-92-91
> http://secretariat.efta.int
>
> Brussels Office:
> (EEA matters)
> 74 rue de Trèves, B-1040
> Brussels, Belgium
> Tel.: (32) 2-286-17-11
> Fax: (32) 2-286-17-50

European Union
The European Union (EU), formerly known as the European Community, was created after World War II by six Western European countries. Today, the EU has fifteen member states: Austria, Belgium, Denmark, Finland, France, Germany, Greece, Ireland, Italy, Luxembourg, the Netherlands, Portugal, Spain, Sweden, and the United Kingdom. The EU continues the integration of Europe that began in the 1950s with the creation of the European Coal and Steel Community (ECSC) in 1951, followed by the establishment of the European Economic Community (EEC) and the European Atomic Energy Community (Euratom) in 1957.

The European Commission is represented in the United States by a delegation in Washington, D.C. Its Office of Press and Public Affairs is responsible for providing information on the activities, policies, and publications of the EU. It does not have information on specific job opportunities or prospective employers in Europe. General information on EU personnel rules and competitive exams are available on the Commission's website: http://europa.eu.int/en/comm/dg09/dg9home.htm.

Employment with the EU is limited to the nationals of its member states on the basis of a competitive examination. Each institution organizes its own competitions. A general entrance examination for professional staff is given approximately once a year by the European Commission. Competitions for professionals with special qualifications may appear at any time. Competitions are advertised in newspapers and magazines published in member states. The full details and application forms are published in the official Journal, C Section. An annual subscription to *Notifications of Open Competitions* can be placed with EU sales agents. The agent in the United States is:

UNIPUB
4611-F Assembly Drive
Lanham, MD 20706-4888
Tel.: (800) 274-4888
Fax: (301) 459-0056

EU member state nationals should contact the Recruitment Division at the individual institutions.

European Parliament
Centre european
Plateau de Kirchberg
L-2920 Luxembourg
Tel.: (352) 43001
Fax: (352) 4300-4842
www.europarl.en.int/default.htm

Council of the European Union
Rue de la Loi 175
B-1048 Brussels
Belgium
Tel.: (32) (2) 285-6111
Fax: (32) (2) 285-7381
www.ue.eu.int/en/summ.htm

European Commission
rue de la Loi 200
B-1049 Brussels
Belgium
Tel.: (32) (2) 299-3131
Fax: (32) (2) 295-7488
http://europa.eu.int/en/comm/dg09/dg9home.htm

Court of Justice
Boulevard Konrad Adenauer
Plateau de Kirchberg
L-2920 Luxembourg
Tel.: (352) 43031
Fax: (352) 4303-2600
http://curia.eu.int/en/index.htm

Court of Auditors
12 rue de Alcide de Gasperi
L-1615 Luxembourg
Tel.: (352) 4398-45410
Fax: (352) 4398-46430
www.eca.eu.int/EN/job_opportunities.htm

Economic and Social Committee
rue Ravenstein 2
B-1000 Brussels
Belgium
Tel.: (32) (2) 546-9011
Fax: (32) (2) 513-4893

Committee of the Regions
rue Belliard 79
B-1040 Brussels
Belgium
Tel.: (32) (2) 282-2211
Fax: (32) (2) 282-2325

European Investment Bank
100 Boulevard Konrad Adenauer
L-2950 Luxembourg
Tel.: (352) 4379-3142
Fax: (352) 4379-2545
www.eib.org/jobs/index.htm

European Central Bank
Postfach 16 03 19
60066 Frankfurt am Main
Germany
Tel.: (49) 69-13440
Fax: (49) 1344-6000
www.ecb.int/job/job01.htm

Food and Agriculture Organization

The Food and Agricultural Organization (FAO) was established in 1945 to raise levels of nutrition and standards of living, to improve the efficiency of production and distribution of food and agricultural products, and to better the conditions of rural populations. Today, FAO is one of the largest specialized agencies in the UN system and the lead agency for agriculture, forestry, fisheries, and rural development.

Since its inception, FAO has worked to alleviate poverty and hunger by promoting agricultural development, improved nutrition, and the pursuit of food security—defined as the access of all people at all times to the food they need for an active and healthy life. Accordingly, the FAO collects and disseminates technical information relating nutritional needs and improved agricultural techniques and promotes and recommends national and international action.

FAO has more than 4,000 employees, almost evenly distributed between its decentralized offices and field projects in developing countries and its headquarters in Rome. Besides the central administrative functions, such as human resources, finance, and information technology, FAO hires experts in the fields of agriculture, fisheries, forestry, and related areas.

> FAO Liaison Office for North America
> 2175 K St. NW, Suite 300
> Washington, DC 20437
> Tel.: (202) 653-2400
> Fax: (202) 653-5760
> www.fao.org

Inter-American Development Bank

The Inter-American Development Bank (IDB), established in 1959 to promote the economic and social development of Latin America and the Caribbean, is a major source of external public financing for member countries in Latin America. IDB also functions as a catalyst for mobilizing external private capital for development projects in the region by borrowing in international financial markets and promoting cofinancing arrangements with other financial institutions. IDB seeks to foster a more equitable distribution of development benefits by financing social and economic projects designed to improve living conditions among low-income groups in Latin America. The IDB headquarters are located in Washington, D.C., with field offices in each regional member country (except Canada), and offices in Paris and Tokyo.

Most applicants for professional positions at the IDB possess at least eight years of relevant work experience in addition to a graduate degree in such fields as economics, engineering, agriculture, administration, environmental sciences, and so on. Most positions require fluency in at least two of the official languages of the IDB, which are English, Spanish, French, and Portuguese.

The IDB operates a summer internship program for students who are under thirty years old, enrolled in a graduate-level program, and fluent in two of the official languages.

> Employment Section
> Inter-American Development Bank
> 1300 New York Avenue, NW
> Washington, DC 20577
> Tel.: (202) 623-1000
> www.iadb.org

Inter-American Institute for Cooperation on Agriculture

The Inter-American Institute for Cooperation on Agriculture (IICA) is the specialized agency for agriculture within the inter-American system. Its mission is to encourage, facilitate and support technical cooperation among its thirty-four member states in the western hemisphere in order to promote agricultural development and rural welfare. The four strategic areas for such cooperation are policies and trade; science, technology, and natural resources; agricultural health and food safety; and rural development. IICA's highest governing body is the Inter-American Board of Agriculture (IABA), which is made up of the ministers of agriculture of the thirty-four member states. Eighteen additional countries serve as permanent observers to the IABA.

IICA currently has 103 international and 184 national professional staff positions in country offices throughout North, Central, and South America and the Caribbean, including its headquarters in Costa Rica. A branch office was opened in Spain in 2001 for the purpose of increasing contact with European donor countries interested in promoting IICA's goals. IICA also contracts with large numbers of high-level specialized short-term consultants.

Applicants for professional positions should have degrees in agricultural sciences, development, or other related disciplines. Candidates should also have at least five years of relevant work experience and be proficient in no fewer than two of IICA's official languages: English, Spanish, French, and Portuguese.

The Tropical Agricultural Research and Training Center (CATIE), also located in Costa Rica, was begun in 1946 under the auspices of IICA and continues today for the promotion of scientific research and post-graduate education. They maintain a separate faculty and staff.

Instituto Interamericano de Cooperación para la
Agricultura
Dirección General
Apartado 55-2200
Coronado
San José, Costa Rica
Tel.: (506) 216-0222
www.iicanet.org

IICA
1775 K Street, NW
Washington, DC 20006
Tel.: (202) 458-3767

CATIE
Apartado 7170 CATIE
Turrialba, Costa Rica
Tel.: (506) 556-6431
www.catie.ac.cr

International Atomic Energy Agency
The International Atomic Energy Agency (IAEA) serves as the world's central intergovernmental forum for scientific and technical cooperation in the nuclear field, and as the international inspectorate for the application of nuclear safeguards and verification measures covering civilian nuclear programs. A specialized agency within the UN system, the IAEA came into being in 1957, a few years after U.S. President Dwight D. Eisenhower proposed the creation of an international atomic energy agency in his historic "Atoms for Peace" speech before the UN General Assembly. Today, a wide range of IAEA products, services, and programs incorporate the cooperative efforts and interests of the agency's 132 member states.

Details on the different programs of the IAEA are available on the agency website.

At the end of 2000, the Secretariat had a total staff of 2,173, of which 1,629 were in regular authorized posts. Of these, 912 were in the professional and higher categories, representing ninety-three nationalities. The other 1,261 staff members came under the general service category—clerical, secretarial, administrative, and other support staff—and were generally recruited locally. In addition to the 1,629 regular staff members, the Secretariat also employed 456 other staff on temporary assignments, or as cost-free experts and staff funded from extra budgetary sources. For recruitment purposes, the IAEA's Division of Personnel sends vacancy notices to governmental bodies and organizations in member states such as ministries of foreign affairs, or their national counterparts; national energy and/or atomic energy commissions; universities; permanent missions accredited to the IAEA; the World Bank; and to the UN Secretariat, the UN regional commissions, UN specialized agencies, offices of the UN Development Programme, and UN Information Centres. In addition, advertisements are placed in specialized journals, websites, or international newspapers as required. They are also sent to professional associations. In general, posts at the IAEA are for a fixed term of three years. Fluency in English is essential, and often knowledge of other official languages—such as French, Spanish, Russian, Chinese, and Arabic—is desirable.

Further information on academic background as well as employment experience sought in new hires can be found at www.iaea.org/worldatom/Jobs/.

> International Atomic Energy Agency
> Wagramer Strasse 5
> P.O. Box 100
> A-1400 Vienna, Austria
> Tel.: (+43 1) 2600
> Fax: (+43 1) 26007
> www.iaea.org

International Maritime Organization

The International Maritime Organization (IMO) is the specialized agency of the United Nations with responsibility for the safety of shipping and the prevention of marine pollution by ships. IMO's 158 member states and two associate members have adopted more than forty conventions and protocols relating to international shipping.

In addition to a university degree or its equivalent, considerable experience and expertise in international shipping is required for appointment to the IMO staff. Information on the very limited vacancies is posted on the IMO website, under the section "About IMO."

International Maritime Organization
4 Albert Embankment
London SE1 7SR
UNITED KINGDOM
Tel.: +44 (0) 20-7735-7611
Tel.: +44 (0) 20-7587-3210
www.imo.org

International Telecommunications Union

The International Telecommunications Union (ITU), a specialized agency of the United Nations, is a worldwide organization that brings governments and industry together to coordinate the establishment and operation of global telecommunication networks and services. It is responsible for standardization, coordination, and development of international telecommunications, including radio communications, as well as the harmonization of national policies.

The ITU adopts international regulations and treaties governing all terrestrial and space uses of the frequency spectrum as well as the use of all satellite orbits that serve as a framework for national legislations. It develops standards to foster the interconnection of telecommunication systems on a worldwide scale regardless of the type of technology used. It also fosters the development of telecommunications in developing countries.

The ITU (TELECOM) organizes worldwide and regional exhibitions and forums bringing together the most influential representatives of government and the telecommunications industry to exchange ideas, knowledge, and technology for the benefit of the global community and, in particular, the developing world.

Headquartered in Geneva, ITU's permanent bureaus are the Radiocommunication Bureau (BR), the Telecommunication Standardization Bureau (TSB), and the Telecommunications Development Bureau (TSB).

Candidates for professional posts are required to have a university degree or its equivalent in one or more of the following fields: engineering, telecommunications, electronics, physical sciences, computer sciences, mathematics, statistic, languages, business administration, human resources, communications, or Internet technology. In addition, two (grade P2) to fifteen (grade D1) years of progressively responsible work experience in the field related to the advertised post is requested. Fifty-three posts were advertised in the past year. Applications for vacant posts may be submitted through the telecommunication administration of the country of which the candidate is a national or directly to ITU. Vacancy notices and the Personal History Form are posted on ITU's website.

> International Telecommunication Union
> Place des nations
> CH-1211 Geneva 20
> Switzerland
> Tel.: +41-22-730-51-11
> Fax: +41-22-733-73-56
> Fax: +41-22-730-65-00
> www.itu.int/employment

North Atlantic Treaty Organization

The North Atlantic Treaty Alliance (NATO) is a defensive alliance consisting of twenty-six sovereign nations in Europe and North America. Its objectives, as stated in the Washington Treaty of 1949, are to safeguard the freedom, common heritage, and civilization of their peoples, based on democracy, individual liberty, and rule of law; promote stability in the North Atlantic area; unite efforts for collective defense; and preserve peace and security. To this end the alliance draws up collective defense plans, establishes required infrastructure and logistical support for those plans, and arranges joint training and military exercises. The organization also pursues closer cooperation in the political, social, economic, cultural, and scientific fields. Since 1992 and 1994, respectively, the North Atlantic Cooperation Council and the Partnership for Peace Program at NATO headquarters primarily seek to increase cooperation and consultation between NATO and the democratic states to our east.

NATO staff positions are open only to citizens of an alliance nation; positions for U.S. citizens are usually filled by the Department of State by seconding U.S. government personnel to NATO or by direct hire with concurrence of the U.S. government. A useful publication is the NATO handbook available from the U.S. Liaison Office.

> North Atlantic Treaty Organization
> 1110 Brussels
> Belgium
> www.nato.int

> U.S. Liaison Office
> U.S. NATO
> PSC 81
> Box 200
> APO AE 09724

Organization of American States

The Ninth International Conference of American States (Bogota, 1948) established the Organization of American States (OAS) by adopting the Charter (succeeding the International Union of American Republics, founded in 1890). The Charter was subsequently amended by the Protocol of Buenos Aires (creating the annual General Assembly), signed in 1967, enacted in 1970, and by the Protocol of Cartagena de Indias (concept of integral development), signed in 1985, enacted in 1988.

The OAS is the preeminent political setting for multilateral action in the Americas. Moreover, it is becoming a forum for dialogue in which the member states can develop general standards, principles, and rules of understanding; a forum for assisting governments in developing long-term strategies on shared objectives; and a forum for receiving and imparting the flow of vital information.

The purpose of the OAS is to strengthen the peace and security of the continent; to promote and consolidate representative democracy, with due respect for the principle of nonintervention; to prevent possible causes of difficulties and to ensure the peaceful settlement of disputes that may arise among the member states; to provide for common action in the event of aggression; to seek the solution of political, juridical, and economic problems that may arise among them; to promote, by cooperative action, their economic, social, and cultural development; to achieve an effective limitation of conventional weapons; and to devote the largest amount of resources to the economic and social development of the member states.

> Organization of American States
> 17th Street and Constitution Avenue
> Washington, DC 20009
> www.oas.org

Pan American Health Organization

The Pan American Health Organization (PAHO), founded in 1902 as an independent, inter-American organization, works to promote and protect the health of the peoples of the western hemisphere. In 1949, PAHO became the regional office for the World Health Organization (WHO) in the Americas while keeping its status as part of the inter-American system. Together, PAHO and five other WHO regional offices plan and coordinate health activities on a global basis, with projects including implementation of health programs in member states, strengthening of health services, and training of health workers. Guided by the core principles of equity and pan-Americanism, PAHO is currently focusing on the promotion of high-quality vaccination and immunization programs; the prevention and control of the spread of communicable diseases, noncommunicable diseases, sexually transmitted diseases, and veterinary diseases; the evaluation, prevention, and control of environmental risks for public health (with special emphasis on the most vulnerable populations); the promotion of health systems and services that ensure universal access to quality health care; the provision of humanitarian and technical assistance to areas struck by disasters; and the promotion of services for mental health, nutrition, family health, aging, and other concerns. Acknowledging and reinforcing the idea that health and development are closely related, PAHO advocates treatment of sensitive health issues, promotes inclusive agendas, provides technical advice, and supports resource mobilization efforts aimed at ameliorating specific health unbalances. In order to do so in the most effective way, PAHO has established close cooperation with other development actors in the region of the Americas, including other international organizations of the inter-American system, member organizations of the UN system, and other multilateral organizations, bilateral agencies, and nongovernmental organizations.

PAHO continually seeks physicians, nurses, sanitary engineers, and health administrators. Medical officers and technicians serve as advisors to governments, as professors in universities, or in teams combating specific public health problems. PAHO/WHO needs staff competent, inter alia, in epidemiological analysis; policy analysis and priority determination; program planning and management; resources mobilization; management information systems; health systems research; international communications; and public information.

Approximately fifty positions are open annually in the field of international public health. Requirements vary depending on the position sought but an advanced degree in public health is highly valued as is at least seven years of experience at the national level and at least two years of participation in technical cooperation programs and activities, preferably in the Americas. Knowledge of Spanish and English is required; Portuguese and French are highly desired. As a part of its commitment to strengthen leadership in the area of health, PAHO has also established a training program in international health. Every year, this program receives between eight and ten health professionals from the Americas, who demonstrate leadership and interest in delving more deeply into the international dimensions of health.

The training process is based on the participants becoming involved in the work of the PAHO through a work-study format for a period of eleven months. Participants are expected to possess the autonomy, enthusiasm, and initiative necessary to become involved in projects that are under way and to take advantage of the available institutional resources inside and outside of PAHO.

> Pan American Health Organization
> Pan American Sanitary Bureau
> Regional Offices of the World Health Organization
> 525 Twenty-third Street, NW
> Washington, DC 20037
> Tel.: (202) 974-3000
> Fax: (202) 974-3663
> www.paho.org

United Nations Children's Fund

The United Nations Children's Fund (UNICEF) is the only UN agency devoted exclusively to the promotion of the needs of children and their families. The organization also plays an important role in the promotion of the basic rights of children embodied in the Convention on the Rights of the Child and in the achievement of the goals set at the 1990 World Summit for Children. UNICEF was created in 1946 as the United Nations International Children's Emergency Fund to help the children of war devastated Europe. In the early 1950s its mandate was expanded by the General Assembly to address the problems of children in both the industrialized and developing world. UNICEF is a semiautonomous agency of the United Nations.

UNICEF has a diverse workforce of more than 5,500 staff. About 49 percent of the UNICEF staff is located in sub-Saharan Africa; 23 percent in South Asia, East Asia, and the Pacific; 10 percent in Latin America and the Caribbean; and 9 percent in the Middle East and North Africa. The remaining serve in New York, Geneva, Copenhagen, Florence, or offices in Central and Eastern Europe and the Baltic states.

About 2,000 UNICEF staff are in the professional category, both international and national. Candidates interested in this category must have a first university degree and postgraduate degree in development-related disciplines such as public health, nutrition, primary education, economics, social welfare, sociology, accounting, civil engineering, public administration, or information systems. Candidates are also expected to have several years of professional work experience in a developing country and fluency in English and another UN language.

UNICEF
3 United Nations Plaza
New York, NY 10017
Tel.: (212) 326-7000
www.unicef.org

United Nations Conference on Trade and Development

The United Nations Conference on Trade and Development (UNCTAD) is a subsidiary organization of the United Nations General Assembly and forms part of the United Nations Secretariat. UNCTAD was created at the request of the developing countries for the establishment of a forum in which they would have a larger voice and that would consider international economic issues with particular attention to the impact on those countries and upon the development process.

Posts at the junior professional level are filled through examinations open only to nationals of member states inadequately represented on the staff of the United Nations Secretariat. Posts above the junior professional levels usually are advertised worldwide. Given equal qualifications, candidates from underrepresented member states and women are given preference. There are about 250 professional posts at UNCTAD, most of which require advanced training and experience in economics and a few that require a legal background. Journeymen candidates usually have a Ph.D. or the equivalent and up to five years of relevant experience. Recruits typically are drawn from advanced university research programs or government positions in an appropriate field.

United Nations Conference on Trade and Development
Palais des Nations
CH-1211 Geneva 10
Switzerland
www.unctad.org

United Nations Development Program

The United Nations Development Program (UNDP) is the United Nations' largest provision of grant funding for development and the main body for coordinating UN development assistance. UNDP has more than 7,000 staff members working throughout a global network of more than 136 country offices in every major developing region and its headquarters in New York.

UNDP's purpose is to help developing countries and countries moving from centrally planned to market economies build capacities for "sustainable human development"—development that centers on people.

UNDP has annual resources of more than U.S. $1 billion at its disposal for development operations, which stimulate approximately nine times that amount in collaborative funding. Since its inception, UNDP has established a far-reaching network of resources—human, technical, and financial—drawing on the U.S. system of specialized agencies, governments, nongovernmental organizations (NGOs), and the private sector. It provides a managerial umbrella for a wide range of funds and activities covering major development initiatives, and especially for special measures for the Least Developed Countries (LACS), round tables for country aid planning and coordination, management services for projects financed by bilateral donors and the World Bank, promotion of technical cooperation among developing countries, collaboration with NGOs, support for the private sector, and strengthening public-sector management.

> United Nations Development Program
> One United Nations Plaza
> New York, NY 10017
> Tel.: (212) 906-5558
> Fax: (212) 906-5364
> www.undp.org

United Nations Educational, Scientific and Cultural Organization
The United Nations Educational, Scientific and Cultural Organization (UNESCO) promotes collaboration among member states in the fields of education, science, and culture. Its programs are organized into five major departments: education, science, social sciences/ humanities, culture, and communication. In addition to its own activities in these fields, UNESCO frequently acts as an executor for UNDP and World Bank projects, often cooperating with UNICEF and other UN agencies.

Competition for permanent, professional positions on UNESCO's staff is very fierce and subject to considerations of geographical distribution. Most candidates must have a Ph.D. and extensive professional experience in one of UNESCO's fields of expertise. Fluency in either English or French is mandatory; field posts may require additional languages. Employment opportunities also exist for short-term contract work with UNESCO. Citizens of member states should apply through the National Commission for UNESCO in their country's capital.

UNESCO Office for Liaison with the United Nations
2 United Nations Plaza
Suite 900
New York, NY 10017
Tel.: (212) 963-5995
Fax: (212) 963-8014
www.unesco.org

Bureau of Personnel
UNESCO
7 Place de Fontenoy
75700 Paris
France
Tel.: (33) 1-45-68-10-00
Fax: (33) 1-45-67-16-90

United Nations Environment Program

The United Nations Environment Program (UNEP), established in 1972, works to encourage sustainable development through sound environmental practices everywhere. Its activities cover a wide range of issues, from atmosphere and terrestrial ecosystems and the promotion of environmental science and information, to an early warning and emergency response capacity to deal with environmental disasters and emergencies. UNEP's present priorities include environmental information, assessment, and research, including environmental emergency response capacity and strengthening of early warning and assessment functions; enhanced coordination of environmental conventions and development of policy instruments; fresh water; technology transfer and industry; and support to Africa.

UNEP is headquartered in Nairobi, Kenya, and has regional and outposted offices in Paris, Geneva, Osaka, The Hague, Washington, New York, Bangkok, Mexico City, Manama, Montreal, and Bonn. There are approximately 260 professional posts in UNEP with about 70 job openings annually. The academic and employment experiences required vary by position, but an advanced degree is usually necessary.

Information networks and monitoring systems established by UNEP include the Global Environmental Information Exchange Network (INFOTERRA); the Global Resource Information Database (GRID); the International Register of Potentially Toxic Chemicals (IRPTC); and the recent UNEP.Net, a web-based interactive catalogue and multifaceted portal that offers access to environmentally relevant geographic, textual, and pictorial information. UNEP.Net is being developed in partnership with the Environment Systems Research Institute (ESRI) and National Geographic. In June 2000, the World Conservation and Monitoring Centre (WCMC) based in Cambridge, United Kingdom, became UNEP's key biodiversity assessment center. UNEP's latest state-of-the-environment report is the *Global Environment Outlook 2000* or GEO 2000. GEO 3 was published in 2002. For other publications and information concerning UNEP, please visit their website at www.unep.org.

> United Nations Environment Programme
> P.O. Box 30552
> Nairobi, Kenya
> Tel.: (254-2) 621234
> Fax: (254-2) 226886, 622614
>
> Washington Office
> 1707 H Street, NW, Suite 300
> Washington, DC 20006
> Tel.: (202) 785-0465
> Fax: (202) 785-2096
> www.unep.org

United Nations High Commissioner for Refugees

The United Nations High Commissioner for Refugees (UNHCR) is charged with providing international protection for all refugees, defined as persons who have left their native country "owning to a well-founded fear of being persecuted for reasons of race, religion, nationality, or membership in a particular social group, or political opinion," and with facilitating their voluntary repatriation. Although the organization's responsibilities include the provision of interim care for displaced persons and the search for permanent solutions for refugee problems, it generally is occupied with the provision of legal services as regards, for example, difficulties with the granting of asylum or forced repatriation.

Much of UNHCR's demand is for people with backgrounds in protection law, social sciences/community services, health, logistics, security, water and sanitation, finance, and administration. Applicants should preferably have a master's degree and at least three years of postgraduate experience with emphasis in humanitarian work. Preference will be given to women applicants and to applicants who are proficient, at a minimum, in English and one other UN language.

A high degree of mobility is required in accordance with UNHCR's mandatory rotation policy. Initial recruitment often takes place during emergency operations, which require a willingness to take up assignments at short notice and for a short duration in hardship and nonfamily duty stations located in a remote area where living conditions are often difficult.

UN High Commissioner for Refugees
Case Postale 2500
CH-1211 Geneva 2 Depot
Switzerland
Tel.: (44) 22-739-8111
www.unhcr.ch

United Nations Industrial Development Organization

The United Nations Industrial Development Organization's (UNIDO) mission is to help countries pursue sustainable industrial development. This is its specialist role in the UN system. Sustainable industrial development is never easy to achieve. It means balancing concerns for a competitive economy, sound environment, and productive employment. UNIDO has been working with governments, business associations, and individual companies to solve industrial problems and equip them to help themselves. Services are customized and have been designed to be easily integrated into packages that will address specific country needs.

From a practical point of view, UNIDO strives to strengthen industrial development in three broad categories: industry's role in the economic structure; production technology, production processes, and production efficiency; and the enabling environment for industrial growth.

UNIDO has approximately 300 professionals at headquarters and 1,200 experts and advisers working in field projects. UNIDO employs professionals with academic studies and related working experience in areas such as industrial policies and research, industrial statistics, information networks, private-sector development, quality management, technology and investments, cleaner production, environment management, industrial energy, and climate change.

UNIDO career opportunities are found under "Jobs" on UNIDO's website. Available working or learning experiences are described in professional and senior management positions, field project experts and consultants, associate experts, junior professional officers, and internships.

Director
Human Resource Management Branch
P.O. Box 300
A-1400 Vienna
Austria
www.unido.org

United Nations Institute for Training and Research

The United Nations Institute for Training and Research (UNITAR) was established by the Secretary-General pursuant to General Assembly resolution 1934 (XVIII) of December 21, 1963, as a UN agency, an autonomous institution within the framework of the United Nations. In April 1993 the General Assembly decided to move UNITAR's headquarters to Geneva, where most training programs are designed and conducted. A liaison office is kept in New York to coordinate training activities. UNITAR's mandate is to enhance the effectiveness of the United Nations in achieving the major objectives of the organization, in particular the maintenance of peace and security and the promotion of economic and social development.

UNITAR has, as its name implies, two main functions: training and research. Recently, however, the main focus has been shifted to training; basic research is only conducted if extra-budgetary funds are provided. The research activities currently undertaken concentrate on training. Training is, according to UNITAR's statute, provided at various levels to persons, particularly from developing countries, for assignments with the United Nations or the specialized agencies and for assignments in their national services connected to the work of the United Nations, the organizations related to it, or other organizations operating in related fields. UNITAR's training programs are comprised of courses on multilateral diplomacy and international affairs management, economic and social development programs, as well as fellowship programs in international law and peacemaking and preventative diplomacy.

UNITAR employs a professional Geneva-based staff of about twenty. In addition, a number of senior fellows and consultants contribute to the completion of UNITAR's tasks. Many training activities also call upon senior staff of the UN Secretariat and specialized agencies.

United Nations Institute for Training and Research
Palais des Nations
CH-1221 Geneva 10
Switzerland
www.unitar.org

United Nations Population Fund

The United Nations Population Fund (UNFPA) helps developing countries find solutions to their population problems. UNFPA began operations in 1969. It is the largest international source of population assistance. About a quarter of all population assistance from donor nations to developing countries is channeled through UNFPA. The fund has three main program areas: reproductive health, including family planning and sexual health; population and development strategies; and advocacy.

UNFPA extends assistance to developing countries, countries with economies in transition, and other countries at their request to help them address reproductive health and population issues. It also raises awareness of these issues in all countries, as it has since its inception.

UNFPA's three main areas of work are to help ensure universal access to reproductive health, including family planning and sexual health, to all couples and individuals by or before 2015; to support population programming; to promote awareness of population and development issues; and to advocate for the mobilization of the resources and political will necessary to accomplish its areas of work.

UNFPA is guided by and promotes the principles of the Programme of Action of the International Conference on Population and Development (1994). In particular, UNFPA affirms its commitment to reproductive rights, gender equality, and male responsibility, and to the autonomy and empowerment of women everywhere. UNFPA believes that safeguarding and promoting these rights and promoting the well-being of children, especially female children, are development goals in themselves. All couples and individuals have the right to decide freely and responsibly the number and spacing of their children as well as the right to the information and means to do so.

UNFPA is convinced that meeting these goals will contribute to improving the quality of life and to the universally accepted aim of stabilizing world population. We also believe that these goals are an integral part of all efforts to achieve sustained and sustainable social and economic development that meets human needs, ensures well-being, and protects the natural resources on which all life depends.

UNFPA recognizes that all human rights, including the right to development, are universal, indivisible, interdependent and interrelated, as expressed in the Programme of Action of the International Conference on Population and Development, the Vienna Declaration, and the Programme of Action adopted by the World

Conference on Human Rights, the Convention on Elimination of All Forms of Discrimination Against Women, the Programme of Action of the World Summit for Social Development, the Platform for Action of the Fourth World Conference on Women, and in other internationally agreed-upon instruments.

UNFPA, as the lead UN organization for the follow-up and implementation of the Programme of Action of the International Conference on Population and Development, is fully committed to working in partnership with governments, all parts of the UN system, development banks, bilateral aid agencies, nongovernmental organizations, and civil society. UNFPA strongly supports the UN Resident Coordination system and the implementation of all relevant UN decisions.

UNFPA will assist in the mobilization of resources from both developed and developing countries, following the commitments made by all countries in the Programme of Action to ensure that the goals of the International Conference on Population and Development are met.

For employment with UNFPA, an advanced degree in a study pertinent to UNFPA's program (e.g., demography, public health, or population studies) and some experience in a developing country, preferably with a development organization similar to UNFPA, are prerequisites.

The applicant should also have the ability to take up assignments in UNFPA field duty stations as part of career development with UNFPA. Fluency in English is required; speaking and reading ability in one other UN language, preferably French or Spanish, is desirable. UNFPA is able to respond only to those applicants in whom is has a further interest.

There were thirty-two international professional-level job openings in 2000.

United Nations Population Fund
220 E. 42nd Street
New York, NY 10017
www.unfpa.org

United Nations Relief and Works Agency

Established in 1949 to assist refugees from the 1948 Arab-Israeli conflict, the United Nations Relief and Works Agency (UNRWA) provides education, health, and welfare services to more than 3 million registered

Palestinian refugees living in Jordan, Lebanon, Syria, the West Bank, and the Gaza Strip. The Agency has 644 elementary and prepara- tory schools, 8 vocational and teacher training centers, and 123 health centers. UNRWA relies on voluntary contributions, mainly from governments, for its funding. The largest contributor is the United States, providing more than a third of the funds, followed by the European Union and its member governments.

The Agency employs more than 20,000 people, almost all Pal- estinian refugees. There are about 170 international positions in the areas of finance, administration, data processing, law, personnel, public relations, and supply. Since 1988, UNRWA has been running emergency operations in the occupied West Bank and Gaza Strip, as well as in Lebanon. These operations account for some of the international positions. Sixty-eight of the international positions are at UNRWA's Vienna, Austria, headquarters; the remainder are at a headquarters unit in Amman, Jordan, Gaza, or in five field offices.

UNRWA had twenty-eight professional vacancies in the past year. Applicants are normally considered only if they have a minimum of three years' work experience in addition to the related educational qualifications.

Chief, Recruitment and Staff Development Division
UNRWA Headquarters
Vienna International Centre
P.O. Box 700
A-1400 Vienna
Austria
www.unrwa.org

United Nations Secretariat
The United Nations Secretariat carries out the substantive and administrative work of the United Nations as directed by the General Assembly, the Security Council, and other UN organizations. It has a total staff of about 8,900, drawn from 160 countries. Duty stations include UN Headquarters in New York as well as offices in Geneva, Vienna, and Nairobi. There are also regional commissions in Addis Ababa, Santiago, Bangkok, and Beirut. Special efforts are made to recruit from as wide a geographic area as possible, in order to achieve, as closely as possible, equitable representation among member states.

Employment opportunities are available in the following occu- pational groups: administration, economics, finance, Internet technology, language and related work, legal, library, social development, and statistics. Staff for entry-level positions are recruited via National Competitive Recruitment Examinations, organized as a matter of priority in countries that are inadequately represented among the staff of the Secretariat. Candidates must possess a first-level university degree and be thirty-two years of age or younger. Fluency in either English or French is required. Interested candidates are encouraged to visit the UN website for more information.

United Nations Secretariat
United Nations Headquarters
First Avenue at 46th Street
New York, NY 10017
www.un.org

United Nations University

The United Nations University (UNU) is an international community of scholars that generates knowledge and builds capacities in areas relevant to the global problems of human security and development, in particular in developing countries. Its position as an academic institution within the UN system offers the university unique opportunities to contribute to the advancement of knowledge as well as to its application in the formulation of sound policies. Current research and capacity building activities focus in five main areas: peace and security, governance, development, science technology and society, and the environment.

The university comprises the UNU Centre in Tokyo, twelve research and training centres, and programs that focus on specific problems and a network of cooperating institutions and scholars the world over. The university currently has a total of 215 positions and advertised for 15 vacancies in the year 2000. UNU advertises all programmatic positions in the international media, particularly *The Economist*. Applicants for such positions should have an advanced degree and a substantial publication record in the relevant discipline, particularly on issues of relevance to the developing world. Further information can be found at the website.

United Nations University Centre
5-53-70 Jingumae, Shibuya-ku
Tokyo, T 150-8925
Japan
Tel.: (81) 3-3499-2811
Fax: (81) 3-3499-2828

UNU Office at the UN, New York
2 United Nations Plaza, Room DC2-1462
New York, NY 10017
Tel.: (212) 963-6387 Fax: (212) 371-9454
www.unu.edu

United Nations Volunteers

The United Nations Volunteers (UNV) program is the fourth-largest multilateral volunteer program in the world. It is an associated program under the administration of the United Nations Development Programme. Since the inception of the program, men and women from both developed and developing countries alike have provided their professional and technical skills within United Nations projects around the world. At the present time, volunteers from more than 80 countries are involved in development work in more than 100 countries.

Approximately 1,970 volunteers currently hold field positions with the UNV program, ranging from agronomists to dentists to engineers to medical specialists to humanitarian and emergency relief workers. Requirements for these positions include the knowledge of one foreign language (English mandatory), a master's degree, and at least three to five years' work experience. This emphasis on experience, coupled with the high degree of commitment and motivation inherent in volunteer service, produces an extremely efficient agency for development on an international level.

United Nations Volunteers
United Nations Development Programme
1775 K Street, NW, Suite 420
Washington, DC 2000
Tel.: (202) 331-9130
www.unv.org

World Bank Group

The World Bank Group works to help developing countries reduce poverty and promote sustainable development. Unlike many international aid programs, however, the Bank does not make grants but rather lends money to developing countries, which must repay the loans. The World Bank Group comprises five organizations.

The **International Bank for Reconstruction and Development** (IBRD), commonly referred to simply as the World Bank, is the oldest and largest international organization devoted to promoting development through direct loans, technical assistance, and policy advice. The bank lends to developing countries with relatively high per capital

Getting Started at the World Bank
ANDREW FOLLMER

It has gotten more and more difficult to get into the World Bank in recent years. Nevertheless, several avenues remain open, and you cannot afford to be shy about taking advantage of any of them.

Although the bank has a formal internship program, winning an internship can be likened to winning the lottery.

For those who are living in Washington, D.C., two other routes may be more likely to get you where you want to go. First, unpaid internships are an option. Only internships obtained through acceptance into the formal program are paid. However, if you make a contact who likes you and is willing to work with you, they might be willing to give you an unpaid internship. This would be the easiest way in the door. You must pursue anything that will get your foot in the door, so even if an unpaid internship isn't what you had in mind, present it to whomever you meet as an option. It is a low-risk way for them to assess the quality of your work and could lead to paid consultancy work.

(Continued)

incomes. The money the IBRD lends is used to pay for development projects, such as building highways, schools, and hospitals, and for programs to help governments change the ways they manage their economies.

The **International Development Association** (IDA), known as the "concessional loan window" of the bank, shares staff with the World Bank but differs in the terms of financing it provides. IDA provides assistance on concessional terms to the poorest developing countries that cannot afford to borrow from the IBRD.

The **International Finance Corporation** (IFC) encourages private growth enterprises in developing countries through its financial services and the provisions of its expertise in legal and technical aspects of private business. IFC lends directly to the private sector; it does not seek or accept government guarantees. IFC, one of the few international development organizations that makes equity investments as well as providing loans, aids the private sector by providing long-term loans, equity investments, guarantees and "stand-by" financing,

Second, consultancy remains the main road into the Bank. You get one assignment, use that as a springboard for other assignments, and so on. If you did an internship, it would give you contacts that could get you some part-time or occasional consulting work, which could parlay into a fuller program once you are out of school. Opportunities to come on board right away as staff are virtually nonexistent. Consultancies are often awarded on the basis of who you know, so it is important to meet with and network with as many people in the Bank as possible. Take an opportunity to get your foot in the door even if it is not the sector or region you have your heart set on.

Other tips include:

- **Resumé.** Much of the conventional wisdom about resumés is better suited to the private sector than the World Bank. Brevity is not an asset here, though you don't want to pad your resumé with lengthy fluff either. It can be as long as necessary to accommodate the substance you have to put into it. A one-page resume looks rather light here. A memo makes for a great writing sample to attach to your resumé, especially on a topic that your addressee can relate to.
- **Buy a World Bank directory.** The World Bank bookstore in Washington, D.C., sells copies of the World Bank directory. I suggest

risk management and "quasi-equity instruments" such as subordinated loans, preferred stock, and income notes.

The **Multilateral Investment Guarantee Agency** (MIGA), the newest member of the World Bank Group, promotes foreign investment for economic development by providing investors with guarantees against "noncommercial risk" such as expropriation and war. MIGA also provides advisory and consultative services to member countries to assist in creating a responsive investment climate and an information base to guide and encourage the flow of capital.

The **International Centre for Settlement of Disputes** (ICSID) promotes increased flows of international investment by providing facilities for the conciliation and arbitration of disputes between governments and foreign investors. ICSID also provides advice, carries out research, and produces publications in the area of foreign investment law.

In addition to technical expertise, the World Bank seeks candidates with the breadth of education and experience to take a comprehensive you buy one, as it will give you contacts for every sector, every region, and so on.

- **Be professional.** Always err on the side of formality. Do not address someone by their first name, even in e-mail, unless they invite you to do so. Because of the diversity of backgrounds and cultures here, some people are quite informal and others are not. No one will ever be offended by your calling them Mr. or Mrs. Smith, but a young student addressing someone they don't know by their first name will turn some people off. Even though we Americans tend to be informal, seven years in this place has made me a bit resistant to such assumed informality. Once inside, we are quite informal with each other, but you have to get inside first!

- **Sell yourself.** We want to know what you can do for us, not the other way around. That is why it is important to expand on the substance in your resumé, and in your cover letter, draw out a few things that are particularly relevant to the individual you are addressing and say, "This is what I have done. This is how it relates to your project. And this is the contribution I feel I can make." Now *that* will hold my interest, and if I don't have anything to offer you I might remember that the woman in the next office is looking for someone who fits your profile or something. At the least, I think most people will give you a

view of the development issues with which it is concerned. The majority of successful candidates for employment with the Bank have many years of experience in the field and normally join the Bank between the ages of 35 and 50.

Through its Young Professionals Program (YPP), however, the Bank does seek younger candidates who show potential for building a successful career in international development. Current and former young professionals comprise about 18 percent of all professional staff in the World Bank Group. To be eligible for consideration, YPP applicants must not have reached their thirty-second birthdays as of July 1 of the selection year, have a master's degree (or equivalent) in economics, finance, or a related field, and either a minimum of two years' relevant work experience or continued academic study at the Ph.D. level. Fluency in English is required and speaking proficiency in one or more of the bank's other working languages (i.e., Arabic, Chinese, French, Portuguese, and Spanish) is beneficial. Work experience in a developing country also is desirable. Competition for the program is name of someone else to talk to, and you just follow that chain until it pays off. But you have to get your resumé read and not tossed in the trash.

- **Be persistent and use national and other contacts.** Don't get discouraged. I knocked on a lot of doors here before I got my first job as a research assistant. Do not be bashful about using your nationality or other common link. Often I have seen people get a meeting with a manager or project manager just by virtue of a shared nationality.

- **Be patient.** Once you have your foot in the door, particularly as a young person, nothing will happen fast, mainly because there are not many young people. Hard work and quality work will eventually pay off. But if you are looking for a meteoric rise to a high-profile position, better to look in the private sector.

Andrew Follmer, a 1994 graduate of the Master of Science in Foreign Service program, is an operations officer for the World Bank's Human Development Division for Eastern and Southern Africa. He has worked with numerous African countries in his seven years at the Bank and currently supervises a portfolio of Public Health and HIV/AIDS operations in Kenya and Tanzania.

strong. Each year the program receives thousands of applications for twenty to thirty positions. Interested and qualified persons should submit a self-addressed envelope requesting application forms for the program by early fall.

In addition to regular staff positions, there are a small number of temporary research and summer positions available at the World Bank.

> Recruitment Division
> Personnel Department
> World Bank
> 1818 H Street, NW
> Washington, DC 20433
> Tel.: (202) 477-1234
> www.worldbank.org

World Intellectual Property Organization

The World Intellectual Property Organization (WIPO) is an international organization dedicated to promoting the use and protection of intellectual property in the world, through cooperation among states.

With a staff of some 760 drawn from around the world, WIPO carries out many tasks related to the protection of intellectual property rights, such as administering treaties; assisting governments, organizations, and the private sector; monitoring developments in the field; and harmonizing and simplifying relevant rules and practices.

With headquarters in Geneva, Switzerland, and one main office in New York, WIPO is one of the sixteen specialized agencies of the UN system of organizations. It administers twenty-one international treaties dealing with different aspects of intellectual property protection. The organization counts 175 nations as member states.

The recruitment of candidates for career posts at various levels with the professional and special categories (marked P or D) is generally reflected through vacancies published on WIPO's website and the International Civil Service Commission (ICSC) Bulletin and also advertised in WIPO periodicals and through the appropriate administrations of the members states of the organization. Most of these posts require staff with a legal academic background and considerable professional experience in the field of intellectual property. Vacancies for posts in the General Category are advertised in WIPO and are in principle filled by local candidates. In 2000, at professional and director levels, fifty-three posts were advertised through competitions, forty-six competitions organized, twenty-seven posts filled through competitions, and twenty-three posts filled through direct recruitment.

WIPO runs a Summer School Internship program and an Ad Hoc Internship program, open to senior students and young professionals wishing to acquire a working knowledge of intellectual property and to be exposed to the work of the organization.

> World Intellectual Property Organization
> 34 chemin des Colombettes
> CH-1211 Geneva 20
> Switzerland
> Tel.: (41) (22) 730-9111   Fax: (41) (22) 733-5428
> http://wipo.int

World Meteorological Organization

The World Meteorological Organization (WMO) is a specialized agency of the United Nations with a membership of 185 states and territories. WMO was established as an intergovernmental organization in 1950 as the successor of the International Meteorological Organization (IMO) set up in 1873 as a nongovernmental organization. The purpose of WMO is to facilitate worldwide cooperation in the establishment of networks in the making of meteorological, climatological, hydrological, and related geophysical observations, as well as their exchange, processing, and standardization. WMO also promotes training, research, and technology transfer. The organization also fosters collaboration between meteorological and hydrological services and furthers the application of meteorology to aviation, shipping, water resources management, agriculture, and other human activities, and to sustainable development.

The total number of professional positions in WMO is 141. In 2000, there were 19 vacancies giving rise to international recruitment, mostly in various specialized fields of meteorology and hydrology. The organization advertises professional post vacancies infrequently. Professional staff are expected to have a university degree, often a Ph.D., and five to ten years of related experience. The best opportunities for Americans have been and will continue to be for those with considerable experience in the fields of meteorology, hydrology, physical sciences, environmental chemistry, electrical engineering, business administration, or similar disciplines, depending on the specifications for the position advertised. Employment opportunities are distributed to the permanent representatives of members of WMO. Thus, they are always available in the National Meteorological Services of member countries. In the United States, information is available from the U.S. National Weather Services of the National Oceanic and Atmospheric Administration (NOAA) in Silver Spring, Maryland (see chapter 4 on U.S. government). It is also available from the American Meteorological Society, 45 Beacon Street, Boston, Massachusetts 02108. The WMO only accepts applications for specific vacancies.

> World Meteorological Organization
> 41, Avenue Giuseppe Motta
> Case Postale No. 2300
> CH-1211 Geneva 2
> Switzerland
> www.wmo.ch

World Trade Organization

The World Trade Organization (WTO), the successor organization to the General Agreement on Tariffs and Trade (GATT), seeks to liberalize and expand world trade. More than 140 member countries now belong to the WTO, together accounting for almost 90 percent of world trade.

The WTO has a professional staff of about 300 and is based only in Geneva. Between fifteen to twenty new officials are hired annually.

Recruitment standards are very high, and competition is keen. Potential candidates need strong academic backgrounds, work experience in economics and international trade policy, and proficiency in at least two of the WTO official languages (English, French, and Spanish) is highly desirable.

Chief, Human Resources Officer
World Trade Organization
Centre William Rappard
Rue de Lausanne 154
1211 Geneva 21
Switzerland
Fax: (41) (22) 731-5772
www.wto.org

Chapter 6

BANKING

Careers in Banking

<small>KELLY CESARE</small>

When I left Georgetown and headed to Wall Street, I had investment banking pretty much figured out—at least I thought so. As with many students I talk to today, I thought of investment banking as advising companies on strategic decisions. I reasoned that such a first job represented the perfect way to gain exposure to a broad number of industries that would help me to choose my "real" career in a few years, after I had mastered finance. Although I had an idea of the type of career that I wanted to pursue, I now realize that I had a very limited idea of the complexity of investment banking and the variety of careers available not only in the industry, but in an individual bank. Twelve years later, I have had various careers although I have never left J. P. Morgan, let alone Wall Street. I originally joined investment banking because it provided exciting, fast-paced, challenging work with intelligent, motivated, and interesting people. Fortunately, this continues to hold true today.

As I reflected on my career to write this article, I thought back to its beginning: the interview process during my last semester at Georgetown. I tried to focus on what type of information would have helped me to pursue a career in banking. Although I made the right decision, it would have helped me to understand the inner workings of the banking organization in more detail. Although I will share a little bit about my personal experience as an example of the wide variety of positions banking offers, I will try to focus on what banks do and what type of person and skills are well suited for this industry.

Kelly Cesare is a managing director in equity derivatives. Ms. Cesare joined J. P. Morgan in 1989 and presently manages the corporate marketing group within equity derivatives. Before joining the corporate marketing group in 1998, Ms. Cesare spent six years in investment banking, including four years in J. P. Morgan's office in Buenos Aires, Argentina, and three years in convertible sales. Ms. Cesare holds a B.A. from Lafayette College and is a graduate of Georgetown University's Master of Science in Foreign Service.

I hope that this article will offer you some insights into the investment-banking world that will help you in your decision-making process.

Recent Industry Events
As informed students, you are aware of the extensive changes that the banking industry has experienced over the past ten years. The lines between commercial banking and investment banking have not only blurred but disappeared. New models such as J. P. Morgan Chase and Citigroup are changing the competitive dynamic. Commercial banks are using their lending capacity as leverage to push into the lucrative investment banking business. Investment banks are responding by seeking larger balance sheets to preserve their dominance in these businesses. In addition, globalization of most industries has been extensive. Clients demand that their banks be able to serve them globally with the product expertise to address their increasingly complex businesses. Banks must be expert in politics and economics; the two are inseparable.

The result has been intense consolidation in the banking industry. Many once-powerful firms no longer exist as separate entities. The list of mergers is long and distinguished:
- J. P. Morgan Chase—Manufacturer's Hanover/Chemical Bank/Chase Manhattan Bank/Hambrecht & Quist/Robert Fleming Ltd./The Beacon Group/J. P. Morgan
- Citigroup—Citibank/Travellers/Salomon Brothers/Smith Barney
- CSFB/DLJ
- UBS/Paine Webber
- Dresdner/Wasserstein Perella
- Fleet/Bank Boston/Robertson Stephens
- Morgan Stanley/Dean Whitter
- Charles Schwab/US Trust
- Nationsbank/BankAmerica

Although consolidation has slowed recently with the stagnant stock market (stock has been the currency of choice for bank mergers because of favorable accounting rules and historically high stock prices), ultimately there will be only a handful of global players who will dominate the industry.

What Do Banks Do?
Banks focus on many different clients and activities, but the core businesses can be summarized as follows:
- investment banking—integrated capital markets and advisory solutions for clients worldwide,

Table 6.1. Major Product Areas

Advisory

Mergers and Acquisitions (M&A) Work with companies on evaluating acquisitions, divestitures, mergers, sales, and other strategic transactions.

Restructuring Restructure or refinance a company's balance sheet while it is going into, coming out of, or trying to avoid Chapter 11. Includes refinancing advisory, M&A opportunities for buyers or sellers or distressed properties, debt capacity and valuation analysis, and structuring and loan syndication advice.

Capital Markets

Equities Market and execute equity transactions for corporate clients. These include initial public offerings, follow-on common stock issues, convertible issues, and private placements.

Fixed Income Arrange fixed-income financing for corporate and government clients.

Instruments include syndicated loans, money market instruments (i.e., commercial paper), high-grade securities, securitized debt (i.e., asset-backed and mortgage-backed securities), emerging markets debt (sovereign and corporate bonds), project finance, private placements, structured finance, collateralized debt obligations, and credit derivatives.
Major departments include:
Investment Grade Debt Capital Markets: Arrange corporate bond issuance for investment grade companies and sovereigns.
Global Syndicated Finance: Arrange bank loan financing for clients. Banks minimize their exposure by arranging loans that can be distributed across many other banks. The lead bank typically keeps a portion of the loan and earns a fee for the amount placed to other banks.
High-Yield Capital Markets: Arrange corporate bond issuance for companies rated below investment grade (BBB). There is a large and relatively liquid market for these types of bonds today.
Private Placements: Raise financing for companies with private investors. This financing is typically in the form of debt but also can be structured as convertible securities or equity.

Sales and Trading

Sales and Trading Sales and trading professionals interact with major investor clients (institutions, governments, hedge funds, and individuals) in day-to-day trading, portfolio recommendations, and marketing of new bond or equity/equity-linked issues. There are many specialized sales and trading desks across the organization focusing on specific instruments (i.e., equities, convertible securities, fixed-income securities). The salesperson is analogous to the client banker and delivers the bank's research, new issue product, and trading capabilities to the clients. The trader is responsible for facilitating client transactions, committing the bank's capital, and managing the bank's risk.

Instruments include money market instruments (i.e., commercial paper, certificates of deposits, loan participations, and bankers' acceptances), corporate securities, high-grade and high-yield government and quasi-government securities, government agency securities and municipal bonds, emerging markets investments (i.e., sovereign and corporate bonds), structured finance obligations and securitized obligations, equities, commodities, foreign exchange and derivatives, exchange-traded futures and options.

Risk Management	
Equity Derivatives	Structure, execute, sell, and trade all equity derivative hedging and investment products (single stock, baskets, index structures) for investors, private banking, and corporate clients.
FX and Interest Rate Derivatives	Structure, execute, sell, and trade interest rate and foreign exchange hedging transactions for companies.
Commodity Derivatives	Structure, execute, sell, and trade bullion, base metals, oil, natural gas, and agricultural derivatives.

- private banking—advice and solutions for wealthy individuals and families,
- research—research on economics, equities, and global markets,
- asset management—managing assets for a wide range of clients worldwide,
- private equity—equity investing in private companies.

Because the scope of this article cannot cover all of these activities, I have chosen to focus on investment banking. Investment banks serve many different types of clients, including corporations, financial institutions, governments, and institutional investors. Due to the complexity of clients' businesses, the range of products and solutions that a bank must provide results in a wide variety of departments that specialize in each industry or product. It is the job of the client bankers to coordinate and direct these resources to service clients.

Generally, a client banker is responsible for managing the bank's relationship with each client and coordinating the services of the various product areas across the bank to have the maximum impact on the client's business and, as a result, generating the most revenue possible for the bank. Client coverage teams typically are organized by sector and region. Although client bankers are not hired as entry-level employees, they do have a number of more junior professionals who help them with this process. This can be a valuable position to gain an overview of the bank's product groups.

The dominant global banks service their clients by advising on corporate strategy and structure, raising and placing capital, making markets in a broad range of financial instruments, and designing risk-management solutions. To accomplish this, banks have a variety of product groups that are responsible for being experts in their field and are charged with the marketing and execution of the investment banking products. I have included the following major product areas with a brief description of each. Of course this is a simplification, but I hope it is useful to orient you.

What Positions Are Available?
Most banks hire analysts and associates into a generalist pool and place them in different departments after a short training program. Banks generally recruit for the analyst program from undergraduate schools and offer three-year positions. At the conclusion of this term, analysts are expected to attend graduate school, although the best are offered permanent positions. Graduate students, or others with significant experience, are hired as associates, which are permanent positions. Most banks hire local nationals to staff overseas offices because of the economic and logistic advantages such hires offer, but an overseas assignment is possible if you are determined and give it some time. Many U.S. banks staff projects out of New York (especially for Latin America), which means that international exposure and travel for New York hires is common. Most of the positions that are described above are also available at foreign banks and can be applied for directly.

Although most banks will not commit to hire for a particular position or group, if you have one in mind, do not let this policy discourage you. Once you are hired, you will learn the system and identify opportunities for movement. However, without flawless execution and diligence regarding the responsibilities you originally receive, you will not be able to take advantage of new opportunities. As long as you are viewed as a valuable employee, your manager will help you move around if that is what you ultimately want to do.

I offer my career path as an example. I began my career at J. P. Morgan as an associate in corporate finance. This group was a generalist pool, drawn on by most groups in the banks. I decided that I liked the Latin American M&A group because it was a diverse, international group—one in which I felt comfortable. Once I let my manager know this, I was staffed on some projects and became friendly with the professionals in the group. Because we were so busy, I was asked to move to Buenos Aires in 1991, just as the privatization program was going into full swing. It was an incredible time to be involved with a nation in the midst of a major transformation (which unfortunately was not successfully completed). My experience being placed abroad, although atypical, is not impossible (I was one of two Americans in the office). In 1995, I was ready for a change. J. P. Morgan was rapidly expanding into the equities business (after receiving underwriting powers a few years earlier), and I thought it would be valuable to understand how the markets worked. Mexico had just devalued, so the Latin American equity group was not hiring. I decided to focus on the United States for a while to get the experience I wanted and took a position in the equity derivatives group selling convertible bonds to major institutional investors.

> Once you are hired, you will learn the system and identify opportunities for movement. However, without flawless execution and diligence regarding the responsibilities you originally receive, you will not be able to take advantage of new opportunities.

As I began to understand institutional clients and the markets side of the business I found that although this experience was valuable, I preferred working with corporate clients. I also missed Latin America. In 1998, I started talking to people about what else was available and was offered a position in the research department as the Latin American equity market strategist. While thinking about that position, I was approached to move to the equity derivatives marketing group that executes structured hedging transactions for U.S. and Canadian investment banking clients. It sounded like the perfect mix between my background advising corporate clients and my newly gained experience in the markets. I decided to take a chance and, three years later, I am still there, now running the group. Most of my business is done in the United States, although our clients have exposure across the globe, so I do travel internationally and stay current on a variety of different markets.

Although I intend to move back to the international side of our business over time, this is the right spot for me for now.

It is important to remember that your career is a progression. You will not be doing your first job (or any job) forever. The important thing is to continue to learn and challenge yourself. Never stand still.

To evaluate which role is right for you, you should talk to as many people as you can. Ask them how they spend their time. Ask yourself whether you like to focus on analysis or clients. Are you driven to see clients execute on ideas? Do you like to be expert in something or would you rather switch topics often and be a generalist? Do you like to run complex models or feel more comfortable with less quantitative analysis?

> It is important to remember that your career is a progression. You will not be doing your first job (or any job) forever. The important thing is to continue to learn and challenge yourself. Never stand still.

How to Find the Right Job

As I am sure you realize, when the market is difficult, most firms on Wall Street are forced to cut staff significantly. However, this does not mean that there are no job opportunities. New talent is always needed, and investment banks will continue to hire in anticipation of turnover and an eventual upturn in the economy.

Investment banks are looking for motivated people who are entrepreneurial and have strong analytical, quantitative, and communication skills. You should be someone who thrives on the challenge of competitive pressures and is able to remain focused on the client and work well with others in a fast-paced environment. The financial services industry is extremely competitive. To be blunt, the lifestyle is grueling. There is a relentless focus on the bottom line and a drive to service demanding clients without delay. If you will not deliver something by tomorrow morning, someone else will. Clients are moving quickly in a fast-paced and complex business environment, and you have to stay one step ahead. There will be months on end when you do not get a day off (especially for the first few years). The travel schedule is unpredictable and hectic. It is important to realize what you are signing up for. To be successful, this job must come first.

With the amount of time that you will spend at the office, you should spend much of your time deciding which type of culture you prefer. It does vary considerably from bank to bank. The people with whom you work can make all of the difference in the world. It is important to get to know as many people as you can to understand what type of professional excels in that organization and how you would fit in.

If you are coming from a program that specializes in international affairs, it is important to demonstrate that you are serious about your interest in finance. The typical degree for entrance into a banking job is finance or an M.B.A. Make it a point to take classes in finance. You have to point to these and demonstrate that you have strong quantitative and analytical skills during your interviews and on your resumé. Emphasize that you have these quantitative skills along with the benefit of a broader perspective. The practice that an international affairs graduate has with short summary briefings (written and oral) will come in handy. Much of your work will be producing succinct and accurate presentations. Further along in your career you will be delivering those presentations to clients, so being comfortable with public speaking is also useful. One word of advice: focus on the details. You will be surprised at the amount of detail that goes into each and every presentation, model, and transaction. Think from the client's perspective and be proactive in thinking about the next steps and you will do well. The senior project leaders will seek you out for more interesting and challenging work if you consistently turn in thoughtful and error-free work. This will be an adjustment from school, where you are used to thinking about the big picture. However, focus on the details while not losing perspective and you will ultimately succeed.

Good luck!

Resource Listings

Banco Santander Central Hispano / Santander Central Hispano Investment

Banco Santander Central Hispano (BSCH) is a financial group that offers asset management and retail, wholesale, and private banking services. Its aim is to become the leader in Europe and Latin America in financial services through a clear focus on profitability and high growth.

The bank is headquartered in Madrid, Spain, and offers consumer credit, mortgage loans, lease financing, factoring, mutual funds, pension funds, insurance, commercial credit, investment banking services, structured finance, and advice on mergers and acquisitions to a worldwide customer base of approximately 24 million. Currently, the bank's principal operations are in Spain, Portugal, Germany, Italy,

Argentina, Bolivia, Brazil, Chile, Colombia, Mexico, Panama, Paraguay, Peru, Uruguay, the United States, and Venezuela.

BSCH has 45,000 employees and 6,000 branch offices in Spain and 50,000 employees and 2,500 branches outside of Spain. As of January 2000, the bank was the second-largest banking group in the Euro zone in terms of market capitalization and the eighth-largest banking group in terms of total assets.

In the United States, BSCH has branches in Miami (offering private banking services) and New York (offering corporate banking and, through Santander Central Hispano Investment, investment banking services). These branches employ 25 and 350 people, respectively. Most of the bank's employees in the United States are bilingual in English and Spanish or English and Portuguese. New recruits usually possess a technical background in business administration, finance, or economics. Candidates with a bachelor's degree apply for analyst positions, whereas those with advanced degrees are generally considered for associate positions.

> Banco Santander Central Hispano or
> Santander Central Hispano Investment
> 45 East 53rd Street
> New York, New York 10022
> Tel.: (212) 350-3500
> www.gruposantander.com/en

BankAmerica Corporation

BankAmerica Corporation and its consolidated subsidiaries provide diverse financial products and services to individuals, businesses, government agencies, and financial institutions throughout the world. With a global presence in more than thirty countries, BankAmerica Corporation is one of the three largest bank holding companies in the United States based on total assets.

The Global Markets Group (GMG) is a customer-driven provider of capital markets products and services positioned to pursue significant growth opportunities from long-term trends in worldwide financial markets. It has a diversified client base with services through its U.S. and foreign securities, foreign exchange sales and trading, emerging markets and financial engineering, and risk management (derivatives) product areas.

Through a twenty-four–hour global market-making and distribution network, GMG meets its clients' investment, financing, risk management, and foreign exchange requirements. GMG also specializes in tailoring and implementing portfolio and balance sheet strategies to optimize clients' investment, hedging, and financing decisions.

The bank offers a Global Markets Associates Program. Global Markets associates will be hired and initially based in either Hong Kong or London. Everyone participates in a fast-paced, intensive twelve-month training program that combines formalized classroom instruction, self-study, travel, and a variety of on-the-job training experiences. Upon successful completion of the one-year program, associates will be placed in any one of the trading room locations around the world.

Candidates must have proven analytical, problem-solving, and quantitative skills demonstrated by a bachelor's degree in business, finance, or economics with a minimum 3.3 G.P.A. The ideal candidate will have demonstrated a successful track record in taking initiative, risk taking, and leadership roles.

This is a fast-paced, highly competitive work environment. Flexibility, creativity, and the ability to deal with ambiguity are key traits of applicants. Candidates must be willing to work flexible hours given the time zone differences of the many markets in which BankAmerica deals in every day.

Global Market—Asia
Bank of America
2/F Bank of America Tower
12 Harcourt Road
Central, Hong Kong

Corporate Headquarters
100 North Tryon Street
Charlotte, NC 28255
Tel.: (704) 386-1845
www.bankofamerica.com

Bank of Montreal

Founded in 1817, Bank of Montreal is Canada's first bank and one of the largest financial institutions in North America. It offers clients a broad range of financial services across Canada and in the United States through BMO Nesbitt Burns and its Chicago-based subsidiary, Harris Bank.

With average assets of $246 billion and more than 33,000 employees, the bank has diversified activities concentrated in retail banking, wealth management, and corporate and investment banking.

Bank of Montreal fosters both personal and professional growth by offering diverse opportunities to its employees as well as the individual support they need to reach their full potential. Its commitment to learning is embodied in the Institute for Learning. The result is a team environment where both new and highly experienced employees work together to achieve goals and learn from each other.

For all the details on the Bank of Montreal Group of Companies and opportunities available, visit www.bmo.com/careers.

Bank of Montreal
430 Park Avenue
New York, NY 10022
Tel.: (212) 758-6336

Bank of Montreal
One First Canadian Place
100 King Street West
Toronto, Ontario M5X 1A12
Canada
Tel.: (415) 359-5001
www.bmo.com

Bank of New York

The Bank of New York, founded in 1784 by Alexander Hamilton and the nation's oldest bank operating under its original name, is the sixteenth-largest bank holding company in the United States. The bank provides a complete range of banking and other financial services to corporations and individuals worldwide through its core businesses: securities and other processing, credit cards, corporate banking, retail banking, trust, investment management and private banking, and financial market services. The Bank of New York is an important lender to major U.S. and multinational corporations and is the leading retail bank in suburban New York. The bank is also the largest provider of securities-processing services to the market and a respected trust and investment manager.

The Bank of New York hires master's degree graduates with a concentration in finance, strong writing skills, and one to three years of previous financial analysis experience for corporate banking associate positions and corporate credit analyst positions. As an associate, new hires work closely in support of the more experienced corporate finance professionals. In addition to financial modeling and credit analysis, associates participate in all aspects of business development and relationship management. They work closely with and gain knowledge of key product groups throughout the bank, including loan syndications, capital markets, securities processing, and cash management. Analysts work with relationship managers, senior credit analysts, and loan syndicators to analyze and structure credit transactions.

> The Bank of New York
> 13th Floor
> One Wall Street
> New York, NY 10286
> Tel.: (212) 635-7717
> www.bankofny.com

Banque Indosuez

Banque Indosuez is the wholly owned subsidiary of Compagnie de Suez, one of Europe's largest financial holding groups. The bank was responsible for the construction of the Suez Canal during the last century and accordingly takes its name from the canal. The bank is international in its scope. Its head office is in Paris, and it has branches and affiliates in sixty-five countries around the world, including all the major financial centers. As a major international merchant bank employing more than 12,000 people in sixty-five countries, Banque Indosuez offers an extensive range of financial services worldwide, with particular emphasis on Europe, the United States, and Asia. The bank primarily serves large corporations, institutional investors, and individuals with substantial funds.

> Banque Indosuez
> 1211 Avenue of the Americas
> New York, NY 10036
> Tel.: (212) 278-2000

Barclays Capital

Headquartered in London, Barclays Capital is the investment banking division of Barclays Bank PLC, with a $518 billion balance sheet, capital resources of more than $36 billion, and an AA credit rating.

Globally, Barclays Capital has approximately 5,700 employees and offices in 34 cities. Barclays Capital looks for talented graduates who can contribute to the success of their fast-growing business. They recruit candidates at all degree levels (M.B.A., doctoral, master's, and undergraduate) for positions within the following areas: collateralized financing, global markets, global financing, technology, operations, human resources, and finance. Depending upon the area, the graduate program duration can last from sixteen months (front office) to two and a half years (back office). Barclays Capital is an equal opportunity employer with positions available in the New York, London, and Asia offices.

For more information on the graduate program, please visit www.barcap.com/graduatecareers.

Barclays Capital
Corporate Headquarters
5 The North Colonnade
Canary Wharf
London E14 4BB
United Kingdom
Tel.: (44) (0) 20-7623-2323

Barclay's Capital
222 Broadway
New York, NY 10038
Tel.: (212) 412-4000
Fax: (212) 412-7300
www.barcap.com

Brown Brothers Harriman & Co.

Founded in 1818, the investment firm Brown Brothers Harriman & Co. serves its clients as corporate bankers, portfolio managers, securities brokers and custodians, as well as mergers and acquisitions advisers through offices in London, Dublin, Hong Kong, Luxembourg, Tokyo, and Zurich. From their base in New York, account managers in international private banking market the firm's banking and investment service to investors in Europe, Latin America, the Middle East, and the Far East.

Brown Brothers Harriman & Co. has a management training program. Graduates are placed in various domestic and international banking and investment departments. B.A., M.A., and M.B.A. degree recipients are accepted for the training program. Following the training program, trainees are assigned to account manager positions in New York or locations abroad. Candidates for overseas assignments must have appropriate language skills and meet residency requirements.

Additional information about Brown Brothers Harriman & Co. can be obtained by accessing the "Career Opportunities" section of their website at www.bbh.com. Resumés also can be forwarded through the website. Resumés sent through the mail should be addressed to

> Brown Brothers Harriman & Co.
> 59 Wall Street
> New York, NY 10005
> Attn: Human Resources Division

Citigroup

Citigroup offers individual and corporate customers a range of quality products and services. As a result, it is able to provide its employees with a breadth of career opportunities.

The creation of Citigroup in 1998 brought together two large companies: Citicorp and Travelers. It is now the most profitable financial services company in the world, with some 100 million customers in more than 100 countries.

Citigroup is a company for people who have a sense of urgency and excitement; who are candid, insightful, and creative; and who thrive in an environment of change, challenge, and competition. Citigroup is composed of four distinct business divisions:

- Corporate and Investment Bank
- Consumer Businesses
- Emerging Markets
- Global Investment Management and Private Banking Group

In almost all of its businesses, Citigroup offers structured programs for professionals joining the banking and insurance businesses. These programs combine on-the-job experience with training modules and other learning tools and are intended to prepare participants for future leadership positions in the organization. In the first years at Citigroup, a new hire would typically be offered two to three rotational assignments in order to develop a broad understanding of a business field or specialty. Many programs include an overseas assignment. During this stage, recruits are called management associates.

For more information, please visit the careers section at www.citigroup.com/newgrads.

> Citigroup
> 399 Park Avenue
> New York, NY 10043
> www.careers.citigroup.com

Credit Suisse First Boston

Founded in 1856 in Zurich, Credit Suisse was the oldest of the three big Swiss banks. As Credit Suisse First Boston, the bank is one of the world's largest securities firms. Operating in nearly ninety locations in thirty-seven countries on six continents worldwide, Credit Suisse First Boston has a presence in all major financial centers, leading industrial nations, and markets with high growth potential. Its businesses include sales and trading, investment banking, venture capital, brokerage services, private equity, financial advising, and securities underwriting. Its clients include businesses, governments, and wealthy individuals.

Candidates for positions with Credit Suisse First Boston should be quick, energetic, flexible, team-oriented, and enthusiastic self-starters with strong communication, quantitative, computer, and problem-solving skills along with a desire to succeed. Graduate students finishing M.B.A.s or other postgraduate programs can apply for associate positions within investment banking, fixed income, equity, and private client services as well as analyst positions within equity research. Undergraduates can apply for analyst positions within investment banking, equity, and fixed income and for associate positions within equity research and information technology.

Credit Suisse First Boston Headquarters
11 Madison Avenue
New York, NY 10010
Tel.: (212) 325-2000
www.csfb.com

Deutsche Bank

Deutsche Bank, the largest bank in Germany, is one of the leading banking institutions in the world. Through its extensive network of domestic and foreign branches and subsidiaries, the bank provides a broad range of financial services, including retail and corporate lending; project finance; trade finance; leasing; foreign exchange trading; primary securities issuance; secondary market trading; corporate finance; mergers and acquisitions advice; asset management; derivatives; and real estate, financial, and economic research.

Deutsche Bank employs nearly 100,000 people worldwide and serves more than 12 million people in more than seventy countries. A great emphasis is placed on promotion from within the bank. Candidates for positions with Deutsche Bank should have an M.B.A. or a master's degree in international affairs or a related discipline, proficiency in German, and be willing to relocate internationally. Previous experience in financial services is preferred.

University Relations
Deutsche Bank
31 West 52nd Street
New York, NY 10019
Tel.: (212) 469-8000
http://group.deutsche-bank.de/ghp/index_e.htm

Dresdner Bank

Headquartered in Germany, Dresdner Bank is one of the world's major banks. U.S. branches of Dresdner North America are located in New York City, Chicago, and Los Angeles. Since Dresdner does not have a formal credit training program, all applicants must have knowledge of finance and fluency in German. Those who possess a bachelor's of business administration are most frequently hired. The bank's training program covers organizations, operations, international banking, and credit training at a money center bank.

Opportunities for American nationals are almost exclusively with the bank's American branches. U.S. citizens may apply, however, to any other office provided they are able to obtain all necessary work permits.

Human Resources Department
Dresdner Bank AG
75 Wall Street
New York, NY 10005-2889
Tel.: (212) 429-2100
Fax: (212) 429-2127
www.dresdner-bank.com

GE Capital Services

With assets of more than $370 billion, GE Capital is a global diversified financial services company grouped into six key operating segments comprised of twenty-four businesses. A wholly owned subsidiary of General Electric Co., GE Capital, based in Stamford, Connecticut, provides a variety of consumer services—such as credit cards, life and auto insurance, mid-market financing, specialized financing, specialty insurance, equipment management, and specialized services—to businesses and individuals in forty-seven countries around the world. GE is a diversified services, technology, and manufacturing company with operations worldwide.

The Global Leadership Development Program (GLDP) is a twelve- to eighteen-month training program created to prepare talented individuals for global careers in GE Capital. It combines real-world work in a global GE Capital business with advanced training in business practices and leadership. Following successful completion, GLDP graduates will have the opportunity to take on a substantial leadership role within their placement country or region. Depending on business needs, opportunities may include general management or senior functional leadership positions.

GE Capital limits recruiting for the program to select U.S. and international business schools and consortiums. Based on anticipated staffing needs, each participating GE Capital business determines the number of GLDP members it will require to meet its global market growth objectives. By design, generally twenty-five members are chosen for each GLDP class.

Requirements for the GLDP program are an M.B.A. with superior academic performance; a minimum of three to five years of relevant work experience outside the United States, preferably in financial services; persuasive communication skills and demonstrated leadership abilities; fluency in business English, as well as the language of the placement country; and current citizenship and/or permanent work eligibility for the country of hire.

GE Capital Services
Corporate Human Resources
260 Long Ridge Road
Stamford, CT 06927-9300
Tel.: (203) 961-2468, 961-2952
www.gecapitalcareers.com

Goldman Sachs

Goldman Sachs is a leading international investment banking and securities firm, providing a full range of investment and financing services to corporations, governments, institutions, and individuals worldwide. Areas of work in this firm include debt and equity trading and underwriting, merger and acquisition advice, privatizations, currencies, commodities, bank loans, corporate banking, asset management, and fundamental and quantitative research.

Founded in 1869, Goldman Sachs is among the oldest and largest of the U.S.-based international investment banks. The firm is headquartered in New York and has forty-one offices throughout the world. The firm seeks to hire a diverse group of individuals with different skills and professional orientations. It values a team approach, creativity, high ethical standards, and a willingness to work hard.

Each year, Goldman Sachs hires individuals from leading universities and graduate schools to work as professionals in a wide range of positions in various geographic locations. Although the firm's needs vary each recruiting season, it hired approximately 550 new M.B.A. graduates and 1,100 undergraduates on a worldwide basis in the 1999–2000 recruiting season.

> Goldman Sachs
> 85 Broad Street
> New York, NY 10004
> Tel.: (212) 902-1000, (800) 323-5678
> www.gs.com

J. P. Morgan Chase & Company

J. P. Morgan Chase & Company is a leading global financial services firm with assets of $799 billion and operations in more than fifty countries. It serves more than 30 million individuals and the world's most prominent corporate, institutional, and government clients. The firm is a leader in investment banking, asset management, private banking, private equity, custody and transaction services, retail, and middle-market financial services. Its competitive advantages include scale in capital, clients, and products; leadership positions in numerous product and services areas; and an outstanding talent base.

Undergraduates and M.B.A.s can choose from a wide range of opportunities in corporate, wholesale financial services, and retail financial services.

For more information on opportunities, including qualifications, training, and assignments, please visit their website at http://careers.jpmorganchase.com.

> J. P. Morgan Chase & Company
> 270 Park Avenue
> New York, NY 10017
> www.jpmorganchase.com

Merrill Lynch

Merrill Lynch is a leading financial management and advisory company with a global network of offices and client assets of nearly

$2 trillion. The company offers a broad range of capabilities to serve the needs of both individual and institutional clients through its principal businesses.

As an investment bank, it is the top global underwriter and market maker of debt and equity securities and a leading strategic advisor to corporations, institutions, and governments worldwide.

Through Merrill Lynch Investment Managers, it is one of the world's largest managers of financial assets, with assets under management exceeding $500 billion.

For private banking customers, its platform of products and services provides access to a robust range of investing and wealth-building tools plus the personal guidance of financial advisors.

As a top-tier financial services firm, Merrill Lynch can offer a wide range of work experience and learning opportunities—opportunities that are constantly evolving and growing to stay ahead of the changing financial services landscape.

For more information on careers at Merrill Lynch, including contact information and recruiting schedules, please visit their website.

www.ml.com/careers

Morgan Stanley International

Morgan Stanley has earned a worldwide reputation for excellence in its financial advice and execution. Truly global, the firm is a market leader in Europe, Asia, and the Americas. Its 62,000 people represent more than 120 nationalities and speak ninety languages; they work in 600 offices in twenty-seven countries. Morgan Stanley's goal is to help individuals, institutions, and sovereign states realize their financial aspirations. To achieve this, it has built leadership positions in investment banking, asset management, credit services, debt and equity underwriting, research, sales and trading, and the provision of financial advice. In each business, it focuses on creating custom-tailored solutions that cut across functions to help clients discover and realize new business and financial opportunities.

Its success is measured by the satisfaction of its clients. It is also measured by the professional and personal achievements of employees and the long-term value they create for shareholders. It rests on shared values held throughout the firm: a common belief in the importance of integrity, excellence, entrepreneurial spirit, teamwork, and a respect for individuals and cultures around the world.

Morgan Stanley
Firmwide Recruiting
1221 Sixth Avenue, 44th Floor
New York, NY 10020
Fax: (212) 762-9242
www.morganstanley.com/careers/index.html

Salomon Smith Barney

A leading global financial firm with offices around the world, Salomon Smith Barney provides investment banking and asset management as well as brokerage services to clients that include individuals, governments, and corporations. Salomon Smith Barney is a subsidiary of Citigroup. Through its partnership with Citigroup, Salomon Smith Barney offers global job opportunities.

Candidates for positions with Salomon Smith Barney should possess a university degree with high academic standing.

Salomon Smith Barney
388 Greenwich Street
New York, NY 10013
www.salomonsmithbarney.com

Standard & Poor's

Standard & Poor's Rating Group (S&P), part of the McGraw-Hill Companies and based in New York with fifteen offices in twelve countries, is one of the world's leading financial rating agencies. S&P's points of financial focus range from public finance to derivative securities, from the asset-backed bonds of structured finance issues to insurance company stability or mutual fund volatility. S&P does not engage in trading or underwriting activities. S&P analysts interact with the world's leading financial intermediaries, banks, corporations, governments, and other capital market participants. They visit the institutions they analyze. For example, they inspect the real estate used as collateral for mortgage-backed bonds and meet with government leaders. S&P analysts work closely in teams that encourage collaborative efforts to arrive at a quality rating.

Candidates for positions with S&P should be energetic team players with a demonstrated record of academic achievement—usually in fields such as business, finance, economics, or mathematics—and possess strong analytical capabilities.

Standard & Poor's
55 Water Street
New York, NY 10041
Tel.: (212) 438-2000
www.standardandpoors.com

Standard Chartered Bank

Standard Chartered Bank (SCB) is an international banking group founded in 1853 and headquartered in London and is now the leading emerging markets bank. The bank employs 30,000 people in more than 500 offices in more than fifty countries in the Asian Pacific region, South Asia, the Middle East, Africa, United Kingdom, and the Americas.

The firm's strategy is to build and grow its strong businesses in East and Southeast Asia, enhance its historical position in the Middle East and South Asia, and develop its African businesses in a focused way. SCB concentrates its operations in the Organization for Economic Cooperation and Development (OECD) countries on those activities that support its franchise in newly industrialized and developing markets.

SCB hires undergraduate and graduate students in a variety of disciplines to work in consumer banking, corporate and institutional banking, global markets, risk management, and other areas. Applying to the bank is a multistep process that involves psychometric testing, numerical testing, and an interview.

Standard Chartered Bank
1 Evertrust Plaza
Jersey City, NJ 07302
Tel.: (201) 633-3400
www.standardchartered.com

Wells Fargo Bank

Wells Fargo has provided a variety of financial services since 1852. With operations across the western half of the United States and more than 660 branches, it is particularly strong in the retail and business banking sector. Its operations are primarily domestic, but it does provide financial products and services to meet the international banking needs of the bank's domestic customers.

Competition for employment with Wells Fargo is high. Although most positions dealing with international matters are filled by those with previous experience in international or commercial banking, some entry-level professional positions do exist. Wells Fargo also offers summer internships and development and training programs lasting a year to eighteen months. Bachelor's and master's degree candidates should have a solid grounding in finance, accounting, economics, or international relations.

University Relations
Wells Fargo Bank
475 Sansome Street
San Francisco, CA 94163
Tel.: (415) 477-1000
www.wellsfargo.com

Chapter 7

BUSINESS

Careers in Business

LUIS A. VIADA

Events over the last few years have dramatized the fact that the post–Cold War issues of national security and the global economic order are far from resolved. Add to this the continuing quiet revolution of the Internet and new technologies gnawing away at the foundations of traditional business models, and you have a landscape that is causing global businesses to make fundamental reassessments of their accepted thinking on risk, asset deployment, target market definitions, and terms of competition. Not surprisingly there is a resurgence of interest in the state of management preparedness for leadership in this rapidly evolving global environment.

In a recent issue of *Strategy & Business,* Jeff Garten, the dean of the Yale University business school and former undersecretary of commerce for international trade, cites the demands on the corporate CEO in a global context of military and ideological confrontation. To respond to these challenges, Mr. Garten calls for American corporations to revise their strategy, leadership development, and management training, highlighting the following:

> *Schools and businesses must focus on producing* broad-gauged leaders *who can run companies that are profitable and progressive agents of change. . . . Undergraduate and graduate schools must train business leaders who can* understand geopolitics as well as finance and marketing (emphasis mine; Booz-Allen publication, [first quarter 2002]: 27).

Luis A. Viada, a 1976 graduate of the Master of Science in Foreign Service program, is managing director of Global Development for the McGraw-Hill Companies. Prior to his current position, he was director of emerging markets for Standard & Poor's. He began his career at Citibank, where he held corporate banking positions in Asia, Latin America, and the Middle East. Mr. Viada received his undergraduate degree from Tufts University, majoring in political science, and later served three years in the Army Security Agency.

The Evolving Role of the International Manager

Garten's observations suggest that graduates from programs such as the Master's of Science in Foreign Service program will be in greater demand by international companies than had been the case in the more recent past. My observation has been that for all their talk of globalization over the last ten to fifteen years, companies have, in fact, unintentionally rolled back the clock in terms of their development of global managers. In the 1960s and 1970s, a period of very aggressive international expansion for U.S. corporations, companies made a point of developing expatriate managers that were sent on foreign assignments early in their careers.

The intention was to create a cadre of managers that could be deployed at a moment's notice to develop new markets or take over troubled overseas operations. Your success in these companies often depended on the extent and quality of your overseas management experience. Another part of the equation was that it was relatively hard to find managers with the appropriate academic and multinational business qualifications in many of the countries in which U.S. companies opened shop. Thus, the backbone of the overseas management team was U.S. expatriate staff.

This began to change by the mid-1980s. A new generation of U.S.- and European-educated managers was emerging that could now move into the senior-most positions in their respective countries. Not only did these new managers offer the advantage of a profound understanding of their home markets, they were significantly less expensive than the average senior expatriate. As a result, the number of expatriate assignments declined rapidly so that by the mid-1990s, only a select number (and usually quite senior) of international positions were available.

> Companies are now coming to the realization that their senior ranks are populated by managers who have had little if any international experience. We can expect changes not only in how corporate career development is managed, but also in recruitment guidelines. This bodes well for graduates of professional schools of international affairs.

Companies are now coming to the realization that their senior ranks are populated by managers who have had little if any international experience. We can expect changes not only in how corporate career development is managed, but also in recruitment guidelines.

As I suggested previously, this bodes well for graduates of professional schools of international affairs.

The Making of the New Global Manager

Numerous studies have examined what combination of personal qualities, skills, and experiences make for a successful global manager. One consistent yet elusive quality cited in these studies is the notion of a "global mind-set." It is a mix of intellectual and behavioral qualities that enables the individual to understand and operate a business in vastly different cultural and environmental contexts. This mind-set is seen as a defining characteristic of top global executives that sets them apart from their domestic counterparts. In their recent book, *Developing Global Executives,* Morgan W. McCall and George P. Hollenbeck made the following observation:

> *We believe that this mind set comes not from home-country leadership challenges, but rather from experiences in other cultures. To reach this level of understanding, executives should be fluent in at least one language other than their own and need to live and work in at least one, and probably two, other cultures* ([Harvard Business School Press, 2002]).

This brings us to the choice between a job that is home country–based with an international focus and one that is foreign-based. Graduates of professional international affairs programs may of course compete effectively with M.B.A.s and other entry-level graduates for the former, but they have a comparative advantage in the latter.

The academic preparation in economics and political science together with the language and cultural perspective that the typical international affairs graduate brings to the equation make them ideally equipped for taking on challenging international assignments in a way that the typical business school graduate does not. Keep in mind that the more a job requires working in a foreign environment, the more you can leverage the unique aspects of your international affairs studies and any prior international working or living experience you may have had.

The Job Search

Some of you will face the last semester of your education serenely, with a clear sense of what you want to do and armed with a short list of companies that you want to approach, perhaps even with a standing offer from one as a result of a stunning summer internship experience. For the rest of us mere mortals there is/was tremendous anxiety. Besides the psychological (and economic) need to have a job when you leave school, one is often plagued with the fear that your first job will somehow define irreversibly the direction of your career. Although it is certainly important that you find an opportunity that will provide you with a meaningful learning experience, you will do much better if you look forward to your international career as a multidimensional body of work, or portfolio of experiences, as opposed to a linear evolution of one particular job or job family.

In my case, I had no intention of going into the private sector. My interest was development economics. I was thinking in terms of the World Bank or the UN Development Program. I heard that the money center banks were interviewing on campus so I signed up. I liked what I heard (particularly the international living component), and nine months later I was on my way to Citibank's Tegucigalpa, Honduras, branch as a trainee. Sixteen years later I had lived in seven different countries with assignments that ranged from setting up business in China to running the regional training center in Asia and managing the corporate banking business in Turkey. An executive search firm then recruited me for Standard & Poor's, where I helped develop their emerging markets strategy and set up their Latin American operations. I'm now in charge of global development for S&P's parent company, McGraw-Hill. There is no way I would have imagined that career path twenty-five years ago!

Given the current economic environment and the corresponding scale-back of entry-level jobs, it makes even more sense to keep your options open and develop an entry strategy that also includes non-international jobs that provide you with key business competencies. It is worth keeping in mind that no matter how appealing your internationalist credentials might be, companies are looking first and foremost for individuals that can bring a specific business talent to the job. To the extent that you can build your credentials in areas such as marketing, sales, or business development, you will be in a much stronger position to bid for international jobs.

In your search for opportunities I would suggest that you think not only in terms of companies that have international operations but also in terms of fields that could have an international component such as advertising, investor relations, marketing, purchasing and, yes, e-business. No matter what may have happened to the stock performance of the "dot-coms," the evolution toward online delivery of products and services and other unconventional media is moving forward inexorably. E-business is by definition a global business. These companies are always looking for talented, technology-savvy individuals who can operate effectively under pressure, uncertainty, and in less structured work environments.

Last Thoughts

Make no mistake, you need to feel passionately about business as you would any other field of endeavor if you hope to be successful and have fun in the process. Even if you have taken basic business courses such as accounting and finance, there is a whole body of understanding about decision making and how businesses operate that you will have to learn on your own initiative—skills and understanding that your M.B.A. brethren were fed intravenously for two years! You have to be interested in business in the first place.

I have found individuals who have taken the business route for all the wrong reasons and have been miserable. The international living or compensation aspects of the job will not be enough to sustain either your interest or your performance. If you're not sure if business is the right direction for you, by all means go for a summer internship in business and try it out. Another approach is to pursue the business option but focus your search on those companies or job types that you think would provide a valuable experience even if you decide to shift to the public or nonprofit sector. Again, if you take a "portfolio" approach to your career, you are unlikely to make bad choices, only different ones.

There are few careers more exciting or challenging than those in international business, and given the multidisciplinary thinking bias of most professional international affairs graduates, international business can feel very much like "coming home."

Resource Listings

Asea Brown Boveri

Asea Brown Boveri (ABB) is a $23 billion global technology company headquartered in Zurich, Switzerland. The company is a global leader in power and automation technologies that enable utility and industry customers to improve performance while lowering environmental impact. Having helped countries all over the world to build, develop, and maintain their infrastructures, ABB has in recent years shifted from large-scale solutions to alternative energy and the advanced products in power and automation technologies. ABB fulfills its commitment to sustainable development by developing and supplying eco-efficient products and systems, sharing state-of-the-art technologies with emerging markets, contributing to common efforts, and continuously improving its own sustainability performance.

ABB has approximately 157,000 employees in more than 100 countries and is a global technology company with many diverse career opportunities around the world. The company aims to provide its employees with the opportunity to use and expand their skills, knowledge, and creative potential both for their own benefit and for that of the company. ABB encourages personal initiative and entrepreneurial behavior and seeks to offer challenging and rewarding work environments.

ABB Group Headquarters
Affolternstr. 44
P.O. Box 8131
CH-8050
Zurich, Switzerland
Tel.: (41) 1-317-7111
Fax: (41) 1-317-7958
www.abb.com

ABB USA
501 Merritt 7
P.O. Box 5308
Norwalk, CT 06856-5308
Tel.: (203) 750-2200
Fax: (203) 750-2263
www.abb.com/us

American International Group, Inc.

American International Group (AIG) is the world's leading U.S.-based international insurance and financial services organization, the largest underwriter of commercial and industrial insurance in the United States, and the second-largest life insurer. Its member companies write a wide range of general insurance and life insurance products for commercial, institutional, and individual customers through a variety of distribution channels in approximately 130 countries and jurisdictions throughout the world. AIG's global businesses also include financial services and asset management, including aircraft leasing, financial products, trading and market-making, consumer finance, institutional, retail and direct investment fund asset management, real estate investment management, and retirement savings products. AIG's common stock is listed on the New York Stock Exchange, as well as the stock exchanges in London, Paris, Switzerland, and Tokyo.

The company employs more than 30,000 employees worldwide. It seeks students who have an interest in international business and who are willing to tackle the problems associated with today's changing environment. Between fifteen and thirty trainees are hired each year.

>   Manager, College Relations
>   American International Group, Inc.
>   72 Wall Street, 6th floor
>   New York, NY 10270
>   Tel: (212) 770-7000
>   www.aig.com/college/

BP Amoco

BP is one of the world's largest petroleum and petrochemicals companies, comprising 140 individual business units. Their main activities are exploration and production, refining, marketing, supply, and transportation of crude oil and natural gas and manufacturing and marketing of petrochemicals. They have a growing activity in power generation using natural gas and in solar-power generation. BP has well-established operations in Europe, North and South America, Australasia, and Africa. BP people are working in more than 100 countries on six continents.

One enduring characteristic of the oil industry has been change. As a company with a long history in oil and natural gas, petrochemicals, and more recently in renewable and alternative energy technologies, BP has learned to be responsive to change and indeed to be at the forefront of the process of change.

>   BP - New York
>   535 Madison Avenue
>   New York, NY 10022-4212
>   Tel.: (212) 421-5010
>   Fax: (212) 421-5084
>   http://bpfutures.com/index.asp

Brunswick Corporation

Brunswick Corporation is the world's leading manufacturer and marketer of pleasure boats, marine engines, fitness equipment, bowling equipment and consumer products, and billiards tables. Brunswick products are sold throughout North America, the United Kingdom, South America, Europe, Asia, and Australia. Brunswick brands include Mercury and Mariner outboard engines; Mercury MerCruiser sterndrives and inboard engines; Sea Ray, Bayliner, Maxum, Hatteras, and Sealine pleasure boats; Baja high-performance boats; Boston Whaler and Trophy offshore fishing boats; Princecraft fishing, deck, and pontoon boats; Life Fitness, Hammer Strength and ParaBody fitness equipment; and Brunswick bowling centers, equipment, and consumer products.

Brunswick Corporation has a growing international presence and has opportunities for both U.S. citizens and foreign nationals throughout its operations. Candidates for these international operations are encouraged to apply for internships that afford international affairs students substantive exposure to that area of the company's operations.

> Brunswick Corporation
> 1 North Field Court
> Lake Forest, IL 60045
> Tel.: (847) 735-4700
> Fax: (847) 735-4765
> www.brunswick.com

C. Itoh & Company

C. Itoh & Co. (America) Inc. is a diversified multibusiness corporation with global capabilities serving more than 5,000 major clients. Established in 1858 as a textile wholesaling concern, C. Itoh has evolved into a broad-based international organization. Their eleven operating groups handle more than 50,000 products and commodities from textiles to machinery, electronics, chemicals, metals, produce, energy, and general merchandise. C. Itoh America's research, management, financial, and technical skills have been servicing industry and commerce in the United States for more than thirty years. Specialists throughout the United States work with the worldwide resources of the parent company, C. Itoh & Co. Ltd. New business is generated for American and foreign clients by developing new markets and processes, coordinating the movement of resources through distribution channels, managing domestic and international business projects, and investing in and guiding joint ventures. As the flagship subsidiary of a leading Japanese "sogo shosha" (general trading company), C. Itoh America offers the business community broad access to world trade.

> Human Resources
> C. Itoh & Co. (America) Inc.
> 335 Madison Avenue
> New York, NY 10017

ChevronTexaco

ChevronTexaco is one of the world's largest integrated oil companies. Its worldwide operations comprise several major activities: exploration, production, refining, marketing, transportation, and research. Offices and operating facilities are maintained at various locations throughout the world. The largest employee centers are in Texas, New York, Louisiana, and California.

Career opportunities with ChevronTexaco are primarily in the fields of engineering (chemical, petroleum, mechanical, electrical, civil, and metallurgical), geology, geophysics, computer science, accounting, chemistry, mathematics, physics, liberal arts, business administration, marketing, and petroleum land management. ChevronTexaco also has high-potential opportunities in a number of specialized areas such as law, economics, finance, employee relations, and public relations.

Although ChevronTexaco's operations are worldwide, new recruits usually are assigned to domestic locations, at least for the first several years. ChevronTexaco and its subsidiaries and affiliates abroad are staffed largely by nationals of the countries where they operate. Opportunities for overseas assignments at the entry level do not occur often, since most assignments call for highly experienced people in specialized fields such as geology, geophysics, engineering, accounting, or marketing. Fluency in a foreign language, especially French, Italian, German, Spanish, or Portuguese, is often a requirement for overseas assignments.

> ChevronTexaco Corporation
> 575 Market Street
> San Francisco, CA 94105
> Tel.: (415) 894-7700
> www.chevrontexaco.com/about/careers/

Coca-Cola

The Coca-Cola Company, founded in 1886, is the world's leading manufacturer, marketer, and distributor of nonalcoholic beverage concentrates and syrups used to produce more than 230 beverage brands. Their corporate headquarters are in Atlanta, Georgia, with local operations in nearly 200 countries around the world. The Coca-Cola brand is one of the most recognized trademarks in the world, but their other local and global brands continue to contribute to its success.

Over the past century, Coca-Cola's people have led its success by living and working with a consistent set of ideals. Although the world and business will continue to change rapidly, Coca-Cola believes that respecting these ideals will continue to be essential to its long-term success. The Coca-Cola work environment combines the fast-paced, creative atmosphere of an emerging company with all the strength and support of a company that has been around for more than 100 years.

At this time the Coca-Cola Company is only accepting resumés via e-mail at careers@na.ko.com.

The Coca-Cola Company
P.O. Box 1734
Atlanta, GA 30301
www.coca-colacareers.com/

DaimlerChrysler

DaimlerChrysler is one of the world's leading automotive, transportation, and services companies. Its passenger car brands include Maybach, Mercedes-Benz, Chrysler, Jeep, Dodge, and Smart. Commercial vehicles are produced under the Mercedes-Benz, Freightliner, Sterling, Western Star, Setra, Thomas Built Buses, Orion, and American LaFrance brands. It offers financial and other services through DaimlerChrysler Services. With 372,500 employees, DaimlerChrysler achieved revenues of EUR 152.9 billion (U.S.$136.1 billion) in 2001.

DaimlerChrysler today has a global workforce, a global shareholder base, a global brand awareness, and a global outlook. With around 416,000 employees worldwide, DaimlerChrysler is one of the biggest employers in the world. Aware that technological progress and commercial success are the result of the skills and motivation of its employees, DaimlerChrysler is extremely committed to continually improving training and furthering education for its staff and to recruiting skilled trainees.

DaimlerChrysler
CIMS 485-01-991000 Chrysler Drive
Auburn Hills, MI 48326-2766
http://company.occ.com/chrysler/

Dell Computer Corporation

Headquartered in Austin, Texas, Dell is the world's most preferred computer systems company, and a premier provider of products and services required for customers worldwide to build their information-technology and Internet infrastructures. The company employs approximately 34,600 team members around the globe.

Dell was founded in 1984 by Michael Dell, the computer industry's longest tenured chief executive officer, on a simple concept: that by selling computer systems directly to customers, Dell could best understand their needs and efficiently provide the most effective computing solutions to meet those needs. This direct business model eliminates retailers that add unnecessary time and cost or can diminish Dell's understanding of customer expectations.

Dell Computer Corporation
RR1 Box 50
One Dell Way
Round Rock, TX 78682
Fax: (800) 816-4643
http://ausoladrpjap1.us.dell.com/careers/students/
index.asp

DuPont

Headquartered in Wilmington, Delaware, DuPont is a research- and technology-based global chemistry and energy company offering high-performance products in chemicals, polymers, fibers, and petroleum. Founded in 1802 to manufacture black powder, the company is today one of the largest and most diversified industrial corporations in the world. With more than 110,000 employees and 200 manufacturing and processing plants in more than forty countries on six continents, more than 50 percent of its $40 billion in annual sales is outside the United States. DuPont serves worldwide markets in the aerospace, apparel, automotive, agriculture, construction, packaging, refining, and transportation industries.

DuPont promotes almost exclusively from within, and most employees start in entry-level positions. Most DuPont managers are transferred outside the Wilmington headquarters. DuPont has an extensive college recruiting program for entry-level engineers and computer and financial systems people in the United States.

DuPont Human Resources
Nemours Building
1007 Market Street
Wilmington, DE 19898
Tel.: (800) 774-2271
Fax: (800) 631-2206
www.dupont.com

Eastman Kodak

Through the years, Eastman Kodak has led the way with an abundance of new products and processes that have made photography simpler, more useful, and more enjoyable. Today, its work increasingly involves digital technology, combining the power and convenience of electronics with the quality of traditional photography to produce systems that bring levels of utility and fun to the taking, making, and utilization of images.

Eastman Kodak is a worldwide enterprise of more than 76,000 employees with operations in more than thirty countries.

Eastman Kodak Company
343 State Street
Rochester, NY 14650
www.kodak.com

Eli Lilly & Company

Eli Lilly, a leader in the pharmaceutical industry, is developing a growing portfolio of best-in-class pharmaceutical products by applying the latest research from its worldwide laboratories and from collaborations with eminent scientific organizations. The company provides answers for often complex, difficult health problems in two ways: through the discovery and development of breakthrough medicines and through the health information they offer.

Lilly is also strengthening its ability to identify high-potential drug candidates by improving its research and development processes, investing in new research technologies, and expanding its research team. Lilly is seeking answers for some of the world's most urgent medical needs.

The company employs more than 41,000 people worldwide and markets its medicines in 159 countries. Lilly has major research and development facilities in nine countries and conducts clinical trials in more than thirty countries. Right now, Lilly is looking for dynamic, hard-working people who are driven to discover answers to the most pressing unmet medical needs facing our world today.

Lilly Corporate Center
Indianapolis, IN 46285
Tel.: (317) 276-2000
www.lilly.com/careers/index.html

Ford Motor Company

Ford Motor Company is a family of consumer-focused vehicle and service brands. Vehicle brands include not only Ford but Mazda, Mercury, and the Premier Automotive Group: Aston Martin, Jaguar, Land Rover, Lincoln, and Volvo. Service brands include Ford Credit, Hertz, Kwik-Fit, and QualityCare. In addition to Ford brands, the company operates three distinct businesses, Automotive Operations, Ford Financial, and Hertz. Automotive Operations sells and services vehicles through well-known brands such as Ford, Jaguar, and QualityCare. Ford Financial is the world's largest finance company dedicated to serving the automotive industry. Hertz is the world's first and largest car rental organization.

As a global company, Ford manufactures and sells vehicles all over the world and has career opportunities in many countries. Hiring at Ford Motor Company is a two-step process designed to be quick yet thorough as well as personal. The first phase is initial recruiting, a review and assessment of your credentials, experience, and background. The second phase is a more in-depth interaction with Ford Motor Company at a leadership conference. Conferences are expenses-paid events at a Ford facility. If you're invited to a conference, you'll know you've made the first cut. Then, based on your performance during the conference, Ford managers will make a hiring decision. Resumés are only accepted online. For more information, visit http://www.mycareer.ford.com/main.asp. If you do not find the answers to all of your questions there, contact Ford at 1-800-300-7222 or via e-mail: hireinfo@ford.com.

Ford Motor Company
1 American Road
Dearborn, MI 48121

Gateway

Founded in 1985, Gateway has grown from a two-person startup in an Iowa farmhouse to a multibillion, Fortune 500 company that employs 12,000 people. Chairman and CEO Ted Waitt started Gateway on his family's cattle farm and took it public in December 1993 (NYSE: GTW). The company, which is headquartered in Poway, California, operates sales and technical support centers throughout the United States. Gateway was a pioneer in the build-to-order PC business. It has since expanded to offer a broad range of peripherals, accessories, software products, and related services such as training, financing, high-speed Internet access, and networking solutions for home and business.

Corporate Headquarters Gateway Inc.
610 Gateway Drive North
Sioux City, SD 57049-2000
http://jobs.gateway.com/search.asp

General Electric

General Electric (GE) is a diversified services, technology, and manufacturing company with a commitment to achieving customer success and worldwide leadership in each of its businesses. GE operates in more than 100 countries and employs 313,000 people worldwide. The company traces its beginnings to Thomas A. Edison, who established Edison Electric Light Company in 1878. In 1892, a merger of Edison General Electric Company and Thomson-Houston Electric Company created General Electric Company. GE is the only company listed in the Dow Jones Industrial Index today that was also included in the original index in 1896. In recent years, GE has moved from a focus on heavy industry to a strong emphasis on services and high technology.

GE is constantly seeking innovative minds to keep its businesses on the leading edge of their respective fields. GE thrives by sharing information across borders and across businesses in working environments that foster open, fluid communications. Another part of the attraction of a GE career is the opportunity for lifelong learning. The company invests nearly $1 billion a year in career development for its employees—both on the job and through leadership programs.

General Electric Company
Corporate Headquarters
Fairfield, CT 06431
Tel.: (203) 373-2211
www.gecareers.com/index.cfm

General Mills

General Mills is a major marketer of consumer foods and a leader in the full-service dinner house restaurant business. Headquartered in Minneapolis, Minnesota, the company is one of the largest corporations in the United States, with more than 97,000 employees and operations in almost every state. The company has about sixty Red Lobster restaurants in Japan and is involved in the cookie and confection business in Western Europe. Cereal Partners Worldwide, the company's joint venture with Nestlé Foods to produce and market General Mills in Europe, Latin America, and the ASEAN markets of the southwestern Pacific, is the world's number 2 cereal company outside North America.

Career opportunities for B.A.s and M.B.A.s exist in marketing, marketing research, finance, human resources, manufacturing, engineering, strategic planning, and analysis.

> Director, Recruitment & College Relations
> General Mills
> P.O. Box 1113
> Minneapolis, MN 55440
> Tel.: (612) 540-2311
> www.generalmills.com/careerOpportunities/

General Motors

General Motors (NYSE: GM), the world's largest vehicle manufacturer, designs, builds, and markets cars and trucks worldwide. Founded in 1908, GM has manufacturing operations in more than 30 countries and its vehicles are sold in about 200 countries. GM's major markets are North America, Europe, Asia-Pacific, Latin America, Africa, and the Middle East. It employs about 362,000 people globally. GM has been the world's automotive sales leader since 1931. In 2001, GM earned $1.5 billion on sales of $177.3 billion. GM sold more than 8.5 million cars and trucks—15.1 percent of the world vehicle market. GM also operates one of the world's largest and most successful financial services companies, GMAC, which offers automotive, mortgage, and business financing and insurance services to customers worldwide.

GM cars and trucks are sold under the following brands: Chevrolet, Pontiac, Buick, Oldsmobile, Cadillac, GMC, Saturn, Hummer, Saab, Opel, Vauxhall, and Holden. GM parts and accessories are marketed under the GM, GM Goodwrench, and ACDelco brands through GM

Service Parts Operations. GM's OnStar is the industry leader in vehicle communications and information services. It provides more than 2 million subscribers with a variety of services, including personalized assistance, emergency aid, and voice-activated access to Internet-based information, including news, sports, weather, e-mail, and stock quotes.

GM's major subsidiaries are Hughes Electronics Corporation, GM Locomotive Group, and Allison Transmission Division. As part of its global growth strategy, the GM Group includes major alliances with Fiat Auto SpA, Fuji Heavy Industries Ltd., Isuzu Motors Ltd., and Suzuki Motor Corporation. GM also has strong technology collaborations with Toyota Motor Corporation and Honda Motor Company and vehicle ventures with Toyota and Renault SA.

GM is one of the largest employers in the United States. GM believes in investing in its employees. As a result, GM offers a variety of continuing education opportunities to further its employees' careers.

General Motors
Renaissance Center
P.O. Box 300
Detroit, MI 48265-3000
Tel.: (313) 556-5000
www.gm.com/company/careers/

GlaxoSmithKline

GlaxoSmithKline (GSK) is a world-leading research-based pharmaceutical company with a powerful combination of skills and resources that provides a platform for delivering strong growth in today's rapidly changing healthcare environment. Headquartered in the United Kingdom and with operations based in the United States, the new company is one of the industry leaders, with an estimated 7 percent of the world's pharmaceutical market. In 2001, GSK had sales of $29.5 billion and profit before tax of $8.8 billion.

The company also has a consumer healthcare division comprising over-the-counter medicines, oral care products, and nutritional healthcare drinks, all of which are among the market leaders.

GSK has more than 100,000 employees worldwide. Of these, more than 40,000 are in sales and marketing, the largest sales force in the industry. More than 42,000 employees work at 107 manufacturing sites in forty countries and more than 16,000 are in Research and Design (R&D). GSK R&D is based at twenty-four sites in seven countries.

With an R&D budget of about $4 billion, the company has a leading position in genomics/genetics and new drug discovery technologies.

GSK offers a competitive benefits package and recognizes the need for a healthy balance between work and family life.

> GlaxoSmithKline, Corporate Headquarters
> 1 Franklin Plaza
> P.O. Box 7929
> Philadelphia, PA 19101
> Tel. (888) 825-5249 (job line)
> www.gsk.com/careers/joinus.htm

Goodyear Tire & Rubber

Goodyear is the world's largest tire company. Together with its U.S. and international subsidiaries and joint ventures, Goodyear manufactures and markets tires for most applications. It also manufactures and sells several lines of power transmission belts, hose, and other rubber products for the transportation industry and various industrial and consumer markets, as well as rubber-related chemicals for various applications. Goodyear is the world's largest operator of commercial truck service and tire retreading centers. In addition, it operates more than 2,000 tire and auto service center outlets. Goodyear employs about 96,000 associates worldwide and manufactures its products in ninety-six facilities in twenty-eight countries. Founded in 1898, Goodyear measures sales in excess of $14 billion today.

New hires to Goodyear can expect challenging assignments in an environment that supports continuous learning. Employment may begin at the Akron corporate headquarters or any of the worldwide facilities.

> Goodyear Tire and Rubber
> Corporate Headquarters
> 1144 East Market Street
> Akron, OH 44316-0001
> www.goodyear.com/careers

Hakuhodo

Established in 1895, Hakuhodo is one of Japan's oldest marketing, advertising, and public relations agencies. Hakuhodo provides market research, media relations, strategy, and concept planning services. The company also sponsors the Hakuhodo Institute of Life and Living, which studies the consumption behavior and social orientation of the Japanese people by examining individuals' day-to-day thoughts and feelings, emotional and intellectual needs, aspirations, concerns, and worries through questionnaires and interviews.

Headquartered in Tokyo, the firm's office network spans forty-eight countries. Hakuhodo has about 3,500 employees worldwide. About forty people are employed in its U.S. offices in New York, Atlanta, and Los Angeles. U.S. hiring is handled through the New York office; other positions are filled through the Tokyo office.

Hakuhodo Advertising America
18th Floor
475 Park Avenue South
New York, NY 10016
Tel.: (212) 684-7000

Hakuhodo
22, Kanda-Nishikicho 3-chome
Chiyoda-ku
Tokyo 101
Japan
www.hakuhodo.co.jp/Jinji/e/index.html

Halliburton Company

Halliburton Company is a global energy services company that supports oil companies in locating, developing, extracting, and processing hydrocarbon resources. Halliburton's businesses are active in most global locations where hydrocarbons have the potential for extraction or processing.

Most professional positions are technical or business-related and require educational background in the sciences and/or business. Ten or fewer positions are available in the international relations area annually.

Halliburton Company
1150 18th Street, NW
Suite 200
Washington, DC 20036
www.halliburton.com

Hewlett-Packard

Founded in 1939, Hewlett-Packard (HP) is headquartered in Palo Alto, California. The company has 88,000 employees worldwide and more than 540 sales and support offices and distributorships in more than 120 countries. The company's growth has been generated by a strong commitment to research and development in electronics and computer technology. That growth has been accomplished by providing a rapid flow of new products and services to markets HP already serves and by expanding into new areas that build upon its existing technologies, competencies, and customer interests. In addition, the company actively pursues emerging opportunities in related fields that it is well positioned to serve.

HP services mission is to help customers transform their business and derive measurable business value from their IT investment. It achieves this by delivering comprehensive support to companies on a worldwide basis, ranging from desktop services to enterprise class consultancy and support. HP services offerings meet all computing environment and IT infrastructure needs through all stages of the life cycle.

Since the turn of the 21st century, HP has focused on three key areas of invention: intelligent, connected devices; an always-on Internet infrastructure; and applications that can be delivered over networks as e-services. The company's vision for the future technology landscape is service-centric computing in which information technologies are delivered, managed, and purchased as services.

In 2002, HP acquired Compaq Computer Corporation, a leading global provider of information technology products, services, and solutions for enterprise customers. Compaq designs, develops, manufactures, and markets information technology equipment, software, services, and solutions, including industry-leading enterprise storage and computing solutions, fault-tolerant business-critical solutions, communication products, personal desktop and notebook computers, and personal entertainment and Internet access devices.

Hewlett-Packard
3000 Hanover Street
Palo Alto, CA 94304-1185
Tel.: (650) 857-1501
Fax: (650) 857-5518
www.jobs.hp.com/

Honeywell

Honeywell has more than 115,000 employees in more than 100 countries. It's a Fortune 100 company with $24 billion in sales in 2001. Honeywell is involved in broad and diverse businesses, technology, and products. Honeywell aerospace products and transportation and power systems go into collision-avoidance and traffic-control systems, wing ice and wind shear sensors, autopilots, and landing systems. Honeywell's automation and control solutions keep homes and offices at just the right temperature. Honeywell chemicals for pharmaceuticals help safeguard health. Space-age fibers make body armor bullet-resistant.

Honeywell's often-benchmarked learning program—really an ongoing education and development process—ranges from forty hours of mandatory, on-the-job experience to executive course work at top schools such as Harvard and Northwestern to a rigorous evaluation process that measures achievement, in part, on fulfillment of educational goals. And these are in addition to classes and other self-improvement programs at on-site learning centers.

> Honeywell Corporate Headquarters
> 101 Columbia Road
> Morristown, NJ 07962
> www.honeywell.com/careers/index.html

IBM

IBM creates, develops, and manufactures the industry's most advanced information technologies, including computer systems, software, networking systems, storage devices, and microelectronics. A worldwide network of IBM solutions and services professionals translates these advanced technologies into business value for our customers. In 2001, IBM revenues reached $89.9 billion. In addition, IBM's worldwide research labs work in all areas of information technology, from physics and cognitive science to leading-edge application research. IBM invents innovative materials and structures and uses them to create exciting machine designs and architectures. IBM creates tools and technologies that will enable the continued evolution of computing and computing services over the network. Work across many disciplines is often done in concert with IBM colleagues in academic and government research centers, as well as "in the marketplace" with customers who provide IBM with challenging research problems.

Industries, education, health care, government—no matter the enterprise, IBM's global presence provides an opportunity for you. IBM has jobs worldwide, with more than 300,000 highly motivated employees in more than 100 countries.

> IBM Corporation
> 1133 Westchester Avenue
> White Plains, NY 10604
> www-1.ibm.com/employment/

International Language and Culture Center

International Language and Culture Center (ILCC) was established in 1976 as a small translation house and has since grown to a registered staff of more than 400 from eight countries. ILCC has expanded to serve international business and culture through communication services, coordination of major events, public relations, and commercial publications. The company's clients include multinational manufacturers, financial institutions, international advertising and human resources companies, and Japanese government agencies.

ILCC seeks bright, articulate people to work in Japan as interpreters, translators, English editors, and rewriters. Bilingual Japanese who are studying overseas and highly proficient, bilingual non-Japanese who plan to reside in Japan are urged to apply. ILCC is especially interested in energetic people with backgrounds in liberal arts, Asian studies, international relations, languages, English, business, marketing, and human relations to work in Japan on a freelance basis. Major study in specific fields will be considered secondary to language proficiency.

> International Language and Culture Center
> 2-17-44, Akasaka Minato-ku
> Tokyo 107
> Japan
> Tel.: (81) (3) 5562-3661
> Fax: (81) (3) 5562-3666
> www.ilcc.com

ITOCHU International Inc.

ITOCHU International Inc.'s parent company, ITOCHU Corporation, is headquartered in Tokyo, Japan. With more than $100 billion in revenue and ranked the worlds thirteenth-largest company by *Fortune* magazine in 2000, ITOCHU is one of Japan's major "sogo shosha," or general trading companies. ITOCHU is active in sales, distribution, financing, importing, and exporting in a variety of sectors—"from soybeans to satellites"—including textiles, automobiles and machinery, aerospace industry, information technology, energy, metals, food, insurance, and logistics. ITOCHU is active worldwide, with thousands of employees in 170 offices in eighty countries. ITOCHU also has more than 740 affiliates and subsidiaries globally, including joint ventures with companies such as General Motors, AOL Time Warner, Dunhill, and Exxon.

III is the wholly owned North American subsidiary of ITOCHU and is based in New York City. With revenues in 2000 of more than $7.5 billion, III is involved in import and export of textiles, machinery, aerospace and electronics, steel and raw materials, metals, food, forest products, chemicals, and energy. In addition, III has amassed a portfolio of more than twenty successful subsidiary and affiliate companies, many of which are leaders in their fields—companies such as Master Halco, the largest manufacturer of fencing materials in North America, and Telerent Leasing Corporation, the exclusive U.S. distributor of Philips healthcare television systems. III also helps introduce American technology products to Japan through ITOCHU Technology Inc., a subsidiary based in Silicon Valley.

> ITOCHU Corporation
> 6-1 Kita-Aoyama 2-chome
> Minato-ku, Tokyo 107-8077, Japan
> Tel.: (81) (3) 3497-7295
> Fax: (81) (3) 3497-7296
> www.itochu.co.jp
>
> ITOCHU International
> 335 Madison Avenue
> New York, NY 10017
> Tel.: (212) 818-8000
> Fax: (212) 818-8378
> www.itochu.com.

Johnson & Johnson

Johnson & Johnson products are sold in more than 175 countries, generating annual global revenues of more than $27 billion. The company produces and sells products to meet a wide range of human health care needs, including anti-infectives, orthopaedics, cardiology and circulatory diseases, urology, diagnostics, women's health, mental health, skin care, and many more.

Johnson & Johnson is comprised of 37 global affiliates with 197 operating units—each of which is highly autonomous and accountable for its individual performance. This unique organizational structure allows the company to effectively support its business strategy of remaining the world's most comprehensive and broadly based health care company.

Johnson & Johnson's many small-company environments create new and expanding opportunities for university students who are ready to establish their careers. At the same time, they offer the world-class leadership development, competitive compensation and benefits, and global impact you would expect from a big company like Johnson & Johnson.

Although educational requirements vary, Johnson & Johnson seeks students with a bachelor's or advanced degree to work in the following functional areas: engineering, finance/accounting, human resources, information management, marketing, operations, quality assurance, research and development, and sales.

Johnson & Johnson
One Johnson & Johnson Plaza
New Brunswick, NJ 08933
Tel.: (732) 524-0400
www.jnj.com/careers/index.htm

Lockheed Martin

Lockheed Martin is a customer-focused, global enterprise principally engaged in the research, design, development, manufacture, and integration of advanced technology systems, products, and services for government and commercial customers. Lockheed Martin operates in the same context as its customers and is deeply involved in solving the problems and meeting the demands and expectations of its customers. Moreover, it leads the way in showing customers new systems-based possibilities and opportunities.

The corporation's core business areas are systems integration, aeronautics, space, and technology services. Lockheed Martin's vision is to be the world's best systems integrator in aerospace, defense, and technology services: to be the company our nation and its allies trust most to integrate their largest, most complex, most important advanced technology systems. Lockheed Martin had 2001 sales of $24 billion and employs approximately 125,000 people.

Lockheed Martin
6801 Rockledge Drive
Bethesda, MD 20817
Tel.: (301) 897-6000
http://lmpeople.external.lmco.com/careers/careers.asp

Marathon Oil Corporation

Marathon Oil Corporation (formerly USX) is engaged in the world-wide exploration and production of crude oil and natural gas, as well as the domestic refining, marketing, and transportation of petroleum products. Headquartered in Houston, Texas, Marathon is among the leading energy industry players, applying innovative technologies to discover valuable energy resources and deliver the highest quality products to the marketplace. With operations that embrace four continents, Marathon strives to be the company of choice for investors, partners, customers, neighbors, and employees in the areas in which we do business.

The January 2002 separation of USX Corporation into two independent businesses saw the creation of Marathon Oil Corporation as a new stand-alone energy company on Wall Street.

Marathon Oil offers a wide variety of internships and employment opportunities in the fields of geology, geophysics, engineering, information technology, finance, accounting, and purchasing. The company seeks talented undergraduates and graduate students who thrive in an environment full of challenges and professional development prospects. Students are encouraged to contact a university relations coordinator via e-mail at explorewithus@marathonoil.com.

Marathon Oil Corporation
5555 San Felipe Street
Houston, TX 77056
Tel.: (713) 629-6600
www.marathon.com/Careers/Career_Opportunities/

Marriott International, Inc.

Marriott International, Inc. is a leading worldwide hospitality company. Its heritage can be traced to a small root beer stand opened in Washington, D.C., in 1927 by J. Willard and Alice S. Marriott. Today, Marriott International has nearly 2,100 lodging properties located in fifty states and fifty-nine countries and territories. Headquartered in Washington, D.C., the company has approximately 153,000 employees worldwide. Marriott Lodging operates and franchises hotels under the following brands: Marriott, Renaissance, Courtyard, Residence Inn, Fairfield Inn, Townplace Suites, Springhill Suites, and Ramada International. In addition, the company develops and operates vacation ownership resorts under Marriott Vacation Club International, Ritz-Carlton, and Horizons brands. It also runs the Ritz-Carlton Hotel Company.

Attracting and retaining talented associates is critical to Marriott's success as a global brand leader.

Marriott International
Marriott Drive
Washington, DC 20058
Tel.: (301) 380-3000
http://careers.marriott.com/

Marsh & McLennan Companies

From its beginnings in 1871, Marsh & McLennan Companies (MMC) has evolved into a Fortune 500 company with revenues of more than $10 billion. Today, some 58,000 employees provide analysis, advice, and transactional capabilities to clients in more than 100 countries. MMC is comprised of three companies: Marsh, Putnam, and Mercer Consulting Group.

Marsh is the world's leading insurance broker and risk adviser, providing advice and transactional capabilities to clients in more than 100 countries. In 2001, combined revenue for the risk and insurance services businesses of MMC was $5.2 billion. In recent years, two major acquisitions have enhanced Marsh's client services around the world. In 1997, the company joined forces with **Johnson & Higgins,** one of the largest brokers in the United States and a respected competitor over many decades. Then, at the end of 1998 MMC completed the acquisition of Sedgwick Group, the leading U.K.-based broker and the third-largest broker in the world.

Founded more than sixty-four years ago, **Putnam Investments** has built a worldwide reputation for investment management. At the end of March 2002, Putnam had $314 billion in assets under management, making it one of the largest money-management firms in the United States. The company manages more than 14 million shareholder accounts and has more than 2,700 institutional and 401(k) clients. It offers a breadth of investment choices: mutual funds, institutional portfolios and retirement plans, including 401(k)s and IRAs as well as variable annuities and variable life insurance.

Mercer Consulting Group is one of the largest consulting firms in the world. It has about 15,000 employees located in more than

---

International Affairs In Business
RAFFAELLA CRISTANETTI

New and different actors continue to transform the world's economic, political, and social systems. In addition to providing products, services, and technology, companies are also now required by the marketplace to consider their role in society and their relationship to the broader world. Decisions are made within a more interactive context in which business, government, and civil society form a single dynamic system. The rules of the game constantly are being reevaluated and, in some cases, rewritten.

The integrated, generalist education of international affairs graduates is an important asset in this context. Their studies have equipped them with an understanding of politics and economics, historical perspectives, and cultural nuances affecting the conduct of international business. Strong oral and written communication, foreign language, and analytical skills are vital, but so are poise and the talent to handle difficult situations diplomatically.

(Continued)

---

forty countries. In 2001, combined revenues for Mercer's subsidiaries were $2.2 billion (see chapter 10 for more information on Mercer Consulting Group).

If you are interested in career opportunities in the fields of insurance and risk management, consulting, or investment management, you should contact Marsh, Mercer, or Putnam directly.

> Marsh & McLennan Companies
> 1166 Avenue of the Americas
> New York, NY 10036-2774
> www.mmc.com/index2.html

MCI
MCI is one of the world's largest and fastest growing diversified communications companies. MCI offers consumers and businesses a broad portfolio of services including long distance, wireless, local access, paging, Internet software and access, online information services, business software, and global telecommunications services.

An internship with a Washington, D.C., consultant taught me how much I enjoyed bridging the business and government communities, but I also learned that I prefer working within an organization rather than providing outside advice. Through university contacts, I learned of a position with Chevron Corporation's Washington office and joined the international lobbyist in developing and advocating policy positions consistent with business interests.

The importance of hard work and high personal standards became evident in our daily contacts with U.S. and other government officials, international financial institutions, and opinion makers in foreign policy, trade, and economics. Just this year, a *Wall Street Journal* article described the first oil shipment from Kazakhstan's Tengiz field reaching the Black Sea via the newly completed Caspian Pipeline B eight years after negotiations began and I first supported Chevron's pipeline team.

Cross-cultural competence—the ability to operate fully in a different culture—is a valuable attribute, both inside and outside a corporation. International business can mean interacting with government officials from various political systems, local or indigenous communities in several countries, and colleagues from

Since its founding twenty-seven years ago, MCI has grown to a $13 billion company. Through a number of key strategic ventures and alliances with companies such as BT, News Corp., and Banacci, MCI is providing new services to its customers around the world.

Today, there are some 40,000 MCI employees working in hundreds of offices around the world from their headquarters in Washington, D.C., to business centers such as London, Paris, Frankfurt, Tokyo, Beijing, Moscow, Mexico City, and São Paolo.

MCI is looking for recent graduates with degrees in such fields as computer science, engineering, finance, business, and international relations.

Human Resources
MCI
1801 Pennsylvania Avenue, NW
Washington, DC 20006
Tel.: (202) 872-1600
www.mci.com

professional backgrounds as diverse as geology and journalism, polymer chemistry and genetics. International affairs graduates' abilities to recognize, balance, and leverage competing perspectives are highly applicable.

As an operations analyst in Chevron's Angola/Zaire unit, I sometimes felt as though my participation in business planning and project management was taking me away from government relations. But being able to bridge disciplines became essential when Chevron hosted President Dos Santos in San Francisco, following the first official visit to Washington by an Angolan head of state.

Nonetheless, such skills are sometimes more difficult to recognize or quantify for many businesspeople used to more specialized courses of study. It is critical for international affairs graduates to demonstrate knowledge and interest in a particular industry or company and to articulate clearly their potential contribution to real-world business needs.

Today, after an assignment in Venezuela and a switch to E. I. duPont de Nemours & Co., I work in Corporate Plans, part of a multidisciplinary team developing integrated strategies for biotechnology across various business sectors, including agriculture, food, and materials. Although the difference in industries

Merck & Company

Merck & Company, Inc., is a leading research-driven pharmaceutical products and services company. Merck discovers, develops, manufactures, and markets a broad range of innovative products to improve human and animal health. The Merck-Medco Managed Care Division manages pharmacy benefits for more than 40 million Americans, encouraging the appropriate use of medicines and providing disease-management programs.

The mission of Merck is to provide society with superior products and services, innovations, and solutions that improve the quality of life and satisfy customer needs; to provide employees with meaningful work and advancement opportunities; and to supply investors with a superior rate of return.

Merck & Company
1 Merck Drive
Whitehouse Station, NJ 08889
Tel.: (908) 423-1000
www.merck.com/careers/

is considerable, the training and experience I brought with me are tested every day as the technology is evaluated by society on scientific, political, and cultural levels.

I have now had the opportunity to discuss genetic engineering, intellectual property rights, trade regulations, and ethics in places as diverse as Mexico City, Geneva, and Hong Kong. International business decisions must appropriately balance market realities with human considerations and changing regulatory structures.

Companies can no longer completely segregate their domestic and overseas activities, or their financial obligations from their environmental and social ones. For those committed to a career in international business, there will be new challenges and many potential rewards ahead.

Raffaella Cristanetti, a 1993 graduate of the Bachelor of Science in Foreign Service and Master of Science in Foreign Service programs at Georgetown University, is currently biotech issues and international policy manager, Business Network for Biotechnology, at E. I. DuPont de Nemours & Co., based in Wilmington, Delaware. Before joining DuPont, Ms. Cristanetti held various positions with Chevron Corporation in the areas of international government relations and business development.

Microsoft

Founded in 1975, Microsoft designs, develops, markets, and supports a wide range of personal computer software systems, applications, development tools and languages, hardware peripherals, and books. The company offers a family of operating system products to satisfy any level of customer need. Microsoft Windows, introduced in 1990, is regarded as the standard operating system for personal computers worldwide. In addition to its offices in the United States, Microsoft has forty-eight international subsidiary offices worldwide and international manufacturing and distribution facilities in Ireland and Puerto Rico. Microsoft software is sold in more than fifty countries and more than thirty languages.

Microsoft employs more than 17,000 people worldwide. Career opportunities with Microsoft exist in software and consumer product (multimedia) design and development, product marketing and sales, technical support, and consulting. For most positions, a bachelor's degree in computer science, computer engineering, or another technical discipline is needed.

Recruiting
Microsoft Corporation
Dept. P8001-9596
One Microsoft Way, Suite 303
Redmond, WA 98052
Tel.: (206) 882-8080 Tel.: (800) 892-3181
www.microsoft.com

NEC Corporation

With global operations, cutting-edge technology in numerous fields and more than 100 years of business experience, NEC has emerged as a leading global Internet solution provider. In each of the three areas most important to the future of the Internet—IT, networking, and electron devices—NEC stands at the forefront of research, product development, and implementation of new services. NEC integrates its strengths from these fields to offer customers new solutions and greater business opportunities in the technological, industrial, and social convergence made possible by the Internet. NEC, headquartered in Japan, operates in twenty-one countries. Last year, NEC's net sales reached nearly $43 million.

NEC Corporation
7-1, Shiva 5-chome, Minato-ku
Tokyo 108-8001
Japan
www.nec-global.com

Nestlé

Nestlé is one of the world's leading food companies, with sales almost exclusively in branded products. Nestlé is a global company, with 45 percent of its business in Europe, more than 35 percent in the Americas, and almost 20 percent of sales generated in the other regions of the world. Nestlé does more than 98 percent of its business outside of Switzerland, its home country, and has more than 490 factories in more than seventy countries.

Nestlé is looking for recent college graduates in a wide variety of disciplines, including business, accounting, finance, marketing, international affairs, and computer science.

College Recruitment Office
Nestlé USA
800 North Brand Boulevard
Glendale, CA 91203
Tel.: (815) 549-6000
www.nestleusa.com/

Nestlé S.A.
Avenue Nestlé
1800 Vevey
Switzerland
Tel.: (41) (21) 924-2111
www.nestle.com/

Panasonic

Panasonic's vision of the digital future is driven by the needs and aspirations of its business customers and millions of consumers around the world who use Panasonic products every day. As Panasonic moves forward into the twenty-first century, its standards are still firmly grounded in the philosophy of company founder Konosuke Matsushita, who began the company in 1918 after inventing a two-socket light fixture.

Panasonic takes pride in being one of the world's premier electronics manufacturers. Not only do they make the DVD players, televisions, and dozens of other consumer electronics products enjoyed by millions, but they are also a supplier of electronics components.

Panasonic
1 Panasonic Way
Secaucus, NJ 07094
Tel.: (201) 348-7000
www.prodcat.panasonic.com/employee/joblisting.asp

PepsiCo

PepsiCo is a world leader in convenience foods and beverages, with revenues of about $27 billion and more than 143,000 employees. The company consists of the snack businesses of Frito-Lay North America and Frito-Lay International; the beverage businesses of Pepsi-Cola North America, Gatorade/Tropicana North America and PepsiCo Beverages International; and Quaker Foods North America, manufacturer and marketer of ready-to-eat cereals and other food products. PepsiCo brands are available in nearly 200 countries and territories.

Many of PepsiCo's brand names are more than 100 years old, but the corporation is relatively young. PepsiCo was founded in 1965 through the merger of Pepsi-Cola and Frito-Lay. Tropicana was acquired in 1998 and PepsiCo merged with the Quaker Oats Company, including Gatorade, in 2001.

PepsiCo's continued growth has created career opportunities for talented professionals in a variety of specialized fields at their corporate world headquarters, located in Purchase, New York. The company is looking for people with a background in information technology, tax, human resources, law, accounting, public affairs, and auditing. For more information, visit the Pepsi Career Center website, www.pepsico.com/pepsicocareers/.

Pfizer International

Pfizer Inc. is a research-based global health care company with operations on six continents. A publicly held corporation with headquarters in New York City, Pfizer recently celebrated 150 years in business. The company's medicines for people and animals and its consumer products are sold in more than 150 countries. Pfizer's drug research and development and its sales and marketing expertise are regularly cited as leading the industry—in current and potential growth and in the level of resources the company commits to building them.

Forbes magazine named Pfizer Inc. its 1998 company of the year. *Fortune* has also named Pfizer as one of its best companies to work for in 2000. Headquartered in New York, Pfizer Inc. is determined to build on its success, investing in its people and resources. The company has the largest sales force in the industry, backed by the largest research budget in the industry, and is continuing to expand. By joining forces with Warner-Lambert, it is bringing together the best people and practices from both organizations.

> Pfizer Pharmaceuticals Group
> 235 E. 42nd Street
> New York, NY 10017
> Tel.: (212) 573-2323
> www.pfizer.com/pfizerinc/career/

Philip Morris/Kraft

Philip Morris Companies Inc. is the largest consumer packaged goods company on Earth. The company has 175,000 talented and diverse employees who keep Philip Morris Companies' business fundamentals strong and its companies growing. The people are the force behind more than four decades of contributions to the communities in which Philip Morris operates. They are also key players in helping to find reasonable solutions to many of society's concerns about the company's businesses.

The success of the company is driven by the power of its global brand portfolio. In 2001, ninety-two of its operating companies'

Prior experience in a related field, either with Rockwell or elsewhere, is required for positions in Rockwell's international functions.

Corporate College Relations
Rockwell International
P.O. Box 4250
Seal Beach, CA 90740-8250
Tel.: (412) 565-2000
www.rockwell.com

SAIC

Founded in 1969, SAIC, a Fortune 500 company, now ranks as the largest employee-owned research and engineering firm in the nation. SAIC and its subsidiaries have more than 41,000 employees with offices in more than 150 cities worldwide.

SAIC is a key source for leading-edge technologies that will carry clients into the twenty-first century. The SAIC Strategies Group—a dynamic multidisciplinary team inside SAIC that provides strategic consulting and policy research and analysis services to a growing number of government and industry clients worldwide—does most of SAIC's work in the international arena. For more than two decades, it has acted as a trusted partner, helping organizations to solve their most complex problems. It is now almost 800 strong and is actively hiring talented candidates in national security policy, arms control policy and analysis, counterproliferation, logistics/transportation, systems security, operations research, and PPBS. The majority of the positions within the strategies group require that an individual either have or be able to obtain a security clearance.

SAIC Corporate Headquarters
10260 Campus Point Drive
San Diego, CA 92121
www.saic.com/career/

Siemens Corporation

Siemens Corporation has international activities in the area of information and communications, automation and control, power, transportation, medicine, and lighting. With a presence in 190 countries worldwide, Siemens has more than 440,000 employees.

Siemens seeks candidates with bachelor's, master's, or doctoral degrees in natural and computer sciences; electrical, mechanical, and software engineering; business administration; economics; finance;

human resources; and other fields. The company has both entry-level and more advanced positions available in the fields of research and development, marketing, manufacturing, logistics, sales, purchasing, finance, business administration, systems engineering, project management, and human resources. The company seeks candidates with adaptability, situational sensitivity, networking skills, communication skills, ability to analyze, ability to implement, creativity, customer focus, and strategic orientation. Siemens filled 5,000 vacancies in 2001.

> Siemens Corporation
> 153 East 53rd Street, 56th Floor
> New York, NY 10022-4611
> Tel.: (212) 258-4000
> Fax: (212) 767-0580
> http://w4.siemens.de/en/career/continent/Europe/
> index.html

Texas Instruments
Texas Instruments Inc. is a leader in the real-time technologies that help people communicate. The company is moving fast to drive the Internet age forward with semiconductor solutions for large markets such as wireless and broadband access and for new emerging markets such as digital cameras and digital audio.

> Company Headquarters
> Texas Instruments Inc.
> 12500 TI Boulevard
> Dallas, TX 75243-4136
> Tel.: (800) 336-5236
> www.ti.com/recruit/index.htm

United Airlines
UAL Corporation is the holding company for United Airlines, the second-largest air carrier in the world. With hubs in Chicago, Denver, Los Angeles, San Francisco, and Washington, D.C., and key international gateways in Tokyo, London, Frankfurt, Miami, and Toronto, United flies to some 119 destinations in twenty-six countries. United's 84,100-plus employees worldwide bring people together safely, conveniently, and efficiently more than 1,650 times a day. United Airlines' customers also enjoy access to more than 890

destinations around the world through Star Alliance, the leading global airline network.

United also leads the way in safety and technological advancements for the aviation industry. The pioneer of systems such as the Enhanced Ground Proximity Warning System (EGPWS), United always focuses on its top value of "safety at all times, in all things." United Airlines has a seventy-five-year history of leadership in the airline industry. The company's dedication to innovation and commitment to its customers and employees enable it to attract and build a talented, highly qualified, diverse workforce.

United Airlines
World Headquarters
P.O. Box 66100
Chicago, IL 60666
Tel.: (847) 700-4000
Fax: (847) 700-5287
www.ual.com

Yamaha

Since 1887 when it began producing reed organs, the Yamaha Corporation in Japan (then Nippon Gakki Co. Ltd.) has grown to become the world's largest manufacturer of a full line of musical instruments and a leading producer of audiovisual products, semiconductors and other computer-related products, sporting goods, home appliances and furniture, specialty metals, machine tools, and industrial robots.

Yamaha now owns forty-four subsidiaries and representative offices in overseas markets in addition to numerous related companies in Japan.

Since Yamaha Music Foundation was established in 1966, it has generated a wide range of music activities throughout global society, including Yamaha music schools and the Junior Original Concert. Strong commitment to promote and support music education and popularization is one of the most significant elements that distinguish it from its competitors.

Yamaha Music Corporation of America
6600 Orangethorpe Avenue
Buena Park, CA 90620
Tel.: (714) 522-9011

Yamaha Motor Corporation, USA
6555 Katella Avenue
Cypress, CA 90630
Tel.: (714) 761-7300
www.yamaha.com/jobs/jobops.htm

Chapter 8

BUSINESS ORGANIZATIONS

Careers in Business Organizations

ANDREW R. PAUL

Practically every industry in the United States is represented in Washington, D.C., by a trade association that has the unique mission of advancing the interests of its member companies before U.S. government policymakers, regulators, and members of Congress. In addition to their government lobbying functions, associations also enhance their industries' commercial interests through annual trade shows and product expositions, continuing education and professional and training programs for their members, national industry marketing programs, as well as research and development in broad areas such as the setting of national standards.

Companies within a given industry become motivated to participate in an industry trade association because of the value of taking concerted action together with their own competitors in order to deal with those issues that impact their industry as a whole. Their effectiveness—what we would call "clout"—is infinitely increased through their joint efforts rather than each company acting individually on the very same issue. As a result, trade associations, and especially the larger ones, have been successful in enhancing the viability of their industries through legal action, legislative and political persuasion, and representation before regulatory agencies.

Andrew R. Paul is a 1967 graduate of the Master of Science in Foreign Service program at Georgetown University. He has spent more than thirty-five years as a Washington, D.C., public affairs and international trade executive. Mr. Paul has served as communications director in the Motorola Inc. Washington, D.C., office; director of government relations for Paramount Communications Inc., a leading television, entertainment, and publishing company; and senior vice president of the Satellite Broadcasting and Communications Association, where he was the principal Washington lobbyist for the U.S. satellite industry. Mr. Paul is currently a consultant for defense and communications companies. Prior to completing his MSFS, Mr. Paul received a B.A. from Dartmouth College and served in the U.S. Army as an intelligence officer.

Associations also utilize both national public relations programs and "grass roots"—that is, lobbying Washington, D.C., from their home states—in order to make their message heard by their congressional representatives. As a result, associations such as the National Association of Broadcasters (television stations), the Motion Picture Association of America (movie studios), the National Association of Manufacturers, the Aerospace Industries Association, and the National Association of Home Builders, to name a few, wield exceptional influence in our nation's capital.

The need for companies to band together to perform these functions is twofold: first, to advance the broad economic interests of their industry so as to improve its potential for succeeding; and second, to deal with government actions—in the form of current or proposed legislation or rules and regulations promulgated by government agencies—that could hinder or advance the progress of the industry, depending on the directions established by the affected company members of the trade association.

Typically, an executive employee of a trade association can be classified as a "jack of all trades." Association staff members are skilled in a broad range of abilities ranging from communications, lobbying, and law to conferences, trade shows, and education programs for company members. They come from a variety of educational backgrounds and workplace experience. Because of the overall political tone that drives the existence of an influential organization, many staff have been previously employed in congressional offices, have worked in a presidential administration, or have a major interest in the political process.

> Association staff members are skilled in a broad range of abilities ranging from communications, lobbying, and law to conferences, trade shows, and education programs for company members. They come from a variety of educational backgrounds and workplace experience.

Career-minded university students can also find trade association positions that deal with international business. The scope of the organization's international programs rests on the international business interests of its members. For example, the Motion Picture Association must deal with major international copyright issues in licensing and protecting from illegal use the films and television programming that its movie studio members produce and distribute around the world. The same holds true for the Recording Industry Association of America and the Association of American Publishers, whose members have a vital stake in the protection of intellectual property rights worldwide. These organizations participate intensively in the deliberations of the World Trade Organization (WTO), negotiations of the General Agreement on Tariffs and Trade (GATT), the Office of the U.S. Trade Representative (USTR), as well as other U.S. government agencies that can assist them in the protected distribution of their products and services.

Trade associations can offer challenging and stimulating career opportunities for individuals who are interested in the American political process and representing a particular industry on a partisan basis either before the U.S. government or in a commercial context through the facilitating of meetings, conferences, trade shows, and expositions. Given the political emphasis and raison d'etre of an association, however, a prospective employee should research carefully the international activities of an association if that is where his or her interests lie.

Resource Listings

Advanced Medical Technology Association

The Advanced Medical Technology Association (AdvaMed) represents the interests of manufacturers of medical devices. Its members control more than 50 percent of the $159 billion world market share. Association members work on regulatory and reimbursement issues. The association works with both the U.S. and foreign governments in the development of public policy on issues of interest to its members.

Most hiring is done out of the ranks of government employees. Although it favors people with policy degrees and experience, the association is not likely to hire recent graduates unless they have considerable experience in the health care industry. The hiring process for the association is informal. The qualifications the association looks for in new hires include analytical skills, experience working in health care (especially in reimbursement systems or managed care), a public policy background, health care economics, and general analytical skills. Member companies occasionally contact the association when looking to fill specific needs—usually these are efforts to fill "hardship" posts. In general, people looking to work overseas have to work in the industry for a period of time.

AdvaMed
Health Industry Manufacturers Association
1200 G Street, NW
Washington, DC 20005
Tel.: (202) 783-8700
Fax: (202) 783-8750
www.himanet.org

American Bankers Association

The American Bankers Association (ABA) acts as a consensus building and lobbying organization for influencing government policy affecting the banking sector. It represents 90 percent of the United States banking industry's assets. Every year the association sponsors an annual convention and numerous schools, conferences, and workshops. Through its American Institute of Banking, it conducts more than 1,000 courses and other educational activities each year. The ABA publishes several periodicals concerning compliance with government regulation, current banking practices, and public information. The ABA is the secretariat for the annual International Monetary Conference.

The association has a staff of more than 350 professionals, of whom 5 work in its international relations division. Its annual budget is about $50 million.

American Bankers Association
1120 Connecticut Avenue, NW
Washington, DC 20036
Tel.: (202) 663-5000
www.aba.com

AeA (formerly American Electronics Association)

Advancing the business of technology, AeA is the nation's largest high-tech trade association. Founded in 1943, AeA has more than 3,500 member companies that span the high-technology spectrum from software, semiconductors, and computers to Internet technology, advanced electronics, and telecommunications systems and services. With eighteen regional U.S. councils and offices in Brussels and Beijing, AeA offers a unique global policy grassroots capability and a wide portfolio of valuable business services and products for the high-tech industry. For fifty-eight years, AeA has been the accepted voice of the U.S. technology community.

Positions become available on a random basis in the Washington, D.C., office in the groups handling domestic policy, international policy, small business, and research and statistics.

Director of Human Resources
AeA
600 Pennsylvania Avenue, NW
North Building, Suite 600
Washington, DC 20004
Tel.: (202) 682-9110
Fax: (202) 682-9111
www.aeanet.org

American Forest & Paper Association

The American Forest & Paper Association (AF&PA) is the national trade association of the forest, pulp, paper, paperboard, and wood products industry. AF&PA represents more than 200 member companies and related trade associations that grow, harvest, and process wood and wood fiber; manufacture pulp, paper, and paperboard products from both virgin and recovered fiber; and produce engineered and traditional wood products.

AF&PA's international activities include influencing trade policy at the state, federal, international, and multilateral level; monitoring international trade developments; collecting, analyzing, and disseminating statistics on the international forest products trade; and promoting exports of U.S. forest products. AF&PA's international staff members have varied backgrounds, with experience in economics, environment, trade policy, law, and/or languages.

American Forest & Paper Association
1111 Nineteenth Street, Suite 800
Washington, DC 20036
Tel.: (202) 463-2700
www.afandpa.org

American Iron and Steel Institute

The American Iron and Steel Institute (AISI) is a nonprofit trade association of North American companies engaged in the iron and steel industry, including integrated, electric furnace, and reconstituted mills. It comprises more than thirty-seven associate member companies who are suppliers to or customers of the industry. Member companies account for more than two-thirds of the raw steel produced in the United States, most of the steel manufactured in Canada, and nearly two-thirds of the flat-rolled steel products in Mexico.

The international trade section monitors legislative and executive actions in import and export trade in steel, organizes research and symposia of North American and global trade law and steel trade practices, maintains contact with government officials concerned with international trade, makes recommendations for action to the institute's governing bodies, and engages in public advocacy of AISI's positions.

American Iron and Steel Institute
Suite 1300
1101 17th Street, NW
Washington, DC 20036
Tel.: (202) 452-7100
www.steel.org

American Petroleum Institute

The American Petroleum Institute (API), founded in 1919, is the U.S. oil and natural gas industry's primary trade association. Its membership consists of a broad cross-section of oil, gas, and allied companies in exploration, production, transportation, refining, and marketing. API's membership currently includes 400 companies.

API is headquartered in Washington, D.C., and is represented in thirty-three state capitals east of the Rocky Mountains. In the other states, API works in conjunction with regional and state oil and gas associations. The institute staff consists of approximately 275 professionals with a broad variety of backgrounds.

American Petroleum Institute
1220 L Street, NW
Washington, DC 20005
Tel.: (202) 682-8000
www.api.org

The Conference Board

The Conference Board is the world's leading business research and membership organization, linking executives from different companies, industries, and countries. Founded in 1916, the Conference Board has become the leader in helping executives build strong professional relationships, expand their business knowledge, and find solutions to a wide range of business problems. The Conference

Board's twofold purpose is to improve the business enterprise system and to enhance the contribution of business to society. A not-for-profit, nonadvocacy organization, the Conference Board has 3,200 members in sixty-six countries in the world; 1,400 of those members are outside the United States.

The Conference Board's Asia-Pacific events focus on our core competencies of knowledge management, corporate branding and image, shared services, economics, corporate governance, and all areas of human resources. In previous years events have been held in Hong Kong, Australia, Singapore, India, and China. With the Conference Board's growing presence in the region, we anticipate the number of events and countries where events are held to increase substantially.

Currently, the international programs division is located in New York City and depends on freelancers to research and program the content of the event, confirm speakers, and recruit organizations to underwrite the events. Individuals in the capacity of program director ideally must be located in the region, have knowledge of the specific subject matter of the event, and have excellent writing skills and sales experience.

In the Asian Pacific, the Conference Board has offices in Hong Kong and New Delhi staffed with sales, logistics, and administrative executives. The Asian Pacific office had two openings in the last year, in conference programming and administration. The Conference Board also has an office in Mexico City staffed with a regional director; there were no openings last year. When hiring for international offices, the Conference Board looks for local individuals who have an international outlook and three to four years of experience in sales, conference programming, or administration, depending on the position.

> The Conference Board
> 845 Third Avenue
> New York, NY 10022-6679
> Tel.: (212) 759-0900
> Fax: (212) 339-0305
> www.conference-board.org

Consumer Electronics Association

Based in Arlington, Virginia, the Consumer Electronics Association (CEA) represents more than 650 U.S. companies involved in the design, development, manufacturing, and distribution of audio, video, mobile electronics, communications, information technology multimedia, and accessory products, as well as related services, which are sold through consumer channels. Combined, these companies account for more than $70 billion in annual sales.

CEA's mission is to support and expand the consumer electronics industry. CEA is the vital connection between consumers, retailers, and manufacturers of consumer electronics. CEA's vision is to be a vibrant, entrepreneurial trade association promoting industry growth and leading the consumer technology industry in events, business development, strategic relationships, and technology policy.

CEA sponsors and manages the International CES, the annual consumer electronics industry forum that expands, strengthens, drives, and grows the consumer technology industry.

Consumer Electronics Association
2500 Wilson Boulevard
Arlington, VA 22201-3834
Tel.: (703) 907-7600
www.ce.org

Council of the Americas

The Council of the Americas, an affiliate of the Americas Society Inc., is a U.S. business association dedicated to advocacy of the interests of its international corporate members doing business in Latin America. The Council, broadly representative of total U.S. investment in the region, is the private-sector vehicle for promoting positive change and future private-sector-led development in the hemisphere. Its various member constituencies include industrial, financial, and service companies. Consensus and viewpoints are communicated to Latin American government officials and U.S. policymakers as well as to the domestic Latin American private sector.

Applicants should have undergraduate or graduate degrees in international relations, international business, economics, finance, or related fields. Language capabilities also are encouraged.

Council of the Americas
680 Park Avenue
New York, NY 10021
Tel.: (212) 628-3200
Fax: (212) 628-1880

Council of the Americas
1310 G Street, NW
Washington, DC 20005
Tel.: (202) 639-0724
Fax: (202) 639-0794
www.counciloftheamericas.org

Council on Competitiveness

The Council on Competitiveness was founded in 1986 to serve as a focal point for leadership efforts aimed at improving the competitive position of the United States in global markets. The council's core agenda is built around four interrelated and interdependent issues: capital formation and investment policies, science and technology, international economics and trade, and human resources. To address public policy issues, the council publishes reports and position statements developed with the assistance of council members, staff, and expert advisers. To promote public awareness, the council publishes a monthly e-mail newsletter that chronicles major trends, policies, and people affecting competitiveness. A Competitiveness Index comparing U.S. performance to that of other nations also is released annually.

At its peak, the council has seventeen staff members. New graduates usually enter at the position of council associate, which is comparable to that of a research assistant. For its council associates, the council seeks master's degree candidates with a concentration in international trade, business, economics, public policy, and/or technology. Work experience in other associations or think tanks specializing in these issues or experience on Capitol Hill is preferred.

Council on Competitiveness
1500 K Street, NW, Suite 850
Washington, DC 20005
Tel.: (202) 682-4292
Fax: (202) 682-5150
www.compete.org

European-American Business Council

Comprised of more than seventy E.U. and U.S. companies, the European-American Business Council (EABC) is a business association active on transatlantic trade, tax, investment, and other policy issues. The council's work includes providing a forum for dialogue on transatlantic issues, preventing E.U./U.S. disputes and roadblocks to desirable policy outcomes, shaping quality and workable issue strategies, and helping member companies achieve business objectives.

The EABC offices are in Washington, D.C.. The council currently has a staff of four, all of which speak at least one foreign language. New recruits typically possess a graduate degree in international relations, political science, and/or have a public policy background as well as overseas experience. Recruitment is done on an as-needed basis.

> European-American Business Council (EABC)
> 1333 H Street, NW, Suite 630
> Washington, DC 20005
> Tel.: (202) 347 9292
> Fax: (202) 628 5498
> www.eabc.org

International Business-Government Counsellors, Inc.

International Business-Government Counsellors, Inc. (IBC) is a Washington, D.C.-based firm that assists companies in international government relations affecting their global operations. IBC's clients include major multinational companies based in the United States, Asia, and Europe. Established in 1972, IBC is the oldest and most prominent international government relations firm in the United States. IBC's staff of international trade and government relations professionals provides clients with monitoring of executive, legislative, and regulatory developments that may affect the client's operations; analysis of U.S. and foreign government policies and regulations affecting the client's trade; investment and international business operations; development and implementation of strategic advice for worldwide corporate responses to government policies and developments; and direct client representations to the U.S. Congress and executive branch, such as the Office of the U.S. Trade Representative and the Departments of Commerce, State, Agriculture, Treasury, and Defense, as well as to foreign governments.

IBC welcomes inquiries from qualified individuals seeking employment. IBC provides a fast-paced international affairs environment and offers excellent employee benefits. Inquiries may be sent to personnel@ibgc.com. Current employment openings are posted on the IBC website.

> International Business-Government Counsellors, Inc.
> 818 Connecticut Avenue, NW, 12th Floor
> Washington, DC 20006-2702
> Tel.: (202) 872-8181
> Fax: (202) 872-8696
> www.ibgc.com

Japan External Trade Organization

The Japan External Trade Organization (JETRO) was established by the Japanese government in 1958 as the nation's principal organization for implementing trade policy on a comprehensive basis.

In the first half of the 1980s, JETRO began promoting imports entering Japan, a primary mission that continues to this day. The organization is also actively involved in helping developing nations to nurture their supporting industries, promoting cooperation between industries in Japan and other developed nations, supporting the development of regional economies in Japan and other nations, and encouraging international exchange on a variety of levels.

JETRO relies on its extensive worldwide network, which comprises JETRO Headquarters in Tokyo, JETRO Osaka, and thirty-five local offices in Japan as well as eighty overseas offices in fifty-eight countries. Out of about 1,600 full-time professionals with JETRO, 47 percent are working at its overseas offices, where additional local staff (about 300), on various levels, is supporting their operations. In fiscal 2001, twenty-nine new staff members joined JETRO, a quarter of whom had master's degrees.

> Japan External Trade Organization (JETRO)
> 2-2-5 Toranomon, Minato-ku, Tokyo 105-8466, Japan
> Tel.: +81-3-3582-5540
> Fax: +81-3-387-0219
> www.jetro.go.jp

National Association of Manufacturers

The National Association of Manufacturers (NAM) is the nation's largest multi-industry trade association representing more than 14,000 companies, of which 80 percent are small manufacturers, plus 350 member associations in all fifty states. NAM's member firms produce 86 percent of the manufactured goods and services in the United States and employ more than 18 million people. Headquartered in Washington, D.C., the NAM has ten additional offices across the country.

The mission of the NAM is to improve the ability of U.S. manufacturers to compete in the global marketplace.

The NAM's international activities focus on developing policy that achieves the mission of the organization, focusing on trade, tariffs, sanctions, border security, exchange rates, and dollar valuation, plus other issues of significance to our members. Staff regularly interact with members of Congress, the administration, the Commerce Department, member companies with international operations, and the media.

Operating with a small staff of only four lobbyists, the International Economic Affairs Department hired only one individual last year: a trade policy director. Such an individual must have substantive expertise in a range of trade matters, a master's degree in international relations or a related field, at least six years of relevant work experience, keen political sense, and excellent written and oral communications skills.

Challenging opportunities are available during the summer and school semesters for students who can receive scholastic credit for work experience with the NAM. Research and writing are the primary tasks, while gaining issue exposure through member and Hill meetings.

Those wishing to submit a resumé or inquiries may contact

Director of Human Resources
1331 Pennsylvania Avenue, NW, Suite 600
Washington, DC 20004-1790
Tel.: (202) 637-3000
Fax: (202) 637-3182
www.nam.org

The United States Council for International Business

The United States Council for International Business (USCIB) promotes an open system of world commerce in which business can flourish and contribute to economic growth, human welfare, and protection of the environment. Its membership includes some 300 U.S. companies, professional services firms, and associations. As the American affiliate of several leading international business groups, USCIB presents industry views to policymakers and regulatory authorities worldwide. It also facilitates international trade by working toward harmonization of international commercial practices.

Total staff is approximately fifty, based in New York City and a small Washington, D.C., office. USCIB has a limited number of openings each year for individuals with backgrounds in international affairs, business, law, and related areas. Managerial positions (approximately one or two openings per year) generally require a master's degree and some specialized work or academic experience in the desired subject area. Experience with international economic policy issues and advocacy is particularly desirable, as is foreign language proficiency (especially French). Entry-level administrative and support-staff positions (two or three openings per year) generally require a bachelor's degree and some work experience. Basic computer proficiency is required for all positions.

For more information or to submit a resumé, please contact

United States Council for International Business
1212 Avenue of the Americas
New York, NY 10036
Tel.: (212) 354-4480
Fax: (212) 575-0327
www.uscib.org

US–China Business Council

Established in 1973, the US–China Business Council is a private, nonprofit business association supported by about 220 American firms engaged in trade and investment with the People's Republic of China. Its primary objective is the promotion and facilitation of bilateral economic relations, and its member activities include general seminars, specialized tailored briefings, and market research.

The council publishes a bimonthly magazine, *The China Business Review;* a members-only newsletter, *China Market Intelligence;* and numerous focused studies on topics of current business interest.

Headquartered in Washington, D.C., the council maintains offices in Beijing and Shanghai. The present staff includes professionals with backgrounds in Chinese, East Asian studies, business administration, and government.

The US–China Business Council
1818 N Street, NW, Suite 200
Washington, DC 20036
Tel.: (202) 429-0340
Fax: (202) 775-2476
www.uschina.org

Chapter 9

LOBBYING

Lobbying in Washington, D.C.

GEORGE A. DALLEY

The First Amendment to the U.S. Constitution states that the people of this nation have a right to make their positions and concerns known to the Congress of the United States. This assumption that all individuals and groups are entitled to address their elected representatives in the Federal Government in the making of their public decisions forms the basis for all lobbying activities. It is at the core of America's participatory government.

"Lobbying" consists of presenting positions, concerns, or opinions in every corridor, committee room, and congressional office on Capitol Hill and throughout the executive branch. This is a unique feature of the American form of public government, where doors are open to all. In its essence, the nation's capitol is a "public market" for opinion, and all opinions, domestic or international, are permitted and encouraged.

Lobbying is an integral and accepted part of the American system of government. Professional lobbyists help to inform the Congress and the general public about problems and issues. Lobbyists stimulate public debate, voice the concerns of the wronged and needy, and educate Congress on the practical aspects of proposed legislation—whom it would help, whom it would hurt, who is for it, and who is against it.

Although the term *lobbyist* often carries negative connotations, a lobbyist is simply someone who voices support for or opposition to a particular issue. In short, a lobbyist is anyone with an interest in

George A. Dalley *is counsel and staff director to Representative Charles P. Rangel (D-NY). Prior to working on the creation of DC Air, he was senior partner at Holland and Knight. Mr. Dalley has extensive experience in international affairs as a congressional staffer and State Department official and in his law practice. He is a founding member of the Corporate Council on Africa and has served as a consultant to the UN Development Program. As chair of the Council on Foreign Relations Advisory Committee on Diversity, he has worked to increase the number and participation of minorities in the council.*

legislation. The method lobbyists use to present their positions is perhaps the most significant factor in determining how effective their lobbying is. Simply writing a letter to a member of Congress will not be as effective as, for example, mobilizing a group of leaders in a community to influence the congressman's opinion or decision. Selecting the proper method of communicating and shaping an articulate message are the two critical elements of effective lobbying.

The presentation of these messages must also be made in the right place, in the proper language, and to the right decision maker. They must be based upon a clear understanding of which considerations are most important to the elected public official and the political and bureaucratic framework in which the elected official is operating. Picking the right political champion of an issue is an art, not an accident. Evaluating the best possible approach for influencing a politician on a particular issue is not simple or obvious. An effective strategy can only come from individuals who are intimately familiar with the Washington "market" and its actors.

Today a lobbyist's influence is directly tied to the effectiveness of the message and advocacy—its candor, its honesty, and the quality of the arguments it is able to present to policymakers. The content and the quality of a lobbyist's arguments are even more important these days, given the ever-increasing depth and complexity of the issues confronting American government—a government specifically designed to give every group an opportunity to participate in the process of making policy and laws.

Who Are the Lobbyists?
Lobbying is an activity that is on the rise in Washington. Washington is filled with an increasing number of people who, as paid professionals, visit the offices of members of Congress with the intention of influencing lawmakers in some way. There are nearly 20,000 lobbyists in Washington, an average of about thirty-five for each member of Congress. Examples of the interests represented by registered lobbyists include business corporations seeking preferential treatment from the U.S. tax code; nonprofit organizations trying to promote public interest of a broader nature; state and local governments seeking new roads, airports, or other public facilities; and labor unions, farmers, and professional workers trying to protect their economic interest.

Most lobbyists in Washington are lawyers by profession. This is probably due to the fact that lawyers are naturally attracted to law-making and the legislative process. As a result, most law firms in Washington have developed legislative practices to serve the needs of clients that require advocacy before Congress. The typical legislative practice includes partners with backgrounds in government service and experience in the legislative process. The firm is usually bipartisan, with partners who are active in both political parties and who enjoy relationships with policymakers in the Congress and within the administration.

In addition to law firms, lobbying organizations come in all shapes and sizes. Many U.S. corporations have their own Washington offices to ensure that if their interests are being affected, their opinion will be heard. Corporations will also pool their efforts on legislative issues common to an industry in trade associations representing an industry or in coalitions consisting of many businesses united on a common set of issues.

Individuals also form lobbying organizations on such issues as promoting better treatment of American Indians or preserving private ownership of hand guns or protesting abortion laws. Lobbying groups also form in response to organizations representing the other side of issues. For example, the defense industry has generated the arms control lobby, which opposes new weapons systems. Presently, almost all domestic interests use some type of professional organization or individual with legislative expertise, and increasingly foreign governments and nongovernmental organizations have become active in asserting their interests in Washington. For twelve years I was privileged to provide government relations advice and counsel as the registered foreign agent of governments of nations in Africa and the Caribbean.

Lobbying for International Interests

The challenge of educating members of Congress about the importance of the bilateral relationship between the United States and nations of Africa and the Caribbean to win support for U.S. policies that will benefit the foreign nations through the strengthening of the bilateral relationship is rooted in the reality that members of Congress are not generally interested in foreign policy apart from those areas where there are identified national security or historic interests, such as Western Europe and the Middle East. More precisely, the vast majority of the members of Congress are primarily concerned with their reelection and may know that the voters they represent are generally most interested in what the Congress can do for them and not how it can benefit foreigners. Thus the Congress gives priority to domestic issues and concerns and, generally, except for support for the nation of Israel, opposes assistance to foreign nations.

In addition, to win congressional support for enhanced relationships with the nations of Africa and the Caribbean, it is necessary to convince the members of Congress that supporting these nations results in tangible benefits for the United States and, as specifically as possible, benefits for congressional districts.

In my firm's work on behalf of the interests of the Caribbean nations on issues of trade, for example, we have stressed that the nations of the Caribbean are a proven market for U.S. goods and services, pointing to the record of the Caribbean Basin Initiative (CBI) which, since its inception, has shown the propensity of the Caribbean to purchase U.S.-produced goods and services. The United States enjoys a healthy surplus in its trade with the Caribbean, selling considerably more to the region than we purchase. Typically, Caribbean nations import 60 to 65 percent of the goods and services they import from abroad from the United States. These exports to the Caribbean produce jobs in the United States and thus provide a rationale for members of Congress to support enhanced trade and commerce with the nations of the Caribbean.

We have sought to convince members of Congress that strengthening the economies of nations in the Caribbean strengthens our economy at home by using information on the trade between the United States and the Caribbean region since the inception of the CBI in 1983, which reflects the healthy trade surplus that the United States and individual states enjoy with the Caribbean.

Influence and Access—The Role of Campaign Fundraising

Lobbyists are active participants in fundraising and campaign giving, and it is increasingly apparent that such engagement is a prerequisite for gaining the access needed to make a case. The financial demands of running for and remaining in office are so great that members of Congress are having to spend an inordinate amount of time raising money from the interests who have the most at stake in the decisions they will be making. Thus the imperative of having to raise ever-increasing amounts of campaign funds give members a reason for accessing lobbyists that is almost as compelling as the interests of the lobbyists in accessing them.

Lobbyists can and do organize political action committees (PACs) to contribute money to election campaigns. They are also generally active contributors to political campaigns and organizers of political fundraising events. As the cost of conducting political campaigns for public office escalates as the result of increasing use of the media, elected officials have to raise more money and spend more time in raising funds. Members of Congress value the friendship of those who support their political careers and, therefore, the lobbyist who seeks access and influence will often want to contribute to the campaign of the lawmaker in order to evidence friendship and support.

Much has been written about whether lobbyists "buy" influence through their political contributions. Contributions do help provide access, but members of Congress are, in the great majority, people who are in public life to do what they think is the best for the country and thus are not susceptible to having decisions influenced by money. Those who advocate campaign finance reform worry, however, that the high cost of campaigns forces members of Congress to spend so much time raising money that they are forced into the company of contributors and potential contributors to the exclusion of those who do not have the resources to provide significant funds to political campaigns.

Dalley's Twelve Rules of Effective Lobbying

1. Decide what it is that you want to achieve and define what you need to get done to succeed.
2. Identify the elected or appointed officials with the power to provide what you are seeking.
3. Identify the staff persons who advise the member or official in your area of interest and remember that they are as important as the person for whom they work. Always give the staff due respect and deference.
4. Determine how the elected or appointed officials you are approaching can help you achieve your objective.
5. Develop an effective argument in support of your objective and become totally familiar with your issue.
6. Indicate in your brief why it is in the interest of the public and in the interest of the official to be of assistance in achieving your objective.
7. Never overstate your case or misrepresent. Your credibility is vital to persuading others to support your position, and your reputation for truthfulness is your greatest asset.
8. Obtain an appointment to make your case to the official or appropriate staff; always be willing to meet with staff. Include in the meeting, if possible, constituents of the elected official.

9. Tell the member or staff person what you are asking for as specifically and succinctly as possible, and leave your request in writing.
10. Know the legislative calendar and process so that you make your request at the appropriate time.
11. Offer to work with the elected or appointed official and staff to develop a constituency in support of your objective.
12. Be persistent as well as persuasive. See everyone—staff and members of every legislative committee and all of the executive branch officials who can affect the outcome, and remain in contact as the process unfolds.

Chapter 10

CONSULTING

Careers in Consulting

Mark Buening

The consulting profession continues to thrive and grow as the pace of change in business and government increases. There appears to be no end in sight for technological, economic, and political change. All this ensures the ongoing need and role for consultants to help businesses and governments adapt. Consultants have increasingly been called upon to help solve wide-ranging and complex problems in every area of business or government activity, including (but not limited to) strategy, operations improvement, organizational design, change management, information systems design and implementation, marketing and public relations, performance measurement and management, benefits and compensation planning, balance sheet restructuring, litigation support, and security planning.

The consultants' task is to assist their clients in solving problems or seizing advantages—related to business, competition, or technology—when clients need or want to augment their own internal resources. Providing clients with the best, most appropriate advice on the problem or opportunity at hand is of utmost importance. Clients can be domestic or foreign government agencies, international organizations, corporations, or public institutions. Most consulting work is done on a fee basis, and consulting success depends in large part upon the client receiving value in excess of the consulting fees paid.

Mark Buening, a 1986 graduate of Georgetown University's Master of Science in Foreign Service degree program and an International Business Diplomacy honors certificate holder, is director of strategic planning at Ernst & Young Global Limited in London. He heads their internal strategic planning group, which serves the firmwide industry, functional, and geographic business leaders of this integrated professional services firm. He now focuses on strategic and organizational issues of importance to the Ernst & Young organization worldwide. Prior to joining Ernst & Young, Mr. Buening was an associate with McKinsey & Company, Inc., in their Cleveland, Ohio, and São Paulo, Brazil, offices. He graduated with honors from DePauw University in 1980 with a B.A. in political science.

Clients look to consultants for an objective viewpoint, specialized knowledge or expertise, and the ability to focus on a problem or opportunity in a way and with a time commitment that the client themselves cannot, given their need to manage the many varied activities of their businesses. Because of experience gained while serving other clients, consultants bring an ever-broader understanding and perspective of potential solutions to each case. Often, they have dealt with the same issues in several organizations and have first-hand knowledge and experience in state-of-the-art approaches and methodologies. A career in consulting is fast-paced, challenging, and varied. Such a career offers the opportunity to see the world and to address important strategic, operational, and organizational issues facing business and government leaders.

The expectation that a consultant will address particular problems or opportunities for their clients has generally meant that consulting work is project-based. In most cases, a project team of consultants is assembled to address the particular client problem or opportunity, and consideration of the specific skills and talents of individual consultants is often vital in determining the makeup of the team. Team sizes depend upon the complexity of the issues involved, the scope of the project, and the time allotted for completion. In most large consulting firms, the team includes one or more partners who oversee the client relationship, a project manager who monitors day-to-day project activities, and a few associates or analysts who do data gathering, analysis, and hypothesis testing. In other situations, especially in smaller firms, one consultant may work independently. However, even when part of a team, consultants often work independently on assigned areas of analysis or research.

Consulting firms exist in a wide variety of sizes and flavors. They range from sole practitioners to organizations of several thousand consultants worldwide. There are even in-house consulting groups, which serve the rest of their own company as clients. Some consulting firms focus solely on providing consulting services; others offer an integrated package of business advisory services including consulting, audit, accounting, tax, and other services. Some focus on particular areas of expertise in certain industry or business activities, whereas others strive to be "one-stop shops" that offer services across a variety of industries and activities. The general consulting classifications (notwithstanding a myriad of specialist or niche classifications) are:

- management and strategy consulting (performance improvement),
- information systems consulting,
- economic development or public policy consulting.

Thus, the nature of consulting advice can cover international business and finance, trade and investment, marketing and promotion, project feasibility and design, acquisition or divestiture planning and implementation, economic analysis and forecasting, public policy, international affairs, process design, information systems design and/or development, and competitive analysis.

Individual consultants can be generalists or specialists, and each is essential in particular situations. Generalists usually act as diagnosticians or problem solvers focusing on broad-ranging and integrated management issues. They probe the inner workings of an organization or do external research to define the scope of a problem or opportunity by using a range of analytic tools and frameworks to shape a solution and design an action plan. Most generalist consultants have some in-depth knowledge of a particular industry and/or functional area, but they normally use insights and experiences across companies or industries to address client-specific situations. Specialists, on the other hand, bring a greater degree of technical knowledge of a particular industry or function to a project. Specialists supply the details necessary to customize generalist solutions for cases in which specific content is important to the implementation of the solution.

Like its client industries, the consulting profession itself is undergoing and reacting to more rapid environmental change than it has experienced in the past. The industry is increasingly competitive as companies maneuver to define their competitive advantage. Older firms are facing new competitors as some firms expand their services from either management, information systems, or development consulting into the other areas. Particularly illustrative of this trend has been the movement of computer manufacturers into information systems design and implementation consulting and, more recently, into management consulting. Likewise, several management consulting firms have also acquired information systems firms to develop capabilities in that area.

Despite the increased competitiveness and changing consulting landscape, consulting as a whole has generally experienced impressive growth rates. This is often attributed to the increasing pace of change and the fact that certain consulting services will be important whatever the current state of the business cycle (expansion or recession). In a state of expansion, an organization may need consultants to help identify how to best take advantage of growth opportunities; while in a state of recession, organizations will have an increased need for cost reduction, market protection, and other appropriate advice. Given these trends, most analysts expect continued growth and change for the consulting profession, even though the pace of growth is increasingly affected by business cycles more than has been the case in the past.

The international aspects of and opportunities in consulting are numerous, particularly in the larger international consulting firms or whenever the client is a global or multinational organization. For example, there are always international aspects and considerations involved in the development of a strategy, operations improvement, or organizational redesign for an international organization, such as a Fortune 500 company. Even smaller companies will often use consultants to help them expand into international markets. In the public sector, the role and geographical breadth of the institution being served will often add a heavy international component to the consulting work. Finally, almost any consulting expertise, however narrowly defined, is applicable to other international organizations in the same industry or in the same situation. In my case, I have worked on consulting projects for several international corporations where a perspective and understanding of international issues was extremely important: for example, I was also assigned to a six-month manufacturing facility consolidation project in Brazil. In my current position, I also consult for my company on issues of international strategy and operations, and this work requires international travel and expertise. For the internationally minded consultant, most international consulting firms provide ample opportunities for their consultants to work on projects in foreign offices for a short-term, long-term, or even permanent transfer basis.

The skills required to be a successful consultant include strong analytical capabilities, an ability to work independently and within given deadlines, problem-solving skills, ability to work in a team environment, and outstanding written and oral communications. Beyond this, a generalist is hired largely for insight, whereas a specialist is sought for unique knowledge. Although most consulting firms have in-house training programs designed to build and hone required skills, most training is done on the job.

In hiring, most major consulting firms seek candidates with advanced degrees in business or other specialty areas. In addition, most consultants hired as specialists have years of specific industry or functional experience. In some cases, more experienced consultants with unique expertise are hired on retainer to fulfill a specific contract within a specified time frame instead of being asked to join the firm full time. For most foreign assignments, previous international experience and language proficiency are usually required. Some firms offer summer positions to students who are obtaining their advanced degrees. Many large firms also offer candidates with B.A.s positions as business analysts or interns. Most such programs last two years, after which the individual usually pursues a graduate degree. In some cases, a firm offers financial assistance and/or makes an offer of employment after successful completion of graduate studies.

The point of entry into a consulting firm will be influenced by the focus of the firm and the nature of the position. Many firms have active recruiting programs to attract candidates from undergraduate and graduate schools for full-time associates, business analysts, and internship positions. Alternatively, ask a reference librarian for Dunn's or other consulting directories that list, geographically and by specialty, the thousands of consulting firms in the United States and abroad, and use this information to contact the firms directly. For experienced hires, many of the major consulting firms retain executive search firms that refer candidates to meet specific personnel needs. For consultants on retainer positions, leads on contracts for specialist consulting needs can be found in publications that list U.S. government contract awards at the Department of Commerce, the Agency for International Development, and the Department of State. For other international contracts, the United Nations and World Bank have similar registries of outstanding contracts pending award. In addition, international and trade periodicals such as *The Economist* and *Oil and Gas Digest* frequently advertise government contract bid solicitations.

It is difficult for most consultants to describe a typical day succinctly. There is a high degree of variability from project to project, and this is one aspect of the job most consultants highly value. There is also a high degree of ambiguity and uncertainty. There may be frequent and extensive travel requirements and long hours. There are few careers as stimulating, diverse, demanding, and potentially lucrative as consulting. Many find consulting a rewarding experience, whether it is for a few years or a lifetime. If it is for a few years, the experience gained and the skills developed are well suited and sought after by many organizations and for a variety of positions.

Resource Listings

Accenture

Accenture is a $10 billion global management and technology consulting organization whose mission is to find innovations that improve the way the world works and lives. Accenture is the world's leading provider of management and technology consulting services and solutions, with more than 75,000 people in forty-six countries delivering a wide range of specialized capabilities and solutions to clients across all industries. Accenture operates globally with one common brand and business model designed to enable the company to serve its clients on a consistent basis around the world. Under its strategy, Accenture is building a network of businesses to meet the full range of any organization's consulting, technology, outsourcing, alliances, and venture capital. The company generated revenues of $9.75 billion for the fiscal year ending August 31, 2000, and $5.71 billion for the six months ending February 28, 2001. For more information, visit their website at www.accenture.com.

Accenture works in a wide range of industries, including automotive and industrial equipment; food and consumer packaged goods; pharmaceutical and medical products; retail, transportation, and travel services; communications; electronics, media, and entertainment; chemical; energy; natural resources; utilities; government; banking and financial services; health services; and insurance.

Accenture seeks applicants who demonstrate leadership, enthusiasm, and solid analytical and interpersonal skills. For up-to-date employment opportunities, refer to the website.

Washington, DC:
Accenture
800 Connecticut Avenue, NW, Suite 600
Washington, DC 20006
Tel.: (202) 533-1100 Fax: (202) 533-1111

New York City:
1345 Avenue of the Americas
New York, NY 10105
Tel.: (917) 452-4400 Fax: (917) 527-9915
www.accenture.com

American Management Systems
American Management Systems (AMS) is an international business and information technology consulting firm with 2000 revenues of $1.28 billion. Founded in 1970, AMS leverages cross-industry expertise to manage mission-critical IT, e-business, and systems integration projects for clients including forty-three state and provincial governments, most federal agencies, and hundreds of companies in the Fortune 500. AMS's core strength is its deep pool of talented consultants with expertise in systems development and implementation, large-scale technology integration, change management, and e-business reinvention.

AMS is headquartered in Fairfax, Virginia, and has more than 7,000 employees in fifty-one offices around the world. *Forbes* magazine ranked AMS among "America's 400 Best Big Companies" and *Fortune* placed AMS forty-fourth on its list of the "100 Best Companies to Work for in America." AMS is traded in the NASDAQ under the symbol AMSY.

AMS consultants work side by side with clients, using advanced technologies to analyze business functions, design and develop applications using state-of-the-art tools, and provide systems implementation services.

> AMS Corporate Headquarters
> 4050 Legato Road
> Fairfax, VA 22033
> Tel.: (703) 267-8000
> www.ams.com

Andreae, Vick & Associates
Andreae, Vick & Associates is a government relations consulting firm that specializes in U.S. foreign policy. The firm monitors and analyzes policy developments in both the executive and legislative branches to keep clients abreast of actions that could impact their international trade and investment objectives. Through its understanding of the decision-making process in Washington, the firm provides strategic counsel on how clients' interests can be most effectively supported in Washington. Andreae, Vick & Associates also assists clients in obtaining financial support from Washington-based trade finance institutions and actively works with U.S. government and nonprofit organizations to promote the creation of democratic government systems and political parties in developing countries.

The firm was established in 1990 and currently employs seven full-time staff people. Recently, it has had one to two openings each year. Associate candidates should have a master's degree in a related field such as international relations, international business, government, or public policy. A strong understanding of the U.S. government and other foreign policy actors is required, and Capitol Hill experience is strongly preferred.

> Andreae, Vick & Associates
> Human Resources
> 1250 I Street, NW, Suite 1105
> Washington, DC 20005
> Tel.: (202) 682-5151

A. T. Kearney

A. T. Kearney is an international, multidisciplined general management consulting firm with offices worldwide. The firm has worked for clients in every industry in both mature and newly market-oriented economies. A. T. Kearney has had a continuous presence in North America since 1926, in Europe since 1964, and in Asia since 1972. The firm's mission is to help its clients gain and sustain competitive advantage, now and in the future. A. T. Kearney strives to excel by delivering tangible results, providing a strong process orientation that focuses on implementation, providing service enhancements, and practicing total quality management.

Recruiting takes place primarily for consulting positions and for business associates. Consultants must have a master's degree, which is usually but not necessarily an M.B.A. Business associates must have an undergraduate degree in such areas as engineering, mathematics, economics, business, or management.

> Corporate Recruiting Department
> A. T. Kearney
> 222 West Adams Street
> Chicago, IL 60606
> Tel.: (312) 648-6030
> www.atkearney.com

Bain & Company

Founded in 1973, Bain & Company is one of the world's leading strategy consulting firms. Bain is dedicated to helping major international corporations improve bottom-line results and achieve significant increases in the market values of their companies. Bain employs nearly 2,800 people in twenty-seven offices in twenty countries.

Candidates should be top graduates of leading colleges and universities and should possess excellent academic credentials, strong analytical skills, and high levels of motivation. Online applications are preferred.

> Bain & Company
> Two Copley Place
> Boston, MA 02117-2000
> Tel.: (617) 572-2000
> Fax: (617) 572-2427
> www.bain.com

BearingPoint
BearingPoint's Barents Group is the sector within its Public Services Consulting organization that is focused on the emerging market countries of the world. Much of the work performed by Barents Group is funded by the U.S. Agency for International Development, the World Bank, and other International Funding Institutions. Foreign government counterparts include ministries of finance, planning, privatization, health, and economy; central banks; government-owned banks; and other institutions. BearingPoint assists foreign government counterparts in designing and implementing sound fiscal, financial, and economic policies and in implementing modern processes, procedures, and technology. BearingPoint has more than 9,100 professionals worldwide and $2.856 billion in revenue for fiscal year 2001.

Recruits usually possess ten years of professional experience, a background in economics, utilities, tax, or law and five years of overseas experience. For more information on career opportunities, visit the "Careers/Join Talent Network" section of www.bearingpoint.com.

> BearingPoint
> 1676 International Drive
> Tyson's Tower
> McLean, VA 22102
> www.bearingpoint.com

Booz-Allen Hamilton

Booz-Allen Hamilton, an international management and technology consulting firm with more than 100 offices around the globe, serves most of the largest industrial and service corporations in the world, the departments and agencies of the U.S. federal government, and major institutions and government bodies across the globe. The firm's diverse assignments range from strategic planning and acquisitions to global markets, energy policy design, and technological advancement. Through its Worldwide Commercial Business and Worldwide Technology Business, Booz-Allen provides services in strategy, systems, operations, and technology. The firm combines its integrated service base with specialized expertise in more than twenty industry practices.

Although most of the Booz-Allen professionals have an M.B.A., a wide variety of academic backgrounds and employment experiences exists among its staff, including training in international affairs. Although professionals hired from the industry enter at all levels, M.B.A.s usually join the firm as associates, and recent college graduates are typically hired as consultants.

> Booz-Allen Hamilton
> Corporate Headquarters
> 8283 Greensboro Drive
> McLean, VA 22102
> Tel.: (703) 902-5000
> www.bah.com

The Boston Consulting Group

The Boston Consulting Group's (BCG) reputation in management consulting derives from forty years of experience. The firm's mission is to help clients attain success by guiding, developing, facilitating, and enriching the client's strategy development process. BCG's professional expertise spans more than fifty industries, including consumer and industrial, financial and nonfinancial (including utilities). The majority of BCG's clients rank among the 500 largest companies in each of its three major locations—North America, Europe, and Asia. In addition, the firm works with a number of public and private medium-sized companies and smaller, growing firms. More than 90 percent of BCG's top clients continue to work with the firm from one year to the next.

Founded in 1963, BCG now has more than fifty offices worldwide. A majority of consultants with BCG hold M.B.A.s or other advanced degrees from leading business schools; most have held previous managerial positions in a broad spectrum of private- and public-sector organizations. Most assignments involve one or more teams of three to six BCG professionals, including one or two officers, a project manager, and several consultants, working with a similar group of client staff. The team incorporates a mix of seniority and skills to balance the capabilities needed for the project. Individual assignments can last anywhere from two to twelve months or more, depending on the complexity of the challenges and the client's needs. BCG encourages its consultants outside the United States to spend a portion of their careers in the United States and urges its U.S.-based consultants to do the same abroad.

> The Boston Consulting Group
> Exchange Place, 31ˢᵗ Floor
> Boston, MA 02109
> Tel.: (617) 973-1200
> Fax: (617) 973-1339
> www.bcg.com

Chemonics International Inc.

Chemonics International Inc., headquartered in Washington, D.C., is an international consulting firm focusing on development and project and consultant management. Initially established in 1975 to provide technical assistance to developing countries in agriculture, natural resources, and rural development, the firm has expanded to include several practice areas: business solutions for agriculture, environmental management, resource conservation, private-sector development, environmental responsibility services, finance and banking, law and governance, and humanitarian response and health.

Today, Chemonics manages many projects funded by bilateral donors and multilateral financial institutions such as the U.S. Agency for International Development (USAID), the World Bank, the Asian Development Bank, the African Development Bank, and the Inter-American Development Bank. Chemonics also provides advisory services to foreign governments as well as private clients. Broad experience in project implementation, paired with best-practice management and technical expertise, has equipped Chemonics to deliver management services tailored to the needs of individual projects. They cite as the key pillars of their management approach tested project management systems, comprehensive oversight and backstopping, home-office support services, and focus on efficiency

Getting Started in Consulting
GARGEE GHOSH

Thinking about how best to describe my career choice and my experience as a McKinsey & Company associate, I believe I should start with my immediate surroundings. I am on a plane returning from Ghana on a Sunday night. I have spent a week in meetings with government officials discussing terms for my client—a U.S.-based multinational—to expand operations in West Africa. I traveled 8,000 miles by myself and also conducted the meetings alone. When I land at JFK I will go straight to team meetings to prepare a client debriefing for tomorrow morning. My body hasn't adjusted to any time zone, which explains why I wanted sushi in Heathrow airport at 5:45 A.M.. I am anxious because I have four hours of work to do before landing and only 61 percent of laptop battery life. I forgot to bring a spare.

Some version of the previous example is typical, but there is no "typical management consulting experience." It was precisely the prospect of variety, challenges, and opportunities that brought

and results. With project offices in Africa, Asia, Europe and Eurasia, Latin America and the Caribbean, and the Middle East, the firm maintains subsidiary, affiliate, regional or representative offices in Cairo, Bucharest, Damascus, Guatemala City, Jakarta, Kampala, La Paz, London, Manila, Mexico City, Moscow, Panama City (Panama), Ramallah, Washington, D.C., and Waterford (Ireland).

For home-office positions, Chemonics encourages interested individuals to visit the Career Opportunities page on its website at www.chemonics.com. Chemonics, an equal opportunity employer, encourages individuals with experience overseas and at least five years of professional experience or a graduate degree relevant to Chemonics' work to e-mail their resumés for contract positions to resume@chemonics.com or to mail their resumés on disk to

Recruitment
Chemonics International Inc.
1133 20th Street, NW
Washington, DC 20036

me to this career. Since joining McKinsey, I have served an investment bank, an online brokerage, a pharmaceuticals company, a government, and an economic development organization on issues ranging from designing a competitive strategy to launching a new global product. In the past year, I have learned more about business, acquired more professional confidence, and discovered more about my career interests (and earned more air miles) than in any other year. With the possible exception of the air travel, this was exactly what I hoped to gain.

I didn't start with those clear goals. Prior to graduation, I was facing the typical *generalist's dilemma*—no idea where to begin my career. I was interested in business and economic development and had a strong academic background and aptitude in both. I wanted to work in international development eventually, and believed the private sector should be the engine of economic growth in the developing world. Yet, I wasn't sure how to translate that aspiration into job applications. I never wanted to feel as if I had stopped learning or challenging myself, and several friends and mentors recommended management consulting as a way to continue learning and being challenged—and most of all—a way to *determine and decide* exactly what I wanted to do.

(Continued)

Corporate Executive Board

The Corporate Executive Board is the premier membership organization for senior executives of leading institutions worldwide to discover innovative strategies for addressing their most pressing challenges. In general, Corporate Executive Board serves a group of clients (a membership) as opposed to focusing on the needs of any one specific client. Their dedicated membership programs focus upon increasing the effectiveness of leaders within member organizations. To that end, they provide a variety of services—best practices research, executive education, and decision support tools—designed to accelerate the implementation of new strategies and to help members avoid reinventing the wheel as they address problems shared with their peers.

Corporate Executive Board is a business-to-business content firm serving the world's largest network of senior executives from more than 1,700 companies. The company's research focuses on cutting-edge strategy, operations, and general management issues; through

So, I applied to several management consulting firms and traveled to New York, meeting management consultants, reading about the profession, and preparing for the dreaded case interviews.

Recruiting at McKinsey is rigorous. I interviewed with more than ten people in three rounds of interviews. *Cracking the cases* played a significant part in the process—I highly recommend Wet Feet Press, other case interview guides, and your economics textbooks to prepare. I quickly learned three guiding principles. (Consultants always have "three key points!") First, the case interview is a test of how you approach a problem, not whether you can solve it. As a non-M.B.A., I found that it is important to know business basics, but equally important to structure your thoughts and show off your analytical thinking. The rest you will learn on the job! Second, problem-solving skills and people skills go hand-in-hand. There is no personality blueprint, but you'll get a version of the "airport test": what would happen if you were stuck in an airport for four hours with a client? And, equally important, could your colleagues stand being stuck with you in the same situation? Confidence, poise, energy, enthusiasm, and an interesting "non-consulting" personality

this it can identify the most innovative and effective management initiatives, processes, tools, and frameworks for its clients.

United States:
The Corporate Executive Board
2000 Pennsylvania Avenue, NW
Washington, DC 20006
Suite 6000
Tel.: (202) 777-5000
Fax: (202) 777-5100
www.executiveboard.com

United Kingdom:
166 Piccadilly
London, W1J9EF
United Kingdom
Tel.: 44-0-20-7499-8700
Fax: 44-0-20-7499-9700

count for a lot. Third, their interview process is incredibly effective at finding the right people for McKinsey. It's also a great opportunity to see if they are a fit for you.

I decided management consulting and McKinsey were right for me—the perfect way to learn private sector best practices that I could eventually apply in the economic development arena. Ultimately, it was the people at McKinsey who sold me on consulting. I found they were intelligent, dynamic individuals with varied interests from whom I could learn and with whom I wanted to work.

The past year has been fast, busy, and exhausting. But it has also been extremely rewarding. I have seen the impact of working at McKinsey on my own professional development and the impact of my work on clients and on the firm. I am acquiring tools that will be useful wherever my career takes me from here.

And now I am almost out of battery life.

Gargee Ghosh, a 2002 graduate of Georgetown University's Master of Science in Foreign Service degree program, is an associate with McKinsey & Company in New York. Prior to joining McKinsey she held part-time positions with the OAS, the United Nations, and the government of the province of British Columbia. Ms. Ghosh graduated in 1997 with honors from the University of Victoria in British Columbia, Canada, and holds an M.Sc. in Economics (International Development) from Oxford University.

Deloitte & Touche

Deloitte & Touche, one of the world's leading professional services firms, provides accounting, assurance and advisory, tax, management, and financial and human capital consulting services. Known as an employer of choice for innovative human resources programs, Deloitte & Touche has been recognized as one of the "100 Best Companies to Work For" in America by *Fortune* magazine for four consecutive years.

Deloitte & Touche employs 95,000 people in more than 140 countries—30,000 people in more than 100 U.S. cities alone—and serves nearly 21 percent of the world's largest companies as well as large national enterprises, public institutions, and successful fast-growing companies. The firm believes that helping clients excel demands the most diverse range of skills, talent, experiences, and backgrounds, and therefore, the broader their employee's experience and education, the deeper the firm's collective understanding.

Deloitte & Touche
1633 Broadway
New York, NY 10019-6754
Tel.: (212) 489-1600 Fax: (212) 489-1687
www.deloitte.com

The Delphi Group

The Delphi Group provides strategic advice on climate change and health and environment issues. The Delphi Group assists Canadian and other companies to penetrate the Latin American market, suggests strategies for international development assistance in climate change, and works in partnership with governmental agencies and other stakeholders. The business units involved in Latin America are climate change, health and environment, and sustainable energy. The Delphi Group also does international development climate change work in Asia (China, Pakistan, Bangladesh, etc.).

The Delphi Group is a small consulting group; opportunities are limited. New hires usually have previous training and/or work experience in either climate change economics or policy (in the North American context), or health and environment. Fluency in Spanish is desirable. Applicants should be self-motivated, enjoy working alone as well as in groups, have passion for the work, be willing to take risks and take on challenging tasks, and be outgoing. Candidates must also be eligible to work in Canada. Team players are valued, as are those with communication skills.

The Delphi Group is still a relatively small organization and has an informal hiring process. All applicants under serious consideration will have an informal interview and opportunity to meet with all Delphi staff.

The Delphi Group
428 Gilmour Street
Ottawa, Canada, K2P OR8
Tel.: (613) 562-2005
Fax: (613) 562-2008
www.delphi.ca

Development Associates, Inc.

Development Associates is a management and government consulting firm specializing in educational, social, and economic development programs in the United States and overseas. The company's international projects largely focus on the fields of education, democracy and governance, nutrition and public health, family planning and population, developmental administration, rural development, and urban and regional planning.

Development Associates, with regional offices in San Francisco and Honolulu and offices abroad in Egypt, Senegal, Ukraine, Zimbabwe, and Puerto Rico, can draw on a staff of about 250 active consultants and specialists worldwide. More than 75 percent of their staff speaks one or more foreign languages. New recruits usually possess a technical background (such as economics) and generally apply for research analyst positions; those with advanced degrees are considered for professional slots. There are about 125 people involved on a full-time basis in professional, international capacities. Up to an additional 120 persons are recruited annually for short-term consultancies.

> Development Associates, Inc.
> 1730 N. Lynn Street
> Arlington, VA 22209
> Tel.: (703) 276-0677
> Fax: (703) 276-0432
> www.devassoc1.com

Environmental Resources Management

Environmental Resources Management (ERM) is widely acknowledged as one of the world's leading providers of environmental consulting services. ERM operates with a global business model that enables the company to serve its clients with the highest levels of professionalism, flexibility, and consistency. ERM provides results for hundreds of leading industry and government clients by helping them improve their business and environmental performance.

ERM achieves this by determining the potential implications of key issues such as new environmental regulations, consumer concerns, supply chain issues, corporate reputation, and cost. Dedicated global teams within ERM also provide expert services on climate change, biodiversity, waste management, and corporate social strategies.

Through the provision of strategic and business value, new site development, remediation or site cleanup, and facility operations, ERM achieved net revenues in fiscal year 2001 of U.S.$200 million. The company's annual gross revenues are $300 million.

ERM's philosophy embraces excellence, diversity, creativity, quality, efficiency, and service. With more than 120 offices in more than thirty countries and a staff of more than 2,400, it offers many opportunities for career development.

For more information about ERM and to find out about career opportunities, visit the website.

Environmental Resources Management
855 Springdale Drive
Exton, PA 19341
Tel.: (610) 524-3500
www.erm.com

Ernst & Young

Ernst & Young LLP is the U.S. member firm of Ernst & Young International, a leading international professional services firm dedicated to helping companies identify and capitalize on business opportunities throughout the world. Practice areas include accounting and auditing, tax, management consulting, corporate finance, restructuring and reorganization, capital markets, cash management, valuation, benefits and compensation consulting, and outsourcing services. Ernst & Young has more than 680 offices in more than 125 countries. The firm's professional expertise is engaged by a broad range of organizations, including multinational corporations, owner-managed companies, governments, and nonprofit institutions operating in both developed economies and emerging markets worldwide. Significant international opportunities exist in all practice areas and are enhanced by international residencies and exchange programs.

The mission of Ernst & Young's Management Consulting practice is to contribute to clients' long-term success and competitive strength. This is accomplished by helping clients to identify solutions that improve performance, by assisting in implementing those solutions, and by aiding in managing the subsequent change.

The Management Consulting practice offers both performance improvement and information technology services. The overall objective of the performance improvement (PI) practice is to enhance the performance of all or part of a client's business. Improvements are measured by both marketplace criteria and financial results and against operating benchmarks. PI engagements fall into four categories: strategic management, performance measurement, change management, and process improvement. By combining specific approaches, techniques, tools, benchmarks, and information from their most successful engagements, Ernst & Young consultants bring added value to clients whose challenges in the competitive marketplace continue to grow. PI issues include profitability, globalization, customer focus, quality, time, cost competitiveness, innovation of products and services design and delivery, people and organizational capabilities, and post-service and support.

In addition to recruiting for the U.S. firm, coordination is also provided for Ernst & Young offices in other countries. Management Consulting candidates must have strong academic performance, first-rate analytical skills, excellent interpersonal abilities, a willingness to travel, and a career goal of helping companies make and implement better business decisions. Management Consulting graduate degree candidates should have at least two years of work experience after their bachelor's degree. Preferred are undergraduate degrees in engineering, accounting, finance, information systems, or other strong quantitative or business degrees.

Management Consulting
Director of Campus Recruiting
Ernst & Young LLP
1 North Charles Street
Baltimore, MD 21201
Tel.: (410) 783-3725
www.ey.com/global/content.nsf/International/Careers

The Futures Group International

The Futures Group International is a management, marketing, and strategic planning organization that helps clients make critical decisions in the presence of future uncertainty. Futures is committed to enhancing sustainable development through the transfer of technologies to global experts and institutions and through the creation of appropriate project designs. Areas of program concentration include child survival, family planning, reproductive health, population policy, nutrition, and prevention of HIV/AIDS and sexually transmitted infections (STIs).

Since its founding in 1971, Futures has worked in more than fifty developing countries for more than 600 clients, including the U.S. Agency for International Development (USAID), the African Development Bank, the Asian Development Bank, the World Bank, the United Nations Population Fund (UNFPA), the United Nations Children's Fund (UNICEF), Kreditanstalt für Wiederaufbau (KfW), and the World Health Organization (WHO).

The Futures Group International
1050 17th Street, NW
Washington, DC 20036
Tel.: (202) 775-9680 Fax: (202) 775-9694
www.tfgi.com/career.asp

McKinsey & Company

McKinsey & Company is an international management consulting firm. Founded in 1926, the firm has maintained continued growth and currently has eighty-five offices in forty-four countries, with more than 7,700 consultants. The firm serves organizations in most industrial nations and in some developing countries on matters of strategy, organization, and operations. The firm's mission is twofold: to help clients make substantial and lasting improvements in their performance and to build a firm that is able to attract, develop, excite, and retain exceptional people. McKinsey takes an integrated, general management approach to client work, addressing business problems and challenges from the broad perspective of senior management. The firm also devotes considerable time and effort to pro bono work for nonprofit organizations worldwide.

Associates join teams of two to five other professionals (partners, associates, business analysts, or specialists) and play an active role in all aspects of a project: fact gathering, analysis, development of recommendations, and implementation. Associates are normally involved in presentations to and discussions with top management and are expected to raise issues and express opinions throughout. The associates must work effectively with client teams, adhere to strict professional standards, put the client's interests and needs first, and be prepared for a demanding lifestyle.

McKinsey & Company seeks candidates with outstanding intellect, leadership, work experience, initiative, and proven ability to work effectively with people at all levels in an organization. The firm looks for individuals with strong records of academic and managerial/ professional achievement who have the capacity for continuous development. Although most associates hold an M.B.A., others have graduate degrees in economics, engineering, law, medicine, public policy, and other professional fields. New hires usually have three to five years of work experience. Candidates must have citizenship or permanent working papers for the country to which they apply and meet language requirements.

McKinsey & Company
600 Fourteenth Street, NW, Suite 300
Washington, DC 20005
Tel.: (202) 662-3100
Fax: (202) 662-3175
www.mckinsey.com

Mercer Management Consulting

One of the leading international management consulting firms, Mercer Management Consulting helps major corporations around the world address their most critical strategic challenges. Mercer works in partnership with its clients to identify and seize the most attractive opportunities for accelerated value growth and strengthened prosperity. Mercer takes an integrated, customer-driven approach to the challenges of strategic change. The firm is committed to growing rapidly throughout the world to solidify its leadership position. Recently, Mercer has enhanced its presence in Europe, the Pacific Rim, and Canada and plans to aggressively continue its expansion worldwide over the next five years.

Mercer has more than 1,000 consultants working in twenty-one offices worldwide. The firm interviews and hires candidates primarily from leading undergraduate and graduate business schools in North America, Europe, and Asia. The firm is a member of Mercer Consulting Group, the global consulting organization of Marsh and McLennan Companies.

Mercer Management Consulting
1166 Avenue of the Americas, 32nd Floor
New York, NY 10036
Tel.: (212) 345-8000
www.mercermc.com

Monitor Company

Monitor Company, one of the world's preeminent consulting firms, is headquartered in Cambridge, Massachusetts, and has offices in Amsterdam, Frankfurt, Hong Kong, Johannesburg, London, Los Angeles, Madrid, Milan, New York, Paris, Seoul, Tokyo, and Toronto. Founded in 1982, it has grown from three employees to a global firm. Monitor has relationships with one-third of the Fortune 500 companies—and many of their international equivalents—in such diverse industries as electronics, telecommunications, aerospace, energy, retailing, and financial services.

Monitor's practice focuses on strategy consulting. Most projects fall into one of the following areas: competitive strategies for business units in individual industries; corporate strategies for diversified companies; strategies for entering new businesses, or acquiring them; and organizational redesign to support continuous strategic action. Increasingly, Monitor consults with state and national governments about their competitive prospects.

Monitor believes that a person's background or educational degree—years on Wall Street or an M.B.A., for example—does not translate into consulting success, so apart from the firm's directors, all members of the consulting staff have the same title: consultant. Candidates should be creative, analytical, and like to work in teams. Requirements include a superior academic record, a willingness to take initiative and assume responsibility, and a desire to learn.

> Recruiting Coordinator
> Monitor Group
> Two Canal Park
> Cambridge, MA 02141
> www.monitor.com

Nathan Associates Inc.

Nathan Associates Inc., an economic consulting firm headquartered in Arlington, Virginia, has served developing countries and international development agencies for more than fifty-five years. Known for the quality of its advice and services and for project management skills, the firm's hallmarks are decision support and capacity building for government and private sector leaders. Nathan Associates offers these services to public and private sector clients in the United States and around the world. Its current portfolio of assignments features projects that demand a broad range of services including:

- Analysis of the economic impacts of public policy
- Analysis of and testimony on economic issues in regulatory proceedings
- Expert testimony on liability and damages in antitrust, financial markets, intellectual property infringement, and trade litigation
- Development and analysis of national growth strategies and provision of support to small and medium enterprises
- Analysis of infrastructure planning, policy, and investment needs and feasibility
- Analysis of the economic costs and benefits of recognizing and enforcing intellectual property rights
- Supplementing and building professional, analytical, and negotiating capacity in trade policy

The permanent staff, including Nathan teams in resident service overseas, represent a wide range of specialties. These include macroeconomic analysis and policy formulation, urban and infrastructure development, national and regional development planning, taxation and municipal finance, bank reform, privatization, industrial development, management information systems, telecommunications, monitoring and project evaluation, sectoral studies in agriculture, transportation and energy, international trade and investment, and institutional development.

Overseas and professional staff are supported by persons with graduate-level degrees in economics, business administration, or public policy. The firm looks for quantitative skills and work experience in a developing country as well as fluency in a second language.

> Nathan Associates Inc.
> 2101 Wilson Boulevard, Suite 1200
> Arlington, VA 22201
> Tel.: (703) 516-7700
> Fax: (703) 351-6162
> www.nathaninc.com

The Pragma Corporation

The Pragma Corporation is a private international development consulting firm headquartered in Falls Church, Virginia. With offices throughout the world, Pragma provides technical and management consulting services for development projects worldwide. With a large international staff of senior technical advisors, Pragma has, since 1977, completed more than 500 projects in sixty-five countries for clients ranging from bilateral and multilateral donors to U.S. and international private firms, nongovernmental and private voluntary organizations, and academic institutions.

The number of professional openings in the international field varies yearly with projects, but the firm has approximately two vacancies in Falls Church, Virginia, and ten to fifteen internationally.

Pragma seeks professionals with international experience and relevant degrees. The degrees vary depending on the needs of the project, but include degrees in development, business, agriculture, law, and education. Opportunities for overseas consulting work usually require a minimum of a master's degree and relevant international work experience.

> The Pragma Corporation
> 116 East Broad Street
> Falls Church, VA 22046
> Tel.: (703) 237-9303
> Fax: (703) 237-9326
> www.pragmacorp.com

Pyramid Research

Pyramid Research provides market analysis and consulting services to the telecommunications, Internet, and media industry. It helps clients to develop sound international business strategies by providing rigorous, in-depth analysis and advice on markets that span the globe. Pyramid is the only company whose core competence is covering emerging markets around the world. It has spent more than two decades building a solid understanding of the intangibles that make these markets particularly difficult to navigate, providing clients with guidance in markets filled with regulatory uncertainty, economic instability, and unclear business practices. Its coverage includes North America, Latin America, Central and Eastern Europe, Western Europe, Africa and the Middle East, and Asia-Pacific. Headquartered in Cambridge, Massachusetts, Pyramid Research also has offices in London and Hong Kong and has a network of 100 specialized professionals, including consultants, analysts, and associates.

Pyramid offers a bridge between strategic consulting and proprietary research that assesses clients' individual business issues in emerging and developed countries worldwide. Companies use its services to assist with market analysis and sizing, customer segmentation and targeting, competitive tracking, global benchmarking of opportunities and risk, new license valuation, market entry strategies, and partner identification.

All of Pyramid's analysts and consultants speak one or more foreign languages fluently and have had extensive experience living and working abroad. Although industry experience is not required to apply, a good understanding of international business issues and superior intellect are a must. Candidates with bachelor's degrees usually fill associate positions, whereas analyst and consultant positions are reserved for candidates with graduate degrees in business and international affairs.

> Pyramid Research
> 58 Charles Street
> Cambridge, MA 02141
> Tel.: (617) 494-1515
> Fax: (617) 494-8898
> www.pyramidresearch.com

SRI International

Founded in 1946 as the Stanford Research Institute, SRI International is a nonprofit, independent, problem-solving corporation that provides a broad spectrum of basic and applied research and consulting services to business and government clients throughout the world. SRI's Center for Science, Technology and Economic Development (CSTED) conducts the majority of the company's international development and consulting work, focusing on the fields of economic development and competitiveness, industry clustering, corporate strategy, technology development, and workforce development. Based in Washington, D.C., CSTED has conducted research and consulting assignments in more than sixty states, provinces, and communities in North America and in more than 110 nations worldwide.

Nearly two-thirds of SRI's 1,400 staff members have professional and technical expertise, including economists, management consultants, scientists, and other specialists. CSTED employs about twenty-five full-time staff with a technical background in international affairs, economics, public policy, business, science and technology policy, and education policy. New recruits usually possess a master's degree in one of these areas, as well as work experience in public policy, development, or consulting; strong research, writing, and analytical skills; and some overseas experience. Annual job openings vary based on project and staffing needs.

> Center for Science, Technology and Economic
> Development
> SRI International
> 1611 North Kent Street
> Arlington, VA 22209-2111
> Tel.: (703) 524-2053
> Fax: (703) 247-8410
> www.sri.com/policy/csted

Chapter 11

INTERNATIONAL DEVELOPMENT

Careers in International Development

PATRICIA L. DELANEY

I remember the exact moment when I decided that international development was the field for me. It was in Recife, Brazil, in September of 1986. As I walked out the door of an upscale, all-you-can-eat *churrascaria* (Brazilian barbecue) on a Sunday afternoon, I noticed a small child standing outside and peering in. As I looked closer, I realized that she was doing a pantomime—rubbing her belly and gesturing as if to put food in her mouth. The little girl was probably six or seven, wearing tattered clothes and no shoes. Behind her were several other children, some holding younger siblings and cousins with matted hair and distended bellies. They were *favelados* (slum dwellers) from a nearby encampment. In contrast, my Brazilian host family and I were dressed in trendy jeans and hip shoes. We lived in an upper middle-class suburb in a three-bedroom house, with a lovely garden and an armed guard who spent the night outside the walled compound.

As a North American raised in relatively comfortable middle-class surroundings, I was shocked by the stark contrast between gluttony and hunger, rich and poor. I later learned that poor children in Brazil, like most of the poor around the world, do not have access to safe drinking water or adequate health care. For most, the typical activities of childhood—school and play—are impossible dreams since they spend most of their time begging for food, picking through garbage, or selling trinkets in traffic.

Later still, I learned the academic and professional words to explain this situation—words like *structural poverty, stratification, wealth*

Patricia L. Delaney, a 1990 graduate of the Bachelor of Science in Foreign Service program at Georgetown University and a Ph.D. in anthropology from the University of California, Los Angeles, is currently on the adjunct faculty in the MSFS Program. A social anthropologist, as an AAAS Diplomacy Fellow, Delaney served as the social science advisor to USAID's Office of Foreign Disaster Assistance and as technical advisor to USAID's Office of Population, Health, and Nutrition.

distribution, and *Life Quality Index.* Those words, and the development projects that are designed to address them, now form the basis of my toolkit for doing something about the brutal reality that I observed firsthand. In the time since that Sunday in Brazil, I have worked in more than twenty countries in the developing world. I have garnered skills, learned different languages, worked in virtually every sector of development, and drawn on a range of academic and applied experience. I have never forgotten those children. That initial emotional, almost visceral, response is my motivation, and the desire to do something is my goal. That experience has greatly shaped my professional decisions and career choices in development.

Overview of Chapter

Each of us has our own reason and rationale for entering the always rewarding, often frustrating, and sometimes heart-breaking field of international relief and development. I believe that the first step is to think deeply about your personal, or perhaps even emotional, motives. The second step is to look carefully at the institutions in international relief and development to find the best possible fit for you and the organization with which you chose to work. The purpose of this chapter is to help you with that second step. This essay will provide an overview of the current structure and reality of the field, the types of professional positions, the necessary skills, and likely future trends in relief and development. The field of international relief and development is incredibly varied and there are many different ways to make a contribution. As you read through this summary, I encourage you to remember your own personal motivations and desires before deciding where you fit.

What Is the Field of International Development?

The development field is fundamentally about addressing basic human needs, such as water, food, and shelter, and working toward an improved quality of life for peoples in the nonindustrialized world. Although the actual activities that are implemented by practitioners are incredibly diverse, ranging from agricultural research on drought-resistant seed to HIV/AIDS prevention campaigns, the core issues remain the same.

Chief among these in the field of development is the desire to work toward the eradication of poverty. The slogans of two of the largest actors in relief and development confirm this objective. Whereas the World Bank declares that "Our Dream Is a World Free of

Poverty," the United Nations Development Program highlights its "Partnerships to Fight Poverty." Poverty, however, is not defined simply as the lack of income but also a lack of access to the many other goods and services that provide quality of life. These include health care, education, water and sanitation, housing, the natural environment, political voice, and basic infrastructure. This is adapted from the definition of poverty presented in Deepa Naryan's *Voices of the Poor* (Washington D.C.: World Bank Publications, 2000).

Sectors in Development
This multilayered definition of the goals of development has led to the creation of a variety of specialized sectors that seek to address each of the issues in turn. Although the specific names for sectors vary across the different organizations, the major categories remain the same. They include

- *Health*. This sector usually includes programs and projects in maternal and child health (MCH), child survival, family planning, and infectious disease. Organizations working in this sector implement activities ranging from vaccination campaigns to the improvement of public health infrastructure. Water and sanitation (Wat/San) is sometimes included in this sector or sometimes as its own sector. Many, but certainly not all, of the people who work in the health sector have a master's of public health degree.

- *Democracy/Governance*. Although it is one of the newest sectors in development, donor support for democracy and governance (DG) programs has grown tremendously. This sector features projects such as civil education campaigns, good governance training, and support for constitutional reform of police and legal institutions. Conflict resolution is also sometimes included in this sector. Many of the staff in this sector have an educational background in law, political science, or conflict resolution.

- *Agriculture/Environment*. Although agriculture is one of the longest-standing sectors in development, the addition of environment and natural resource management (NRM) is a comparatively new phenomenon. In agriculture, projects range from seed multiplication and germ plasm research to agricultural extension and vegetable gardening. Many projects aim to introduce improved technologies or encourage crop diversification and market-oriented production. In the environment, many projects focus on preserving biological diversity and promoting environmentally sensitive development such as ecotourism.

Increasingly, implementing agencies are realizing that the two subfields need to be better integrated in order to guarantee both ecological preservation and food security for people in the developing world. Some of the folks who work in this area have specific degrees in agricultural or environmental sciences (such as biology).

- *Economic Growth*. A portion of this sector has traditionally been focused on the micro-level and often aims to empower small producers to increase their income. Activities such as micro-credit, pioneered by the Grameen Bank in Bangladesh, and micro-enterprise fall within this sector. The other component of this sector works on macroeconomic policy formulation and implementation including topics such as free trade, intellectual property rights, and technology transfer. Many of the people working in this sector have a background in both finance and business and "softer" issues such as community organization.
- *Education*. The primary focus in this sector has historically been on elementary education, especially among underserved populations (such as girls, rural peoples, or slum dwellers). Activities include teacher training, curriculum development, supplemental feeding programs in schools, and infrastructure (building schools). In recent years, many projects have also been addressing adult education, literacy, environmental education, and nonformal education such as vocational education. Some staff have training as formal educators, but many of the development practitioners in this sector are also generalists.
- *Infrastructure*. This sector is concerned with creating the infrastructural conditions that will enable a country to reduce poverty and promote economic growth. This can include physical infrastructure in the transportation (roads, bridges) or energy (power lines, hydroelectric dams), as well as the "software" of policy, regulation, and enforcement. People with training in economics, engineering, and public policy most often work in this sector.

What Is the Field of International Relief?

The humanitarian relief field is based on a desire to address the basic and life-saving needs of people who are the victims of disasters and emergencies. For example, the Office of Foreign Disaster Assistance (OFDA), one of the relief arms of the U.S. Agency for International Development (USAID), has a stated mission of "saving lives and alleviating human suffering."

The two subfields in relief seek to provide assistance to victims of natural disasters such as hurricanes and earthquakes and complex humanitarian emergencies (CHEs) such as war and low-level conflict. Although some organizations work in both subfields, most organizations choose to specialize in one or the other. For example, the International Rescue Committee (IRC) focuses on CHEs and seeks to provide "relief, protection, and resettlement services for refugees and victims of oppression or violent conflict."

Sectors in Relief

Although there are major differences between the impacts of natural disasters and those of CHEs, the major sectors of assistance are largely the same. They include:

- *Search and Rescue.* This activity takes place during the first hours or days after a disaster event. Typically, highly trained professionals such as firefighters and emergency medical technicians are involved in this phase. As in any emergency situation, logisticians must also insure the rapid arrival of staff, equipment, and supplies.
- *Health Care.* The provision of emergency health care can take the form of triage, providing immediate assistance to combatants and noncombatants during conflict. It also includes the temporary provision of regular health care for those persons who are temporarily relocated (in evacuation centers, refugee camps, or other shelters). Water and sanitation are especially important components in these situations. Many emergency health workers are trained as nurses, doctors, or MPHs, although other support staff are often needed to provide logistical, financial, or information-gathering assistance.
- *Shelter.* The provision of emergency shelter (tents, plastic sheeting, communal facilities) also takes place in the immediate aftermath of a disaster. People who are displaced from their homes due to political violence or natural events such as earthquakes and floods receive shelter or the materials to construct shelter. They often also receive necessary household goods such as linens and cooking supplies. Shelter staff workers tend to need a strong background or skill-base in logistics and often have some training in construction or engineering.
- *Food Security.* The provision of emergency rations, cooking oil, grains, and supplemental feeding for the malnourished are the most typical activities in the food security area. In some long-term emergencies, food security programs often resemble agricultural development projects, with the distribution of seeds and tools. Many of the staff who work in food distribution are generalists, although persons with skills in logistics and social

assessment (to determine the types of rations and culturally appropriate mechanisms for distribution) are also needed.
- *Conflict Resolution/Protection*. These projects are most often seen in the wake of CHEs, although protection of women and girls from sexual violence and prevention of looting and the like also take place after natural disasters. Typical projects include community workshops in conflict resolution, counseling services for victims of violence, and the capacity building of local security enforcers. Many staff in this sector have experience in law, law enforcement, counseling, or political science. Protection is also a cross-cutting theme that many generalists incorporate into all projects.
- *Long-Term Relief*. These are the development activities such as education or capacity-building that often take place in protracted emergencies such as civil wars. Quite often, the target population is refugees or internally displaced persons (IDPs). Although these activities are implemented by relief agencies, they often more closely resemble development rather than traditional relief. They aim to decrease dependency on external assistance and to ease the transition for beneficiaries after the emergency ends. Many staff working on these projects have been trained as development practitioners and may have little experience with the provision of relief per se.

Cross-Cutting Themes in Relief and Development

In addition to the various sectors in relief and development, there are a variety of cross-cutting themes that are important in virtually every development project. Sometimes organizations rely on technical experts to integrate these important issues. More often, however, generalists are expected to incorporate these principles themselves or to call on colleagues who can do so. Some of the most common such themes are:
- *Gender*. In years past, this issue was often addressed as Women in Development (WID), an approach that aimed to correct past mistakes of exclusion through the explicit inclusion of women. Some programs, such as girl's education and women's empowerment projects, continue to follow this model. Increasingly, however, development practice is moving toward the inclusion of a Gender and Development (GAD) approach. Projects using a GAD lens look carefully at the roles and responsibilities of women *and* men, girls and boys, before and during project activities. The goal is to include culturally and gender-appropriate activities. In one example, this has meant the training of both men and women to serve as peer educators about family

planning (instead of the previous pattern of only working with women). In relief work, GAD activities have included distribution of food relief to women, because they are likelier than men to provide resources to children and the family. Technical experts in this area do things such as gender analysis and gender training.

- *Participation.* This issue is sometimes also referred to as stakeholder consultation (by groups such as the World Bank) or client-oriented design (by USAID, for example). This issue is a result of the growing awareness that earlier development activities often failed to reach their objectives because they did not meet the real needs of people on the ground. Most development projects now include some form of stakeholder involvement and participation, although the quality and quantity of such participation vary widely. The goal of participation is both to increase "buy-in" on the part of beneficiaries and also to better target interventions. Activities stemming from this concept include participatory rural appraisal (PRA) and other participatory diagnostic tools. Although direct participation is often difficult during the acute emergency phase, relief agencies are increasingly incorporating participatory methods in disaster planning and disaster prevention activities. Technical experts in this area often conduct institutional analyses for implementing agencies and also conduct training sessions for field and headquarters staff.

- *Sustainability.* The need for sustainability, or ability for programs to continue to operate after donor agencies have finished their work, is increasingly seen as a given in international development. Donors and implementing agencies now regularly incorporate mechanisms such as cost recovery (e.g., fees for services at health clinics) in order to work toward long-term sustainability. In the relief field, most agencies have worked toward building national capacity in disaster-prone countries including things such as Famine Early Warning Systems (FEWS), climatological forecasting, and the training of local search-and-rescue teams.

Actors in International Relief and Development

Although there are a plethora of actors and institutions in international relief and development, this section will simply describe the different types of actors in the field. The latter portion of the chapter provides an illustrative list of actual development institutions.

- *Donors.* These organizations are either bilateral, providing direct assistance from one nation-state to another (e.g., USAID or the UK Department for International Development [DFID]), or multilateral, providing assistance from a collective group of countries (e.g., UN Development Program [UNDP] or the European Union). Many donor organizations, especially the bilateral ones, provide the financial resources for development but leave the actual implementation of projects to nongovernmental organizations (NGOs) and others. Many of the staff at donor agencies are generalists who need to be familiar with many sectors and regions. Typical duties for employees include monitoring and oversight, policy formulation, and macro-level project design.

- *Implementing agencies.* These organizations are on the front line of development, working in the direct provision of assistance. Most often, they are NGOs or private sector firms that receive contracts or grants from donor agencies. The majority of implementing agencies have both a field and a headquarters presence, with differing staff in these locations. Headquarters staff tend to handle the more administrative and policy-oriented functions such as budgeting and strategic planning. Field staff are more likely involved directly in the actual development projects, with activities such as workshop facilitation, training of health-care workers, or delivery of emergency food provisions. Many organizations are structured in parallel fashion to their major donors, and staff are recruited based on sectoral or regional expertise.
- *Advocacy groups.* These groups are often comparatively small and tend to focus on research and outreach in the attempt to influence development policy, donors, and implementing agencies. Some take the form of think tanks with a specific sectoral or topical focus. Others lobby on behalf of general categories of people, such as women or refugees or indigenous peoples. Staff skills often include marketing, writing, public relations, and data analysis.

What Skills Do You Need? Generalists versus Experts

The two basic categories of staff in international relief and development are generalists and experts (sometimes referred to as technical experts). Virtually every development organization needs both generalists, who are flexible and adaptable, and experts, who tend to have a depth of knowledge in a specific sector or skill area. The ratio of generalists to experts often depends on the nature of the organization. The larger donors and implementing agencies often have sufficient resources to hire many different technical experts, whereas smaller NGOs sometimes rely almost exclusively on generalists, with periodic input from technical consultants.

As the name implies, generalists are expected to a have a wide range of general knowledge about the field of international relief and development. Generalists should be conversant with the major sectors, geographic regions, and institutional culture of the field. The functions that generalists fulfill vary according to the organization and the phase of the project cycle. Thus, flexibility and adaptability, as well as a certain comfort level with ambiguity, are important for generalists. A generalist might be helping to prepare a proposal for a girl's education project in Kenya one month and overseeing (or "backstopping") the budget process for a health project in Brazil the next month. The most common types of work include stakeholder analysis, project cycle management, proposal writing, budgeting and oversight, monitoring and evaluation (M&E), and training. The common skill set for virtually all of these activities encompasses writing, data synthesis, oral presentations, meeting facilitation, and ability to pay attention to detail while multitasking. Most organizations look for individuals who have an appropriate educational background in virtually any field of international affairs, and the organizations are also interested to see people who speak multiple languages and/or have field experience in a variety of contexts.

Experts, technical experts, or specialists are expected to have long-term detailed knowledge of and experience with a particular sector, region, or cross-cutting theme in development and relief. Although experts are expected to have some familiarity with the big-picture issues in an organization, they are usually utilized in fairly narrow ways and often do not assume overall responsibility for project management. Instead, they are brought in to design an element of a project or to evaluate a single component. There are hundreds of different types of specialists but some examples include gender and development experts, shelter experts, environmental assessment experts, infectious disease specialists, and trainers. Regional, cultural, or linguistic expertise is also often sought by both donors and implementing agencies. The skill set for experts includes the ones listed for generalists (writing, analysis, etc.) but also demands a high degree of specialized skills in the technical area. For example, water and sanitation experts are expected to have skills in the areas of architecture, engineering, and biology. Although educational background is one important way to become a skilled expert, skills and experience gained through internships, field experiences, and early job experiences can also qualify one as an expert.

Where Is Your Base? Headquarters versus the Field

Virtually every actor in international relief and development maintains a presence both at the field level and at headquarters. Not surprisingly, the work that staff are expected to do and the skills that are required vary greatly in these different environments. Despite the differences, many workers move back and forth between headquarters and field positions over the courses of their careers. Some development agencies explicitly require this kind of rotation so that people have a chance to see both perspectives.

Although they are sometimes located at the village or community level, staff working in the field are most often located in the national capital or in a provincial center or town. Nonetheless, these positions usually feel much closer to the field, and most staff spend extended periods of time immersed in the culture in which they are working. Staffing profiles usually include both expatriates and local hires. Daily work is often conducted in the local language, although reports to headquarters are usually in the official working language of the home organization (often English). Field workers typically report that their biggest challenges are managing relationships with headquarters and adapting to frequent scarcity of resources. On the other hand, they report that the biggest benefit to working at this level is their deep relationship with beneficiaries and other stakeholders. They also enjoy seeing the often immediate positive impact of their work at the local level. There is no such thing as typical work in the field, and good problem-solving skills and flexibility are key. Field level staff are expected to do everything from receiving and processing equipment and supplies (e.g., making sure computers for a training project make it through customs) to conducting periodic evaluations of ongoing projects.

Staff at headquarters tend to find themselves in a larger, more specialized and compartmentalized environment. Although staff members sometimes feel somewhat removed from the field, they are much closer to the decision-making and policysetting processes. Staff spend most of their time at headquarters, attending meetings and preparing reports. They also conduct periodic visits to the field for training, oversight, and new project development activities. Headquarters staff often report that their biggest challenge is managing what is often a vast bureaucracy and staying focused on the ultimate client—the beneficiary. Conversely, they report that the most rewarding part of working at headquarters is the ability to closely observe, and sometimes influence, the policymaking process. The greater scale on which most headquarters staff works guarantees that any decisions they do make are likely to have an impact on far greater numbers of people than their colleagues in the field. Important skills for headquarters staff include excellent writing and data synthesis skills, strong oral presentation skills, and adeptness at navigating the complex institutional environment. Typical duties include strategic planning, monitoring and evaluation, workplan development, and oversight of portfolios of development projects.

What Do You Actually Do? The Project Cycle in Relief and Development

The actual cycle of a relief of development project depends on many things, including the sector, region, and previous experience of development. Nonetheless, there are several key steps that are common to most development projects. They are:

- *Needs assessment.* This is the first step in the problem analysis process for relief and development projects. Assessments can take a variety of forms such as epidemiological studies for child health projects, detailed participatory appraisals for natural resource management activities, or "windshield" assessments of damages immediately following a natural disaster. Stakeholder analysis is a critical component in any needs assessment.

- *Project design.* Following the needs assessment process, staff members, usually working in teams, complete the actual project design, work plan, and budget. They work to reach consensus among the many stakeholders on topics such as project objectives, risk assessments, and performance monitoring plans.

- *Implementation.* This is usually the longest phase in the development cycle, the period in which services or benefits are actually delivered to clients and beneficiaries. For health projects, this phase might include both training of HIV/AIDS outreach staff and refurbishment of laboratory facilities in a local hospital. Important elements of any implementation include realistic scheduling and budgeting, clear roles and responsibilities, and open mechanisms for feedback and readjustment.

- *Monitoring and evaluation.* Monitoring generally refers to the oversight of activities during the actual phase of project implementation, whereas evaluation refers to the ex-post analysis of impacts, challenges, and lessons learned. M&E work can be either qualitative or quantitative or both. The work in this phase is often conducted by a combination of field and headquarters staff as well as objective outsiders such as consultants.

Future Trends

Where is the field of international relief headed? More importantly, where do your skills, perspectives, and motivations fit in? Where should you start and where would you like to end up? Although each individual must answer those questions alone, the following important trends should help with that calculation.

- *Lessons learned.* Many relief and development organizations are increasingly realizing the value and importance of learning from past successes and failures in the field of relief and development. It seems likely that more and more actors will be moving toward the model of a "learning organization" in which all staff are constantly gaining new perspectives and acquiring new skill sets.
- *Multidisciplinarity.* More and more organizations are recognizing the tremendous value of multidisciplinary work and teamwork in general. As a consequence, people with good group facilitation and consensus-building skills will likely become even more valuable in the relief and development field.
- *The relief to development divide.* Although there has been a historic disconnect between relief and development activities, many organizations are beginning to bridge that gap and are seeking creative and flexible individuals who can help with that process. For development agencies, this often means incorporating awareness about natural disasters and conflict prevention into their projects. For relief agencies, it often means taking a more holistic and long-term view of the impacts of relief and their relationship to development.
- *Institutional change and flexibility.* Perhaps the most significant trend in the field of international relief and development is the tendency toward almost constant institutional restructuring and reformulation. Part of this can be explained by the demise of the Cold War as an organizing principle in development, whereas another part is due to the renewed emphasis on accountability and results in the field. This trend means that future professionals will need to be flexible and agile in order to respond quickly to the changing nature of development institutions.

Final Thoughts

As you move forward in your career as a relief or development professional, I encourage you to remember that one feeling, event, or experience that led to your involvement. For me, the image of that young girl in northeastern Brazil is the thing that keeps me centered, focused, and motivated. Your work as a professional will be much easier, and in my experience, far more rewarding, if you are true to your ideals, hopes, and aspirations, for both yourself and the development endeavor.

In the words of development practitioner and critic, Robert Chambers:

> *Basic to a new professionalism is the primacy of the personal. This recognizes the power of personal choice, the prevalence of error, and the potential for doing better in this thing called development. The personal, professional, and institutional challenge is learning how to learn, learning how to change, and learning how to organize and act* (Robert Chambers, *Whose Reality Counts? Putting the First Last* [London: Intermediate Technology Publications, 1999]).

Getting Started in International Development
MICHELLE D. CARTER

I have very much enjoyed my past five years working with CARE International in Haiti and Rwanda. There is no doubt that international development is challenging, fascinating, and satisfying.

Many people want to enter international development because of a desire to help others, for the adventure of living in developing countries, to experience new cultures, and to share their technical skills with people who need them. They often don't realize how difficult it is to break into the field.

Traditionally, most development organizations have hired former Peace Corps volunteers, or those who have completed two years of "living among the people," but such experience is no longer sufficient. Development organizations can now be choosy. Not only do we require at least two to five years of field experience, but we also look for the following skills:

- A technical skill such as public health, agriculture, or natural resources. The current trend is microfinance, HIV/AIDS, human rights, and education.
- An advanced degree (M.A. or doctorate, in some cases) in a technical field (i.e., MPH).
- Analytic, policy, and advocacy skills (particularly for Oxfam, Médecins sans Frontières).
- Fluency in foreign languages.

Development work is not confined to the field—there are other arenas. A person can work from a (bilateral or multilateral) donor's perspective (i.e., USAID, the Canadian International Development Agency, EU, and World Bank), from a development organization's perspective (i.e., CARE, Catholic Relief Services, Save the Children), and from some policy think tanks (i.e., Brookings Institution, Asia Foundation). Even within those categories, a person can work in fund-raising, project management, financial aspects, policy development, and so on.

It goes without saying that people must have good to excellent management and interpersonal skills in intercultural contexts—this includes coaching and mentoring national staff.

(Continued)

My advice to those who want to break into the field is:

- *Get field experience.* Nobody will take you seriously if you talk about addressing problems in developing countries without having worked and lived in one.
- *Do internships.* I broke into international development—with MSFS's help—in CARE's fellowship program. CARE and Catholic Relief Services (CRS) have yearlong programs that provide training while you work overseas. It requires serious persistence to convince an organization to take on interns, but it is an ideal way to circumvent the "catch-22" of needing field experience when no one will give you field experience in the first place.
- *Financial sacrifices.* If you just want to break in, you have to prepare for financial sacrifice. Although organizations such as Concern, MSF, or GOAL pay small stipends, many organizations don't, but if you make the investment for one year, you will earn experience for your CV.
- *Do emergency work.* If you have no family responsibilities, work in an emergency situation. If you can handle a year in Afghanistan, Democratic Republic of Congo, Angola, Somalia, or Kosovo, it is almost guaranteed that other doors will open for you.
- *Learn more than one language.* If you speak Spanish and want to work in Latin America, remember that there are fewer jobs and you're competing with people who are completely bilingual. Learn Portuguese or Arabic or Russian. For a bonus, learn "exotic" languages such as Kiswahili, Bengali, or Thai.
- *Be persistent.* We all know human resources offices are typically overworked and underappreciated. They receive hundreds of applications a day, so get the HR person's name, follow up, and make sure your resumé doesn't disappear in a filing cabinet.
- *Be flexible and adaptable.* You may decide to focus on one country, but if so, you must realize you are limiting your options. Organizations value the willingness and ability to work in several different regions of the world. Certainly there are advantages to being the Central Africa or Eastern Europe specialist, but it also helps to broaden your experience.
- *Be deep and wide.* Development organizations recognize the need for technically strong programs. Thus, technical assistance is required—whether it is consultants or technical "backstops"— so the more you specialize, the more valuable you are. And at the same time, it helps to have a holistic, interdisciplinary view.

Given the challenges of globalization and the global economy, the international development field requires talented and committed people. Those in developing countries deserve nothing less.

Michelle D. Carter, a 1996 graduate of the Master of Science in Foreign Service program at Georgetown University, began her career as a fellow with CARE in Haiti. She was promoted to assistant regional director, and then posted again with CARE, to Rwanda, where she served first as a suboffice team leader and then was promoted to civil society technical coordinator. She expects to be posted back to the United States in 2002.

Chapter 12

MEDIA

Careers in Media

Marc Ballon

I have never been a big dog lover. My next door neighbor's St.
Bernard mauled my friend when I was about ten, and ever since
then I have been a bit wary of big furry animals with sharp teeth.

When I arrived in Bucharest, Romania, in September 1995 to begin
a seven-month journalism fellowship partly underwritten by the U.S.
State Department, I thought I had prepared myself well for my journey.
I came armed with a pocket knife to slice up fruit, vegetables, and
cheeses, an oversized bottle of antacid, and an English-Romanian
dictionary. I had also read history books and stacks of newspaper
and magazine articles about the country, located deep in the heart
of the Balkans. Having visited Romania just a year and a half earlier, I
felt like an old pro.

Imagine my surprise, then, when my Tarom jet landed at Otopeni
airport and I saw a few stray dogs milling about the runway. No big
deal, I thought, until I saw packs of the beasts patrolling my new
neighborhood. And we're not talking Lassie or Snoopy here. These
dogs were mangy, dirty, and menacing. Worse, they all seemed to
hunger for a taste of one frightened American journalist, who managed to keep them at bay by wildly swinging a backpack to and fro
whenever they approached him. What to do? The answer was easy. I
decided to find out why and how wild dogs had commandeered the
streets of Bucharest and turned it into their own private playground.
I wanted to write an article.

Predictably, Romanian governmental officials ducked, dismissed,
and dodged my questions. But after incessantly pestering several of
them, I discovered Bucharest had about 200,000 stray dogs and that

*Marc Ballon, a 1989 graduate of the Master of Science in Foreign Service program at
Georgetown University, has been writing about the retail and restaurant industries for the*
Los Angeles Times. *He previously worked for* Forbes Inc. *and* People *magazines, among
other publications.*

8,000 city residents had been bitten the previous year, with most victims requiring painful rabies shots to the abdomen. My reporting uncovered some equally surprising information. Romanians, far from wanting them wiped out, adored the dogs. They even fed them. Years before, many Bucharest residents had to give up their animals involuntarily after the late dictator Nicolae Ceausescu leveled their spacious homes, replacing them with faceless concrete apartment blocs with no room for pets. So by giving stray dogs bread and fatty meat, people somehow felt like they were maintaining a connection to the pets they once loved. On top of that, Romanians told me their Orthodox Christian faith encouraged kindness to animals. The dogs, it seemed, were here to stay, much to my chagrin.

Within a week of my arrival in Romania, the *St. Petersburg Times* in Florida ran my dogs piece on the front page. A couple of months later, the Romanian government began tapping my phones and intercepting my mail after I wrote a widely published story arguing that Romania's much heralded plan to privatize state-owned industries was nothing more than a cynical attempt to keep Western aid flowing to its Communist rulers. Needless to say, I wasn't Mr. Popularity among Romanian officialdom. No matter. I was having fun.

I have been a journalist for more than a decade and hope to continue plying my trade for a long, long time. I am currently a business writer at the *Los Angeles Times,* where my beats have included small business, biotech, and the restaurant industry. I hope to one day become a foreign correspondent. During my career, I have worked at publications ranging from the semiweekly *Alameda Journal* in Northern California to the *Prague Post* in the Czech Republic to *Forbes* in New York City. I have interviewed porn stars about sex-positive feminism (they think making dirty movies emancipates them), the late Sonny Bono about why he wanted to become a U.S. senator (he didn't really have an answer, although his aides had plenty of explanations), and Tom Cruise's business partner about the actor's alleged infertility (as with Sonny, I never got a good response).

Journalism has allowed me to travel the world, constantly learn new things, and, best of all, get paid doing it. I'm also proud to be a member of a profession that functions as democracy's guardian by keeping close watch on politicians, CEOs, and generals. Sounds exciting, sexy, and kind of cool, doesn't it? It is. And it isn't. Don't be fooled by the propaganda: Journalism, for all its glamour, is a difficult way to eke out a living. The pay is poor. The hours are long. The stresses are great.

Allow me to share some of the dirty little secrets of a reporter's lot.

Like professional sports and the movie industry, there are far more people who want to become reporters than there are positions. The *L.A. Times,* for instance, has 10,000 resumés on file at any given time, chief recruiter Randy Hagihara said, and added, "It's probably harder to get a job here than to get into Harvard."

Then there's the pay—or lack of it. A new journalist earns an annual salary of about $23,000 at a weekly newspaper, $26,000 at a daily, and $21,600 in TV, according to a survey by the University of Georgia. That's barely enough to pay the bills, let alone buy a decent car or a house. After graduating from Georgetown with an MSFS in 1989, I landed a position at the Maryland Gazette for a whopping $15,000 per year. I subsisted on lots of homemade vegetable soup and turkey sandwiches.

> There are no shortcuts to becoming a journalist and no guarantees that a talented writer will ever hit the big time. It's that fiercely competitive. But the key ingredients, I think, are dedication, a love of the craft, and belief in self.

And then there are the hours. Most journalists, especially at daily newspapers, have little or no control over their work days. Events dictate what they do and when they do it. When news breaks, lunch plans get canceled, dinner dates are postponed, and the laundry has to wait until another day. The incessant stress, along with fifty- to sixty-hour weeks at the office, has led me to hit the bottle nearly every day—I am now a certified Tums addict.

There are no shortcuts to becoming a journalist and no guarantees that a talented writer will ever hit the big time. It's that fiercely competitive. But the key ingredients, I think, are dedication, a love of the craft, and belief in self.

I began my journalism career in 1989 when I won a fellowship at the Poynter Institute of Media Studies, a nonprofit journalism think tank in St. Petersburg, Florida. During my six-week stint, I immersed myself in the basics of news writing, interviewing, and reporting. I also worked hard to forget everything I had ever learned about academic writing, which, according to editors, is bloated, ponderous, and, well, academic.

I had visions of landing a foreign correspondent's position with the *Washington Post* or *New York Times.* Why not? I spoke fluent French, lived in Paris during my junior year at UC Berkeley, and had a prestigious MSFS degree from Georgetown University. Unfortunately, I was more excited about those publications than they were about me. I found a reporter's position at the Maryland *Gazette* in Glen Burnie, Maryland. More than fifty people had applied for it.

I lasted three months. I had a hard time getting too excited about covering PTA meetings and planning commission hearings. What a comedown after having taken courses from the likes of former Secretary of State Madeleine Albright and rubbing shoulders with senators and diplomats during my D.C. days at Georgetown.

Dispirited, I loaded up my rusted-out Honda and drove across the country to my parents' house in L.A. Within four days, I concluded I wanted more out of life than my old room back and free meals with Mom and Dad. Much to my surprise, I missed journalism. I applied to about 100 newspapers. Luckily, I found a job at the *Alameda Journal*, a free semiweekly in a small Bay Area city adjacent to Oakland.

There, I fell in love with reporting. I covered a hard-fought mayoral race, the back-room dealings of a major developer, and an ill-advised attempt by the city to ban soft-core publications from newsstands. What a job, I thought, even if I was only making $18,000, or one-fifth what my lawyer friends earned. After a year, I quickly learned how brutal journalism can be. With California in the midst of a deep recession, I was laid off and faced the prospect of an early career change. Luckily, I found a job within three weeks at a daily newspaper about ninety miles to the east in Fairfield, California.

At the *Daily Republic*, I quickly made enemies after reporting on a city council candidate's drunken driving conviction and a Christian school beset with allegations of sexual abuse. But those same stories helped me get a job at the *Daily News* in Los Angeles. After six months of cranking out more than two stories a day, I quit journalism for the second time. I headed for Prague, joining the throngs of young Americans trying to find themselves in what *Prague Post* editor Alan Levy has called "the second-chance city."

There, I discovered what I was looking for: my voice as a person and as a writer. Away from all those nasty, carping editors, I let the thoughts flow freely, learning to trust my instincts. Within a year, I had become one of Prague's most prolific freelancers, writing stories about everything from the increase of beggars in the city to the popularity of a home-grown methamphetamine called Pervitin. My work appeared in more than a dozen newspapers, ranging from the *International Herald Tribune* to the *Christian Science Monitor* to the *Minneapolis Star-Tribune*.

My success as a writer, combined with lots of Pilsner beer and a couple of torrid romances, made the fourteen months I spent in Prague among the best in my life. None of it would have been possible, if not for Georgetown.

Let me explain. While I was applying to graduate school, my father encouraged me to get an M.B.A., "something marketable," in his words. I told him I wanted to study foreign affairs at Georgetown. "What the hell do you want to do that for? What do you expect to do with that degree?" I smiled: "I want to become a critical thinker."

And I did. At Georgetown, I learned how to write succinctly and coax information from people in a course on negotiations. A debate class taught me how to marshal evidence and the art of persuasion. Statistics gave me a mastery of numbers, a skill that has come in quite handy as a business writer. Professor Seth Tillman deepened my understanding of the U.S. Congress, the Middle East, the world. Simply put, I sharpened my analytical skills, broadened my ken of knowledge, and honed my writing abilities at the School of Foreign Service. I also obtained a stellar credential that impressed several editors who ended up hiring me over the years.

After Prague, I made the transition to magazines, landing jobs at *Forbes* in Boston and *People Magazine* in L.A., with my Romanian fellowship squeezed in between. In 1999, I moved back to newspapers when the *Los Angeles Times* hired me after three rejections.

If I have any words of wisdom, they are those Madeleine Albright spoke when I sought her counsel more than a decade ago as my graduation from Georgetown neared. "You can't plan the future. It just happens and is full of surprises," she said. "The key is to love what you're doing and work hard. Everything else will take care of itself."

Good advice, I think.

Chapter 13

NONPROFIT AND EDUCATIONAL ORGANIZATIONS

Careers in Nonprofit and Educational Organizations

SHERRY L. MUELLER

Many nonprofit organizations are relatively small compared to business, government, or multilateral institutions. Employees play multiple roles and often turn an idea into reality in a relatively short time frame. Therefore, careers in the nonprofit sector often require remarkable flexibility and initiative. For instance, the same day I wrote the first draft of Senate Resolution 87, commemorating the sixtieth anniversary of the U.S. State Department's International Visitor Program, I defrosted the office refrigerator. I have asked a new employee to represent the National Council for International Visitors (NCIV) at a major meeting on Capitol Hill the same day I assigned him the task of sending out a mailing of publications to our members. In a nonprofit organization, you are likely to handle varied duties and have significant responsibilities earlier in your career than you would in more bureaucratic institutions. Nonprofit organizations are relatively "flat" and often without a grade ladder or stair-step type of career trajectory in which responsibilities are more clearly connected to defined tasks in an elaborate set of job descriptions.

When I interview job candidates I tell them that I am looking for versatile self-starters. If you enter a room and you know eight people are expected for a meeting and there are only six chairs, I expect you to find two more chairs. I do not want to hear that "moving furniture" is not in your job description. I also tell job candidates that if they

Sherry L. Mueller, a Friend of Georgetown University's Master of Science in Foreign Service program, is president of the National Council for International Visitors. She holds a doctorate in international affairs from the Fletcher School of Law and Diplomacy, Tufts University, and has served as an adjunct professor at the School of International Service at American University. She is the author of a book titled Careers in International Education, Exchange and Development.

are looking for a "nine to five" job, they should keep looking. Usually pressures are such that one works until a project is completed rather than with an eye on the clock.

In the interview process, I also try to identify potential employees who wholeheartedly embrace the mission of the organization. People who have successful careers in nonprofit organizations are cause-oriented. They are motivated by the need to make a difference. To help appreciate this point, recall the original ad for a Pony Express rider:

WANTED: Young, wiry, skinny fellows under the age of 18. Must be expert riders willing to risk death daily. Wages: $25 per week. Orphans preferred.

If I were to rewrite the ad to recruit people to work in the nonprofit sector, it would read:

WANTED: Young at heart of all ages. Must be well-organized, eager to learn, and willing to risk breaking stereotypes daily. Wages: Won't be discussed. Idealists preferred.

> Those with careers in the nonprofit world tend to be hardworking idealists, service-oriented, and less concerned with financial rewards. Psychological satisfaction, the sense of being a force for good in the lives of others, and a need for autonomy generally outweigh the desire for monetary gain.

Those with careers in the nonprofit world tend to be hardworking idealists, service-oriented, and less concerned with financial rewards. Psychological satisfaction, the sense of being a force for good in the lives of others, and a need for autonomy generally outweigh the desire for monetary gain.

More and more people are finding employment in the nonprofit sector, and that trend will most likely accelerate in the post-September 11 world. Whether referred to as the nongovernmental organization (NGO) sector, the independent sector, the social sector (Peter Drucker's term), or the voluntary sector, nonprofit organizations are growing exponentially around the world. As cutting-edge researcher Professor Lester Salamon of Johns Hopkins University phrases it, we are experiencing a "global associational revolution." For a whole variety of reasons, from South Africa to Poland to the United States, there are more nonprofit organizations than ever before. Competition for philanthropic dollars and for volunteers will intensify. Consequently, excellent writing skills, project-management abilities (including fiscal management), and the capacity to elicit cooperation from diverse constituencies will continue to be in demand. Comfort with ambiguity is a particularly valuable trait as well. Well-honed negotiating skills, too, will help one forge a successful career in an environment where partnerships (to conserve resources, to win new contacts, and for other reasons), consortia, and mergers will increase and thrive.

Most employers want to see a basic building block of international experience on a resumé. Service as a Peace Corps volunteer or Experiment in International Living group leader are good examples. This international experience should demonstrate an ability to communicate effectively with people from other cultures and an ability to complete a substantive project in a foreign environment. It should reflect not only well-developed foreign language skills but an authentic curiosity and desire to learn about other peoples and cultures.

A broad array of organizations are subsumed under the rubric of nonprofit and educational organizations. The descriptions later in this chapter illustrate the range of institutions in this variegated and growing sector. They can be grouped into three major categories according to their general purposes:

- *Assistance organizations*—providing humanitarian relief and fostering economic development through both emergency and long-term efforts (examples are CARE and Save the Children).
- *Exchange organizations*—building intellectual connections and professional networks around the world via cultural and educational exchange programs (such as the Institute of International Education and World Learning).
- *Foundations and associations*—funding or providing information and other services for constituencies (e.g., Carnegie Corporation or the Ford Foundation). This category also includes organizations engaged in advocacy with the U.S. Congress. Interaction and the Alliance for International Educational and Cultural Exchange are excellent illustrations.

Many of the organizations have a regional focus such as the Africa-America Institute; others are global in orientation. Some focus on a particular field, such as the environment, education, management training, human rights, refugee affairs, population and family planning, or educational exchange. Others develop expertise in multiple areas. The headquarters of many of these organizations are often on the East Coast, in New York if the primary sources of funding are foundations and corporations, and in Washington, D.C., if the federal government provides a significant portion of their funding.

A few have regional offices. Some, such as NCIV, have community organization members or chapters throughout the United States. Some have offices around the world. The organizations vary in staff size from those consisting of one or two people to those with paid staffs of hundreds of employees.

Most nonprofit organizations are sustained by the labor of networks of volunteers. Often a primary job requirement is the ability to work well with volunteers and to coordinate their efforts with those of paid staff. Many organizations are short on financial resources. Some exist exclusively because of their government contracts. Some are financed by means of fees for service, membership dues, individual and corporate contributions, foundation grants, or a combination of these funding sources. All receive policy direction from volunteer boards of directors.

In recent years, the U.S. government grant-awarding policies and other factors have fostered increased competition, and many new organizations have accordingly joined the ranks of the traditional organizations that dominated the field for decades. This competitive environment has motivated managers to expend more and more energy on fund-raising, marketing, and public relations as they strive to maintain and improve the quality of their programs and services and to meet burgeoning needs around the globe. Proposal-writing experience is often sought as an essential qualification for a new hire.

Although nonprofit careers will never be as lucrative as business or even government, the notoriously low salaries in the sector are gradually improving as managers increasingly appreciate the cost of recruiting and training new staff members. Because one's effectiveness much of the time is directly dependent on the strength of personal relationships, many executives are better at calculating the true cost of losing an employee's networks and institutional memory. Hence, salaries are going up.

Benefit packages vary. However, for similar reasons, nonprofits have had to increase benefits. Generally, the larger the nonprofit, the better the benefits package. Thanks to technological advances in communication and various forces that have caused power to shift away from nation-states, the nonprofit sector should offer increasing opportunities for hands-on, pragmatic individuals to make a meaningful difference—to build a global civil society.

Resource Listings

Academy for Educational Development

Founded in 1961, the Academy for Educational Development (AED) is an independent, nonprofit service organization committed to addressing human development needs in the United States and in 167 other countries throughout the world. AED's major activity issues include health, education, the environment, and youth development. AED's activities are supported through grants and contracts from international organizations, U.S. and foreign government agencies, foundations, and private contributions. Under these contracts and grants, the academy operates programs in collaboration with policy leaders, nongovernmental and community-based organizations, businesses, governmental agencies, international multilateral and bilateral funders, and schools, colleges, and universities.

In partnership with its clients, AED seeks to meet today's social, economic, and environmental challenges through education and human resource development; to apply state-of-the-art education, training, research and technology, management, behavioral analysis, and social marketing techniques to solve problems; and to improve knowledge and skills as the most effective means for stimulating growth, reducing poverty, and promoting democratic and humanitarian ideals.

When AED hires, it looks for excellent organization and analytical skills, several years of international or domestic experience related to AED's programs, good language ability, solid research and writing skills, and a master's degree in international relations, education, journalism, communications, or similar fields.

> The Academy for Educational Development
> 1825 Connecticut Avenue, NW
> Washington, DC 20009-5721
> Tel.: (202) 884-8000
> Fax: (202) 884-8400
> www.aed.org

Africa-America Institute

The mission of the Africa-America Institute (AAI) is to promote enlightened engagement between Africa and America through education, training, and dialogue. AAI conducts higher education and training programs for Africans, administers exchange and visitor programs related to Africa, and carries out informational programs that seek to shape and inform the debate over U.S. policy toward Africa in ways that highlight African perspectives and promote American engagement.

AAI has offices in New York City and Washington, D.C., and a presence in eighteen African countries. Its U.S.-based staff numbers approximately fifty. Most professional positions require master's degrees. Some entry-level positions require only bachelor's degrees. Travel in or knowledge of Africa is helpful if not required for certain positions. Internships are available in both the New York and Washington offices.

> The Africa-America Institute
> 380 Lexington Avenue, 42nd Floor
> New York, NY 10168-4298
> Tel.: (212) 949-5666
> Fax: (212) 682-6174
> www.aaionline.org

> 1625 Massachusetts Avenue, NW, Suite 400
> Washington, DC 20036
> Tel.: (202) 667-5636
> Fax: (202) 265-6332

Africare

Africare is a private, nonprofit organization founded in 1971 by Africans and Americans to improve the quality of life in rural areas of African countries. The organization promotes development of environmental and water resources, agricultural training, and health care. The AIDS crisis in Africa is of special concern. The organization provides financial and technical assistance to development projects and trains African villagers in everyday maintenance and management.

Africare serves a dual purpose: educating Americans on conditions in Africa and generating American commitment to the development process. Most of Africare's employment opportunities are for overseas positions, including project coordinators and administrative assistants. Most positions require a graduate degree and prior overseas work experience. About half of Africare applicants speak a foreign language.

> Africare
> 440 R Street, NW
> Washington, DC 20001
> Tel.: (202) 462-3614
> Fax: (202) 387-1034
> www.africare.org

AIESEC

The International Association of Students in Economics and Business Management (AIESEC) is the world's largest student organization, with 50,000 members at more than 800 universities in eighty-three countries. AIESEC facilitates the exchange of students and graduates as paid trainees or volunteers at nonprofit organizations. AIESEC's mission is "to contribute to the development of our countries and their people with an overriding commitment to international understanding and co-operation."

In addition to the exchange program, AIESEC organizes conferences and seminars for students and members of the business and academic communities. Applications are limited to students who belong to one of the U.S. local chapters at institutions of higher learning. Overseas traineeships typically last from two to eighteen months.

> AIESEC National Staff
> 127 W. 26th Street, 10th Floor
> New York, NY 10001
> Tel.: (212) 757-3774
> Fax: (212) 757-4062
> www.aiesec.org

American Chemical Society

The American Chemical Society (ACS) is a nonprofit scientific and educational association with more than 160,000 members, including professional chemists and chemical engineers in industry, government, and academia. The organization provides opportunities for peer interaction and career development, regardless of professional or scientific interests. ACS also publishes more than thirty periodicals.

The society maintains a professional staff of around 2,000 people. It has a small Office of International Activities that primarily is involved in administering exchange projects. The office also acts as a liaison between ACS and similar organizations abroad in sponsoring joint international meetings and investigations of alleged violations of scientific freedom.

> American Chemical Society
> 1155 Sixteenth Street, NW
> Washington, DC 20036
> Tel.: (800) 227-5558 (U.S. only)
> (202) 872-4600 (outside the U.S.)
> Fax: (202) 872-4615
> www.acs.org

American Council on Education

The American Council on Education (ACE), founded in 1918, is the nation's coordinating higher education association. ACE is dedicated to the belief that equal educational opportunity and a strong higher education system are essential cornerstones of a democratic society. Its approximately 1,800 members include accredited, degree-granting colleges and universities from all sectors of higher education and other education and education-related organizations. ACE is a forum for the discussion of major issues related to higher education and its potential to contribute to the quality of American life.

ACE maintains both a domestic and an international agenda and seeks to advance the interests and goals of higher and adult education in a changing environment by providing leadership and advocacy on important issues, representing the views of the higher and adult education community to policymakers, and offering services to its members.

> American Council on Education
> One Dupont Circle, NW
> Washington, DC 20035
> Tel.: (202) 939-9300
> www.acenet.edu

American Friends Service Committee

The American Friends Service Committee (AFSC) was founded during World War I in 1917 by the Society of Friends (Quakers) as a public-service alternative for conscientious objectors. Its major purpose today is the alleviation of human suffering and injustice in various parts of the world. AFSC maintains nine regional offices in the United States and is involved in programs in more than twenty countries worldwide. Programs are designed to promote self-help and improve basic living standards and social well-being, emphasizing integrated community development, construction, agricultural production, cooperative organization, public health services, and refugee assistance. The committee sponsors international conferences on world affairs and publishes a variety of reports on its projects at home and abroad.

The majority of positions at AFSC, either in the United States or abroad, require persons with a substantial amount of experience in such areas as community development, community organization, self-help projects, communications, and administration. There are very few entry-level positions.

American Friends Service Committee
1501 Cherry Street
Philadelphia, PA 19102
Tel.: (215) 241-7000
Fax: (215) 241-7275
www.afsc.org

American Society of Association Executives

With more than 23,000 members, the American Society of Association Executives (ASAE) is the leading organization in the field of association management. The membership includes people who manage trade associations, individual membership societies, voluntary organizations, and other not-for-profit associations. ASAE's international section is designed to keep the society's domestic members current on international activities that affect associations and to promote the exchange of ideas and information among colleagues around the world. The international section publishes *International News,* a bimonthly newsletter designed to keep members up-to-date on the latest international issues, with articles on overcoming cultural differences to marketing membership and services globally.

The international staff is very small. Interested people should have a knowledge of international activities in associations as well as experience working with overseas counterparts and designing education programs.

American Society of Association Executives
1575 Eye Street, NW
Washington, DC 20005
Tel.: (202) 626-2723
www.asaenet.org/main/

American Society of International Law

The American Society of International Law (ASIL) is a 4,000-member association committed to the study and use of law in international affairs. As a nonpartisan institution, it provides a forum for an exchange of views among its members from over 100 countries. It publishes books, periodicals, and occasional papers and sponsors research on a broad range of topics in current international law. Outreach to the public on general issues of international law is a major goal of ASIL. ASIL cosponsors the Philip C. Jessup International Law Moot Court Competition.

ASIL has a staff of about twenty people, five or six of whom are in professional-level positions filled by highly qualified individuals with experience in international law. The ASIL internship program enables young professionals to acquire practical experience in international law research and outreach activities.

The American Society of International Law
2223 Massachusetts Avenue, NW
Washington, DC 20008-2864
Tel.: (202) 939-6000
www.asil.org

ARTICLE 19—The International Centre Against Censorship

ARTICLE 19, the International Centre Against Censorship, is a human rights organization concerned with protecting the basic right to free expression and combating censorship. Established in 1986, the organization's name derives from the nineteenth article of the Universal Declaration of Human Rights, which specifically protects freedom of expression. ARTICLE 19 lobbies to change laws that infringe on international human rights law, to prevent restrictive legislation from becoming law, and on behalf of individuals imprisoned for having expressed their views peacefully. ARTICLE 19 also publishes a series of texts on freedom of speech issues.

ARTICLE 19 employs a professional staff of fifteen, most of whom have a regional or country-specific and/or human rights law background. In addition, the organization takes on up to four interns a year and any number of volunteers. The campaigning role of ARTICLE 19 is due to be expanded in the coming years, and individuals with a background in political strategy and media relations will be required. ARTICLE 19 makes use of consultancy services for specialist projects, which currently include satellite television, press laws in South and Southeast Asia, and monitoring the independent media in Central and Eastern Europe. The organization's legal office is located in Washington, D.C.

ARTICLE 19
Lancaster House
33 Islington High Street
London N1 9LH
United Kingdom
Tel.: 44-1-71-278-9292
Fax: 44-1-71-713-1356
www.article19.org

American Baptist Churches in the USA

An evangelical denomination founded in 1814, American Baptist Churches in the USA, through its Board of International Ministries, provides a variety of services designated to help meet basic human needs in developing countries. Assistance is extended in community development, food production, public health and medicine, family planning, social welfare, and disaster relief. The overseas mission programs of the Board of International Ministries utilize approximately $13.5 million and employ about 100 persons in development-related positions. New hires are expected to have at least a master's level academic background plus some professional experience.

> American Baptist Churches in the USA
> Board of International Ministries
> P.O. Box 851
> Valley Forge, PA 19482-0851
> Tel.: (610) 768-2000
> (800) ABC-3USA
> www.abc-usa.org/

American Political Science Association

The American Political Science Association (APSA), with more than 13,000 members, is the major professional organization in the United States for those engaged in the study of politics. Its members, 10 percent of whom reside abroad, are primarily political scientists doing research and teaching at American colleges and universities. One-fourth of its members pursue careers outside academia in government, research organizations, consulting firms, and private enterprise.

APSA sponsors research, reviews current materials, and provides other services to facilitate teaching and professional development. The association publishes two quarterly journals, *The American Political Review* and *PS*. It also operates a personnel service that provides information on available political science positions. APSA administers the Congressional Fellowship Program, a professional-level internship program that places political scientists on congressional staffs.

APSA has a staff of around twenty, primarily editors and administrators with experience in the discipline.

> American Political Science Association
> 1527 New Hampshire Avenue, NW
> Washington, DC 20036-1290
> Tel.: (202) 483-2512
> Fax: (202) 483-2657
> www.apsanet.org/

American-Mideast Educational and Training Services

American-Mideast Educational and Training Services, better known as AMIDEAST, was founded in 1951 as a private, nonprofit organization dedicated to improving understanding between Americans and the peoples of the Arab world through education, information, and development programs. Services include educational advising and testing for Arab students and institutions interested in U.S. educational opportunities (mainly through field offices overseas); education and training program administration (mainly in Washington, D.C.); more than sixty programs for a variety of government, corporate, and institutional sponsors of Arab students; English-language programs for the general public and corporate and government agency clients in Bahrain, Egypt, Kuwait, Lebanon, Tunisia, and Yemen; public outreach services in the form of publications and videotapes to support educational exchanges and materials to improve teaching about the Arab world in American secondary schools and colleges; technical assistance to support institution-building in the Arab world, with an emphasis on educational institutions, public administration, judiciary bodies, legislatures, and nongovernmental organizations.

Headquartered in Washington, D.C., AMIDEAST has a network of field offices in Bahrain, Egypt, Jordan, Kuwait, Lebanon, Morocco, Syria, Tunisia, the West Bank/Gaza, and the Yemen Arab Republic. There are more than 200 staff positions worldwide. Of these, about 90 are professional positions in Washington, D.C.; the remainder are professional positions filled overseas. There are about 10 professional openings a year at AMIDEAST's headquarters. Candidates for employment at headquarters should be U.S. citizens or legal residents of the United States and have at least a bachelors degree, including some U.S. academic experience. Previous cross-cultural management experience, counseling, or related subjects and foreign language skills are preferred. Positions overseas are mostly filled by local professionals.

America-Mideast Educational Training Services
(AMIDEAST)
Attn: Personnel
1730 M Street, NW, Suite #1100
Washington, DC 20036-4505
Tel.: (202) 776-9600
Fax: (202) 776-7090
www.amideast.org/employment/default.htm

Amnesty International

Amnesty International is a Nobel Peace Prize–winning organization dedicated to the defense of human rights throughout the world. It maintains a global network of affiliated volunteer organizations and counts more than 700,000 members and supporters in more than 150 countries. It mounts letter-writing and publicity campaigns, attempts to secure the release of political prisoners, tries to ensure humane treatment of all prisoners, and works to abolish torture and executions.

The organization's headquarters are in London, where researchers write reports based on visits to countries and interviews with government authorities, current and former prisoners, and local people. Offices are maintained in more than fifty countries.

Amnesty International USA has its headquarters in New York where it employs about fifty people. An additional sixty people work in six regional offices and the legislative office in Washington, D.C. A handful of positions are filled annually in the United States. In new employees, the organization usually seeks people with degrees, but for most jobs there are no specialization requirements. Experience in other nonprofit organizations is useful but not required, as is experience in human rights volunteer work.

> Amnesty International
> 322 Eighth Avenue
> New York, NY 10001
> Tel.: (212) 807-8400
> web.amnesty.org/web/HRPJobs.nsf!OpenDatabase

Arms Control Association

The Arms Control Association (ACA), founded in 1971, is a national, nonprofit, nonpartisan membership organization dedicated to promoting public understanding of and support for effective arms control policies. Through its public education and media programs and its magazine, *Arms Control Today*, ACA provides policymakers, the press, and the interested public with authoritative information, analysis, and commentary on arms control proposals, negotiations and agreements, and related national security issues. In addition to the regular press briefings the ACA holds on major arms control developments, the association's staff provides commentary and analysis on a broad spectrum of issues for journalists and scholars both in the United States and abroad.

The ACA is one of the media's primary nongovernmental sources of information on the full spectrum of arms control issues and developments. The association served as the principal nongovernmental source of information on the negotiations of the Intermediate-Range Nuclear Forces (INF), START I and II, and Conventional Armed Forces in Europe (CFE) Treaties and has played a key role in defending the Anti-Ballistic Missile (ABM) Treaty. Since the end of the Cold War, the association has increased its coverage of nuclear nonproliferation as the relative importance of the issue has increased and has provided reliable information on "loose nukes" in the former Soviet Union and the threat of nuclear proliferation in India, Pakistan, Iran, Iraq, and North Korea. The association provided information on and helped build support for the indefinite extension of the nuclear Non-Proliferation Treaty (NPT) and the negotiation of the Comprehensive Test Ban Treaty (CTBT) and has actively supported CTBT ratification.

The association currently has nine full-time positions. Job openings are rare, with only one or two positions filled each year. Applicants should have a demonstrated interest in arms control and foreign policy and should have one to three years of experience in the field. Although a master's degree is preferred, it is not required. Resumés and cover letters may be directed to the executive director of the association.

Arms Control Association
1726 M Street, NW
Washington, DC 20036
Tel.: (202) 463-8270
Fax: (202) 463-8273
www.armscontrol.org

Ashoka: Innovators for the Public

Ashoka is an international organization that identifies experts in their fields who have innovative, entrepreneurial ideas in the areas of health, education, women's issues, human rights, or the environment. Based on submitted proposals or business plans, Ashoka grants these individuals fellowships to pay for the implementation of their plans in foreign countries. Ashoka accepts no government funding; a portion of its funds is generated through the membership fees of businesses that are linked with the organization's fellows. Ashoka has representatives in more than thirty countries in Asia, Africa, Eastern Europe, and Latin America.

Requirements of candidates for the project manager position include a master's degree, fluency in a foreign language, and experience in marketing and development. Ashoka often looks to graduates of international affairs programs to fill these positions. Project managers are stationed abroad and are charged with overseeing the development of initiatives in foreign countries. They monitor a country's political climate and serve as a point of contact for local fellows.

Ashoka: Innovators for the Public
1700 North Moore Street
Arlington, VA 22209
Tel.: (703) 527-8300
Fax: (703) 527-8383
www.ashoka.org/home/index.cfm

Asia Foundation

The Asia Foundation is a private, nonprofit organization founded in 1954. It provides small grants to indigenous institutions and organizations in Asia working toward the development of more open and just societies through projects that contribute to constructive social change, stable national development, and equitable economic growth in the region. The foundation's primary fields of interest are law and public administration, communications and libraries, rural and community development, Asian regional cooperation, and Asian-American exchange. Through its Books for Asia program, the foundation has sent more than 35 million American books and journals to libraries, schools, and institutions in Asia and the Pacific islands.

The foundation maintains twelve field offices in Asia. Total professional staff numbers about fifty in the San Francisco headquarters and twenty Americans overseas. An advanced degree in Asian studies, international relations, or a similar field and work experience in foreign affairs, public service, or educational organization is required for most professional positions. Five to eight professional positions are filled annually.

The Asia Foundation
P.O. Box 193223
465 California Street
San Francisco, CA 94119-3223
Tel.: (415) 982-4640
Fax: (415) 392-8863
www.asiafoundation.org/

Asia Society

The Asia Society seeks to strengthen communication between the countries of Asia and the United States and contribute to a greater understanding of Asia and its inhabitants. It promotes Asian arts and humanities and encourages the examination of current economic, political, and cultural issues in Asian society. The Asia Society administers the Asia House Gallery and assists Asian performing musicians touring the United States. Other activities of the society include meetings and study groups of American and Asian scholars to consider contemporary policy issues. The society publishes the bimonthly journal, *Asia,* newsletters, occasional papers, and various Asian art reviews.

A staff of more than ninety people keep the society functioning. Professionals generally have at least a master's degree in international affairs or Asian studies, and a foreign language (preferably Asian) is sometimes required. If work experience is required, it usually involves travel or living experience in a specific area related to the position.

> The Asia Society
> 725 Park Avenue
> New York, NY 10021
> Tel.: (212) 288-6400
> www.asiasociety.org

CARE

The Cooperative for American Relief Everywhere, or CARE, is a federation of agencies interested in assisting the poor of the world to become self-supporting through organizing and utilizing the resources at their command. Programs focus on providing for basic human needs in primary health care, population and family planning, small economic activity development, nutrition, agricultures and natural resources, education, and effective community organization. CARE maintains programs in more than forty-one countries that provide supplementary food and nutrition education; furnish materials and know-how to help villagers build clinics, water systems, and farm-to-market roads; help villagers improve agricultural methods; train public health officials; and provide swift emergency relief to disaster victims, among many other types of interventions.

International personnel overseas number around 250 and fall into two categories: contract personnel and regular (career) personnel. New employees are hired on a one- or two-year standard contract that may be renewed or changed to career status upon successful completion. Positions may be of an administrative or technical nature. Requirements include a master's degree, at least three years' previous overseas experience, experience in a related field (i.e., nutrition, public health, construction, water resources, administration, etc.), and speaking ability in a foreign language—usually Spanish or French. Emphasis on cultural sensitivity is stressed. There are about fifty openings per year.

CARE
Attn: International Employment
151 Ellis Street
Atlanta, GA 30303-2439
Fax: (404) 589-2651
www.careusa.org/careers/

The Carter Center
The Carter Center is a nonprofit, nongovernmental organization devoted to advancing peace and human rights worldwide. Founded by former U.S. President Jimmy Carter in 1982, it is an independently governed part of Emory University in Atlanta, Georgia. More than 250 staff members implement projects in democracy and development, global health, and urban revitalization in about 130 countries. Areas of specialty include human rights, conflict resolution, disease eradication, African governance, global development, Latin American and Caribbean affairs, democratization and election-monitoring, food production in developing nations, tobacco control, and the environment.

Staff are primarily located in the Center's Atlanta offices; however, field offices are occasionally established, such as those in Guyana and Liberia. Programs are directed by resident experts, many of whom hold academic appointments at Emory University. Program directors have intense, specialized preparation in their specialties. A strong academic background, experience addressing real-world problems, foreign language proficiency, and strong communications skills are desired. In the global health programs, many staff have medical or public health training. In addition, staff work in fund-raising, administration, public information, and conferencing.

The Carter Center
One Copenhill
453 Freedom Parkway
Atlanta, GA 30307
Fax: (404) 420-5145
www.cartercenter.org/

Catholic Relief Services

Catholic Relief Services (CRS) is the relief and development agency of the U.S. Catholic Church. It was established in 1943 to assist people displaced because of war. CRS now funds programs of assistance, both relief and development, in more than seventy-five countries. In more than forty of those, there is resident staff and in the remainder, assistance is directed to local project holders. With an annual budget of more than $300 million, CRS is one of the largest private voluntary organizations in the world.

CRS is continuously seeking to help the poorest, most disadvantaged people in the world with assistance that fosters their self-reliance. Its programs emphasize disaster and emergency relief, mother-child health care, small enterprise development, aid to farmers, and assistance to refugees. All CRS programs seek to build local capacity and enable communities to formulate solutions to their problems.

Each year, CRS usually has about twenty position openings for overseas or headquarters (Baltimore). These can range from short-term to long-term contract positions. Candidates for positions at CRS should generally have a master's degree along with speaking ability in French or Spanish and previous relief or development experience in a developing country. In addition, CRS has about fourteen intern positions for one-year assignments overseas. This intern program focuses on postgraduate applicants with facility in another language (usually French or Spanish). Experience in the developing world is a plus.

> Department of Human Resources
> Catholic Relief Services
> 209 West Fayette Street
> Baltimore, MD 21201-3402
> Tel.: (410) 625-2220
> (800) 235-2772
> www.catholicrelief.org/

CDS International

CDS International, Inc. (CDS) was founded in 1968 as a nonprofit 501(c)(3) organization. CDS is committed to the advancement of international practical training opportunities that stimulate the exchange of knowledge and technological skills and contribute to the development of a highly trained and interculturally competent workforce. This experience helps strengthen global cooperation and understanding among individuals, businesses, organizations, and communities.

Each year, CDS serves more than 1,800 young professionals and students from approximately sixty countries in a variety of work/study, internships, and study tour programs. CDS administers programs ranging in duration from three to eighteen months. Every program consists of an internship component; some have academic or language training elements as well. Internships are possible in any of the following fields: management, business, commerce finance, the sciences, engineering, architecture, mathematics, industrial occupations, media and communications, agriculture, and arts and culture.

CDS offers long- and short-term work/study, practical training, and educational programs, as well as study tours for particular interest groups. CDS administers the following programs: The Congress-Bundestag Youth Exchange for Young Professionals, Robert Bosch Foundation Fellowship, Bayer Summer Internship, Work Immersion Study Program, Culinary Arts and Hospitality Internship Program in Switzerland, the Professional Development Program, and the Automotive Supplier Trainee Exchange Program, as well as internships to Argentina, Turkey, and Singapore. Most internships are paid.

> CDS International, Inc.
> 871 United Nations Plaza, 15th Floor
> New York, NY 10017-1814
> Tel.: (212) 497-3500
> Fax: (212) 497-3535
> www.cdsintl.org

The Citizens Network for Foreign Affairs
The Citizens Network for Foreign Affairs (CNFA) is a nonprofit organization dedicated to stimulating international growth and development in the emerging economies of the world—particularly in the New Independent States (NIS) of the Former Soviet Union. CNFA works with companies, entrepreneurs, farm groups, business alliances, and other groups to create lasting and effective opportunities in international markets. CNFA's approach to international development encompasses food systems restructuring, the expansion of nongovernmental groups in emerging economies, and the involvement of the U.S. private sector in international development.

CNFA's headquarters are in Washington, D.C., with field offices in Moscow and Krasnodar, Russia; Kiev, Ukraine; and Bishkek,

Kyrgyzstan. CNFA has operated since 1986. Among its flagship programs are the Food Systems Restructuring program, through which CNFA coordinates joint ventures between U.S. agribusinesses and Russian and Ukrainian private businesses with funding from the U.S. Agency for International Development; the Agribusiness volunteer program, which arranges for volunteer exchange visits between U.S. agribusiness professionals and their counterparts in the NIS; and the Central Asian Partnership Program, which sets up information and volunteer exchanges between agriculture organizations in Central Asia and similar groups in the United States.

Applicants should have at least a bachelor's degree in international relations or a related field as well as some language expertise (especially Russian or Ukrainian) and/or an agriculture background.

> The Citizens Network for Foreign Affairs
> Suite 900
> 1111 19th Street, NW
> Washington, DC 20036
> Tel.: (202) 296-3920
> Fax: (202) 296-3948
> www.cnfa.com

Church World Service

Founded in 1946, Church World Service (CWS) partners with churches and organizations in more than eighty countries, working to meet human needs and foster self-reliance. CWS works worldwide on behalf of thirty-six Protestant, Anglican, and Orthodox denominations in the United States in programs of social and economic development, emergency response, assistance to refugees, education and advocacy, and ecumenical relationships. With corporate offices and support services in New York City and Elkhart, Indiana, CWS has regional program offices throughout the United States and Southeast Asia, Africa, Europe, and Latin America.

CWS employs about 300 people in positions both domestic and overseas. Currently, 50 to 60 staff are working overseas. A sampling of positions includes caseworkers, who work in refugee processing and resettlement, both within the United States and overseas, and country directors and regional representatives, who work in social and economic program development throughout the world. In addition, CWS partners with the Amity Foundation, providing valuable educational development in China. Overseas experience is often necessary, especially in social and economic development, and, as is appropriate, cultural and multilingual ability and experience. Bachelors and graduate degrees are also preferred.

> Human Resources Department
> Church World Service
> 28606 Phillips Street
> P.O. Box 968
> Elkhart, IN 46515-0968
> Tel.: (219) 264-3102
> Fax: (219) 266-0087
> www.churchworldservice.org

Council on International Education Exchange

The Council on International Educational Exchange, known as Council and often referred to as CIEE, is a nonprofit, nongovernmental organization dedicated to helping people gain understanding, acquire knowledge, and develop skills for living in a globally interdependent and culturally diverse world. Founded in 1947, Council has developed a wide variety of programs and services for students and teachers at secondary through university levels and related constituencies. With 700 professionals in approximately thirty countries working to deliver diverse programs and services, Council has become one of the world's leading operators of international exchange programs and related services. Today, Council operates in six broad business areas: college and university programs, secondary school programs, English language development, work exchanges, voluntary service, and travel services. Regional administrative services are located in North America (New York), Europe (Paris), and Asia (Tokyo).

Council frequently has openings for administrative clerical support staff. Entry-level applicants with excellent organizational and communication skills, foreign language ability, and study or work experience abroad are preferred. Travel opportunities are sometimes available. Council often employs college students for seasonal or short-term jobs. Students able to begin in February or March and continue through August or September are preferred. Most positions are in the Student Services, Work Exchanges, and travel divisions; duties range from selling charter flights and student travel products, processing program applications, and handling information requests. Second languages, overseas experience, and office skills are viewed positively.

Council on International Educational Exchange
633 Third Avenue, 20th Floor
New York, NY 10017-6706
Tel.: (800) 40-Study
Fax: (212) 822-2779
www.ciee.org/jobs.cfm?subnav=utility

Ford Foundation

The Ford Foundation is the largest foundation in the United States. It aims to advance public welfare by identifying and contributing to the solution of problems of national and international importance. It makes grants primarily to institutions for experimental, demonstration, and development efforts that are likely to produce significant advances within the field of interest. The major portion of the Foundation's international budget is devoted to programs in developing countries. These programs include urban poverty, rural poverty and resources, human rights and social justice, governance and public policy, education and culture, international affairs, and reproductive health and population.

The Ford Foundation has assets of over $7 billion and expends more than $285 million annually in program activities. The Foundation's staff in the International Affairs program office numbers around twenty and there are approximately ninety people employed in the Foundation's programs on Africa, the Middle East, Asia, and Latin America.

The Ford Foundation
320 East 43rd Street
New York, NY 10017
Tel.: (212) 573-5000
Fax: (212) 351-3677
www.fordfound.org/

Freedom House

Founded in 1941, Freedom House is a nonprofit, nonpartisan organization dedicated to the promotion of democracy and human rights worldwide. Freedom House conducts research, advocacy, education, and training initiatives that promote human rights, democracy, free market economics, the rule of law, independent media, and U.S. engagement in international affairs. Americans are eligible for hire or volunteer positions in Freedom House activities in Ukraine, Poland,

Getting Started at Nonprofits
CÉLINE GUSTAVSON

Since graduating from the Master of Science in Foreign Service program in 1997, I have worked for three nonprofit organizations overseas and in the United States: Catholic Relief Services (CRS), the Council on Foreign Relations, and Save the Children. The skill sets that international nonprofits seek are fairly similar throughout the sector. The most sought after skills are the following:

- *Writing skills.* These are extremely important because nonprofits must constantly fund raise. Someone who can write proposals and win grants is highly prized.
- *Verbal communication skills in more than one language.* Communication skills are necessary in order to present and defend grant proposals in meetings with donors. Furthermore, a key aspect of work in the nonprofit sector is interfacing with community leaders and communities; you cannot work effectively with these partners or reach your program objectives without the ability to speak and write in more than one language. Without language skills, chances of getting a job decrease significantly.

(Continued)

Serbia, Romania, Hungary, Albania, Bosnia and Herzegovina, Bulgaria, Croatia, Latvia, Lithuania, Macedonia, and Slovakia.

Freedom House typically has a number of openings for experienced consultants and short-term trainers, although the number varies greatly from year to year. Four new hires filled newly created permanent positions in field offices in a recent year. The criteria for new hires vary greatly based on position and location. However, general requirements include a balance of education, work and field experience, and a passion for international affairs, democracy, and human rights issues. Foreign language skills are also highly desirable.

Freedom House
1319 18th Street, NW
Washington, DC 20036
Tel.: (202) 296-5101
Fax: (202) 296-5078
www.freedomhouse.org

- *International work experience.* In the international nonprofit world, overseas work experience is key. It is assumed that you will have obtained some, perhaps through a summer internship, before finishing graduate work. If you haven't, that should be your main objective immediately after graduation.
- *Excellent interpersonal skills and cross-cultural sensitivity.* The ability to work well on teams is highly prized, as is the ability to work in and with other cultures. In the case of relief and development work you should also be able to demonstrate adaptability in hardship situations and stressful environments.

The best way to prepare for a job in the international nonprofit sector is to ensure that, on paper and in an interview, you can demonstrate the skills listed previously. If you do not have them, plan to acquire them.

As you start your search, interview with nonprofit recruiters on campus. A successful interview is the key to getting a job, so the more you interview the better. Here are a few things that helped me:

- Keep up with current events, particularly as they relate to the job, region, and organization to which you are applying. Read the newspaper the day of your interview!
- Know as much as possible about the organization.
- Read your resumé before you go into an interview. If you list your

German Marshall Fund of the United States

The German Marshall Fund of the United States (GMF) is an American institution that stimulates the exchange of ideas and promotes cooperation between the United States and Europe in the spirit of the postwar Marshall Plan. GMF was created in 1972 by a gift from Germany as a permanent memorial to Marshall Plan aid.

Through its work in the United States and Europe, GMF has pursued its founding mission to create a closer understanding between partners on both sides of the Atlantic. GMF's grant making promotes the study of international and domestic policies, supports comparative research and debate on key issues, and assists policy and opinion leaders' understanding of these issues.

GMF has a total grant-making budget of approximately $11 million. Each year almost $1.5 million is spent on GMF-managed fellowships. The remainder is allocated for grants in the following program areas: economics, environment, foreign policy, and immigration and integration.

honors thesis, be prepared to describe it—you'll find you've forgotten a lot of it. Ask a friend to discuss it with you.

These are some of the questions that you could use to practice. I have been asked these, or similar questions, in several interviews:

- Provide an example of when you have worked on a team in a professional capacity. Describe a time when working within a team you had problems, and how you addressed/dealt with those problems.
- Give an example of when you were in a cross-cultural situation where conflict management was required. How did you handle it?
- Describe a situation when you felt it necessary to be very attentive and vigilant to your environment.
- Give an example of how you prioritized multiple tasks under time constraints.
- Provide an example of how you identified, analyzed, and solved a problem.
- Describe a time on any job when you were faced with problems or stresses that tested your coping skills. What did you do?
- Give an example of experience in a hardship or difficult situation. How did you address it?

Working for a nonprofit is challenging and extremely rewarding. In terms of career development, the nonprofit sector is

(Continued)

Total professional staff number about thirty: twenty-one in Washington, D.C., four in Berlin, two in Paris, and three in Bratislava. A bachelor's degree in international relations or a related field and work experience in foreign affairs, public policy, or nonprofit organizations is required or preferred for most positions. Three to five positions are filled annually.

The German Marshall Fund
11 Dupont Circle, NW, Suite 750
Washington, DC 20036
Tel.: (202) 745-3950
Fax: (202) 265-1662
www.gmfus.org

Human Rights Watch

Since its founding in 1978, Human Rights Watch has grown to become the largest and most influential U.S.-based organization seeking to promote human rights worldwide. Human Rights Watch is fairly unique because once you demonstrate your ability to do quality work, you will move rapidly into positions of increasing importance and responsibility. The monetary rewards of the job are less exciting, but they are not as dismal as they are made out to be. For example, when working in a developing country, your salary is probably tax-free, and you are unlikely to spend a great deal since the cost of living is lower than in the United States.

The nonprofit sector is becoming highly competitive, but it is one in which you are well equipped to compete if you have the skills described previously. If you don't, there's still time to get them! My decision to work in the nonprofit sector was one of the best decisions I have ever made, and I hope it will be a decision that you make too!

Céline Gustavson, a 1997 graduate of the Master of Science in Foreign Service program at Georgetown University, is an associate with Save the Children. Prior to this, she worked with Catholic Relief Services in Croatia and Morocco, and at the Council on Foreign Relations in New York. She graduated with a B.A. in International Relations from Mount Holyoke College in 1994 and studied for a semester in Senegal.

known for its impartial and reliable human rights reporting, its innovative and high-profile advocacy campaigns, and its success in affecting the policy of the United States and other influential governments toward abusive regimes. Human Rights Watch conducts regular, systematic investigations of human rights abuses in approximately seventy countries around the world. It addresses the human rights practices of governments of all political stripes, geopolitical alignments, and ethnic and religious affiliations. In internal wars it documents violations by both governments and rebel groups. It is an independent, nongovernmental organization supported by contributions from private individuals and foundations worldwide; it accepts no government funds, directly or indirectly.

Headquartered in New York, Human Rights Watch maintains offices in Washington, D.C., Los Angeles, London, Brussels, and Moscow, with staff based in various other locations around the world. There are five regional divisions covering Africa, the Americas, Asia, the Middle East and North Africa, and Europe and Central Asia. In addition, there are three collaborative projects on arms transfers and land mines, children's rights, and women's rights. In addition, there are individual researchers working on U.S. policy, prisons, academic freedom, corporations, the international criminal court campaign, HIV, and human rights. With a staff of more than 100 worldwide, there are approximately twenty openings each year. Candidates for administrative positions must have a bachelor's degree, preferably in international relations; researchers should have a master's, law, or other advanced degree. Applicants should have a working knowledge of human rights issues; foreign language skills are desirable.

> Human Rights Watch
> 350 5th Avenue, 34th Floor
> New York, NY 10118-3299
> Tel.: (212) 290-4700 Fax: (212) 736-1300
> www.hrw.org

IAESTE United States

IAESTE United States is one member of international organization in more than seventy countries dedicated to placing science and engineering students into paid technical internships abroad. Students can request to be placed almost anywhere in the world; students in previous years have been trained in countries from France and Germany to Tunisia and Thailand. Social activities and housing normally are provided in the host country. The program has sent nearly 100 students abroad in previous years and hopes to increase that number significantly.

To be eligible, students must have attained junior standing by the time the internship begins, be between nineteen and thirteen years old, and be enrolled full-time in a technical field of study at an accredited four-year American university (foreign students currently on F-1 visas welcome). Internships can last between four weeks and one year and typically begin in the summer. Most require only English, though foreign language skills are preferred. In order to be considered for a summer internship placement, students must submit an initial application by January 1 of that year. Applications are available on the website.

> IAESTE United States
> 10400 Little Patuxent Parkway, Suite 250
> Columbia, MD 21044-3519
> Tel.: (410) 997-3069
> Fax: (410) 997-5186
> www.aipt.org/iaeste.html

Immigration and Refugee Services of America

Immigration and Refugee Services of America (IRSA) is dedicated to defending human rights, building communities, fostering education, promoting self-sufficiency, and forging partnerships through an array of programs. IRSA develops and manages education and assistance programs that help refugees recover from past trauma, gain personal independence and economic self-sufficiency, become contributing members of their new communities, and resettle in the United States.

IRSA seeks applicants with a college degree and hands-on experience working with refugees. There were eight professional job openings in the past year. Please refer to the website for up-to-date employment opportunities.

Human Resources
Immigration and Refugee Services of America
U.S. Committee for Refugees
1717 Massachusetts Avenue, NW, Suite 200
Washington, DC 20023-2003
Tel.: (202) 797-2105
Fax: (202) 347-2460
www.irsa-uscr.org

Institute of International Education

The Institute of International Education (IIE) is the world leader in the international exchange of people and ideas. Its mission is to foster international understanding by opening minds to the world. It does this by assisting college and university students to study abroad; advising institutions of higher education on ways to internationalize their student body, faculty, and curriculum; fostering sustainable development through training programs in energy, the environment, enterprise management, and leadership development; and partnering with corporations, foundations, and governments in finding and developing people able to think and work on a global basis.

IIE's programs are managed by professional staff with expertise in such diverse fields as higher education and scholarship administration, energy and the environment, business and public administration, human rights, economic development, and the arts. IIE is currently administering 250 programs through which nearly 18,000 men and women from 175 nations benefit. IIE forges partnerships between the public and private sectors to design and implement international programs.

In addition to its headquarters in New York City, IIE has offices in Chicago, Denver, Houston, San Francisco, and Washington, D.C. International offices are located in Bangladesh, Brazil, China, Egypt, Hong Kong, Hungary, India, Indonesia, Kazakhstan, Mexico, Philippines, Russia, South Africa, Thailand, Ukraine, and Vietnam. Candidates who have a bachelor's degree and possess a minimum of two years' work experience generally apply for program associate and/or program coordinator positions. Overseas experience is preferred. IIE has a staff of more than 475 professionals and relies on the services of more than 6,000 volunteers who serve on regional advisory boards, scholarship screening and selection panels, and program committees.

>Institute of International Education
>809 United Nations Plaza
>New York, NY 10017
>Tel.: (212) 883-8200
>Fax: (212) 984-5452
>www.iie.org
>
>Institute of International Education
>1400 K Street, NW, Suite 650
>Washington, DC 20005
>Tel.: (202) 898-0600
>Fax: (202) 326-7669

InterAction
The American Council for Voluntary International Action, better known as InterAction, is a broadly based coalition of more than 160 private and voluntary organizations (PVOs) dedicated to international relief and development. Members work on a broad range of concerns including sustainable development, refugee assistance and protection, disaster relief and preparedness, public policy, and education of Americans about the developing world. InterAction exists to enhance the effectiveness and professional capabilities of its members and to foster partnership, collaboration, leadership, and the power of the community to strive together to achieve a world of self-reliance, justice, and peace. InterAction serves as an information clearinghouse, works with Congress on international issues, promotes the work of its members, and organizes seminars and conferences. Its biweekly newsletter, *Monday Developments,* contains an extensive listing of job opportunities with international and environmental agencies.

InterAction employs thirty-five to forty professional staff in the United States, who all deal with international issues. On the average, five to ten positions are filled each year. A master's degree is preferred but not required; overseas experience and experience with PVOs or other development agencies are desirable. Strong analytical and writing skills are essential.

InterAction
1717 Massachusetts Avenue, NW, Suite 801
Washington, DC 20036
Tel.: (202) 667-8227
Fax: (202) 667-8236
http://128.121.4.162/

International Executive Service Corps

The International Executive Service Corps (IESC) was founded in 1964 by a group of American businessmen and women to assist enterprises in the developing world and, now, in the emerging democracies by providing technical and managerial expertise and a variety of other services to strengthen the private sector through job creation and building strong civil societies. IESC and its volunteers have completed more than 23,000 projects in 120 countries. IESC's mission is focused on international economic development. Operations in 49 countries include Africa, Asia, Latin America, Central and Eastern Europe, and the Middle East. Its major programs are located in Egypt and Jordan. Another major program is USAID's Global Technology Network (GTN). IESC manages GTN for USAID at IESC's Washington office. IESC's Skills Bank contains the names and qualifications of more than 10,000 American men and women who are ready to volunteer their time and expertise on overseas assignments. IESC also uses paid consultants. Volunteers range in age from twenty-five to seventy. The length of a project ranges from one week to two or three months, but can be up to a year in length for special projects. Visit the website for more detailed information and for job postings.

International Executive Service Corps
333 Ludlow Street
P.O. Box 10005
Stamford, CT 06904-2005
Tel.: (203) 967-6000
Fax: (203) 324-2531
www.iesc.org

International Institute for Environment and Development

The International Institute for Environment and Development (IIED) is an independent, nonprofit research institute working in the field of sustainable development.

IIED aims to provide expertise and leadership in researching and achieving sustainable development at local, national, regional, and global levels. In alliance with others, we seek to help shape a future that ends global poverty and delivers and sustains efficient and equitable management of the world's natural resources.

For information related to our employment opportunities, please refer to the website. Specifics as to academic and professional experience for applicants are detailed in the job description document of the relevant post.

> IIED
> 3 Endsleigh Street
> London
> WC1H 0DD
> Tel.: (44) 20-7388-2117
> Fax: (44) 20-7388-2826
> www.iied.org

International Institute for Sustainable Development

The International Institute for Sustainable Development (IISD) applies research, expert analysis, and information technology to the challenges of sustainable development. IISD's vision is better living for all—sustainably. Their mission is to champion innovation, enabling societies to live sustainably. Their work is focused in the areas of climate change and energy, economic policy, trade and investment, natural resource management, and measurement and indicators. Through its publications, *Earth Negotiations Bulletin* and *Sustainable Developments,* IISD also offers comprehensive coverage of international negotiations on environment and sustainable development.

IISD's head office is located in Winnipeg, Manitoba, Canada. It has satellite offices in Ottawa, New York, and Geneva. IISD draws on the expertise of more than eighty consultants, specialists, and associates in conducting its programmatic activities. The majority of the institute's activities are international in scope. New recruits at IISD typically have graduate degrees and experience working internationally on issues related to sustainable development.

International Institute for Sustainable Development
161 Portage Avenue E., 6th Floor
Winnipeg, Manitoba
Canada
R3Y 0B6
Tel.: (204) 958-7700
Fax: (204) 958-7710
www.iisd.org

International Republican Institute

The International Republican Institute (IRI) is a private, nonprofit, non-partisan organization dedicated to advancing democracy worldwide. IRI conducts programs in thirty countries in such areas as grassroots political organizing, campaign management, polling, parliamentary training, judicial reform, and election monitoring.

IRI maintains a staff of about fifty in Washington, D.C., and approximately twenty international positions available in field offices in Azerbaijan, Cambodia, Croatia, Georgia, Guatemala, Indonesia, Mongolia, Nigeria, Romania, Russia, Slovakia, South Africa, and Ukraine. Trainers and election observers are drawn from among hundreds of volunteers annually.

Human Resources Department
1212 New York Avenue, NW
Suite 900
Washington, DC 20005-3987
Tel.: (202) 408-9450
Fax: (202) 408-9462
www.iri.org

International Rescue Committee

Founded in 1933 at the request of Albert Einstein, the International Rescue Committee (IRC) is the leading nonsectarian, voluntary organization providing relief, protection, and resettlement services for refugees and victims of oppression or violent conflict. The IRC is committed to freedom, human dignity, and self-reliance. This commitment is reflected in well-planned global emergency relief, rehabilitation, resettlement assistance, and advocacy for refugees.

At the outbreak of an emergency, IRC provides sanctuary and lifesaving assistance—rapidly delivering critical medical and public health services, shelter, and food. Once a crisis stabilizes, it sets up programs to enable refugees to cope with life in exile. Through training, education, and income-generating programs, it helps refugees acquire new skills to become self-sufficient.

For those who cannot safely return to their countries and who qualify for entry into the United States, IRC assists in their resettlement. Its network of regional IRC offices makes sure that new arrivals have all that they need to start rebuilding their lives.

IRC serves refugees and the displaced in Europe, Asia, Africa, the Balkans, and the Caucuses.

There were 300 overseas professional positions and professional job openings in the international field last year. The academic backgrounds and experiences looked for in new hires are M.S., M.P.H., M.A., M.D., R.N., civil engineer, C.P.A., and M.S.W.

International Rescue Committee
122 East 42nd Street
New York, NY 10168
Tel.: (212) 551-3000
www.theirc.org

International Research and Exchanges Board

International Research and Exchanges Board (IREX) is an international nonprofit organization dedicated to the advancement of knowledge. Central to its mission is the empowering of individuals and institutions to participate meaningfully in civil society. IREX contributes to the development of students, scholars, policymakers, business leaders, journalists, and other professionals by administering programs between the United States and the countries of Eastern Europe, the New Independent States, Asia, and the Near East. IREX strengthens independent media and academic, public, and nongovernmental institutions and makes the knowledge and skills developed through its programs available to universities, foundations, policymakers, and the corporate sector.

IREX has a staff of 350 employees in twenty-six countries and seventy-one cities worldwide. Its annual operating budget is approximately $35 million.

International Research & Exchanges Board
1616 H Street, NW
6th Floor
Washington, DC 20006
Tel.: (202) 628-8188
www.irex.org

International Schools Services

The Educational Staffing program of International Schools Services (ISS) has placed more than 18,000 K–12 teachers and administrators in American overseas schools since 1955. Most candidates obtain their overseas teaching positions by attending our U.S.-based International Recruitment Centers (IRCs) where ISS candidates have the potential to interview with overseas school heads seeking new staff. Candidates must first apply to establish a professional file with ISS in order to be eligible to register for an IRC.

Applicants must have a bachelor's degree and two years of current K–12 teaching experience. The experience requirement may be waived for those who have overseas living or working experience, teaching certification, and a motivation to work in the developing world. IRC registration materials are provided upon approval of a completed application. Please visit the website for more information, where an application may be completed online.

> International Schools Services
> 15 Roszel Road
> P.O. Box 5910
> Princeton, NJ 08543-5910
> Tel.: (609) 452-0990
> Fax: (609) 452-2690
> www.iss.edu

International Voluntary Services

International Voluntary Services (IVS) works to strengthen the capacities of local organizations and institutions in developing nations through projects that actively help the rural poor through their own efforts and resources. IVS also provides skilled international technicians to fill particular positions at the request of local organizations and governments. The organization's programs focus on community development, small business management and development, food production and agriculture, and medicine and public health. IVS is active in South America, South Asia, and sub-Saharan Africa.

IVS recruits internationally and has approximately fifty full-time staff working in the field. Candidates for program and project manager positions should have degrees in specialized areas of development work, including but not limited to such areas as agronomy, agricultural marketing, irrigation, and hydrology, and previous experience working in developing countries.

International Voluntary Services
1625 K Street, NW, Suite 102
Washington, DC 20006
Tel.: (202) 387-5533
Fax: (202) 387-4291
www.ivs-inc.org/

The Japan Exchange and Teaching Programme

The Japan Exchange and Teaching Programme (JET) seeks to help enhance internationalization in Japan by promoting mutual understanding between Japan, Australia, Canada, China, France, Germany, Ireland, New Zealand, the Republic of Korea, the Russian Federation, the United Kingdom, and the United States. The program is based upon intensifying foreign language education in Japan and upon promoting international exchange at the local level through fostering ties between Japanese youth and JET program participants.

The JET Programme offers two areas of placement. Coordinators for International Relations (CIRs) are engaged in international activities. CIRs are placed in offices of prefectural governments or offices of designated cities. A number of CIRs are placed in municipal governments of nondesignated cities, towns, villages, or other entities through the offices of the prefectures. Assistant Language Teachers (ALTs) are engaged in language instruction. The participants are placed mainly in publicly run schools or local boards of education.

JET Office
Embassy of Japan
2520 Massachusetts Avenue, NW
Washington, DC 20008
Tel.: (202) 238-6772
Fax: (202) 265-9484
www.mofa.go.jp/j_info/visit/jet/

Japan Foundation Center for Global Partnership

Japan Foundation Center for Global Partnership (CGP) provides project grants to nonprofit organizations in order to promote collaboration and improved understanding, as well as to enhance dialogue and interchange between the people of the United States and Japan on a wide range of contemporary issues. CGP is a division of the Japan Foundation, a semi-governmental agency of the Japanese government that supports and promotes cultural exchange between Japan and many other countries through its head office in Tokyo and its eighteen offices overseas.

CGP's operations include general grant-making programs and fellowship programs. The general grant-making programs support policy-oriented research and dialogue, curriculum development, teacher training, public forums, youth exchange and nonprofit organization exchange. The fellowship programs provide research support to individual scholars and support for training to nonprofit sector professionals.

CGP operates its programs through its offices in New York and Tokyo and has a total of twenty-five staff members. Positions for program assistant and program associate, which mostly involve proposal screening and grant management, are occasionally available (once or more per year) in the New York office. Candidates with a bachelor's degree and limited work experience would be considered for the program assistant position. Candidates with either a bachelor's or master's degree and a few years of work experience would be considered for the program associate position. The following qualifications are desirable for either position: experience and knowledge of Japan, experience in the field of U.S.-Japan exchange, knowledge and/or professional experience in academia or the nonprofit sector, experience in the field of grant making, writing and analytical skills, administrative and supervisory skills, and knowledge of the Japanese language.

> The Japan Foundation Center for Global Partnership (NY)
> 152 West 57th Street, 39th Floor
> New York, NY 10019
> Tel.: (212) 489-1255 Fax: (212) 489-1344
> www.cgp.org/cgplink

Maryknoll Mission Association

Maryknoll Mission Association welcomes single people, couples, families with children, and religious and ordained people to serve in cross-cultural ministries in order to create a more just world in solidarity with marginalized and oppressed peoples. As a Maryknoll Mission Association of the Faithful (MMAF) member you could serve in the African nations of Kenya, Sudan, Tanzania, or Zimbabwe; the Asian states of Cambodia, Thailand, or Vietnam; and the Latin American states of Bolivia, Brazil, Chile, El Salvador, Mexico, Peru, or Venezuela. Our first term of service is three and a half years overseas, following a four-month orientation program in the United States. Included in this time is comprehensive language training and an in-country orientation.

Missioners offer their particular gifts and talents in response to people's needs. This can include health, direct service to people with AIDS, education, community organizing, grassroots economic development, and formation of faith communities. Most MMAF members are between the ages of twenty-one and fifty-five years old. Mission volunteers are required to be Catholics active in the U.S. church; singles, couples, and families with children under eight; priests or laypersons; U.S. citizens or permanent residents. Missioners are provided transportation to and from country of assignment, health care, room and board, personal allowance, and language study in country of assignment.

> Maryknoll Mission Association
> Box 307
> Maryknoll, NY 10545-0307
> Tel.: (800) 818-5276
> (914) 762-6364 Fax: 914-762-7031
> www.maryknoll.org

Mercy Corps

Mercy Corps exists to alleviate suffering, poverty, and oppression by helping people build secure, productive, and just communities. With headquarters in the United States and Scotland, Mercy Corps is an international family of humanitarian organizations that includes Mercy Corps; Mercy Corps Scotland; Pax World Service in Washington, D.C.; Proyecto Aldea Global in Honduras; Proyecto Aldea Global Jinotega in Nicaragua; and MerciPhil Development Foundation in the Philippines.

Working in twenty-five countries worldwide and positively affecting the lives of more than 5 million people, Mercy Corps operates programs in civil society and economic development, emergency relief, food resources, health, material aid, and micro-enterprise.

We are searching for those "best of class" candidates who will help grow our vision. We are looking for individuals who are entrepreneurial, creative, positive, team-oriented, personable, bright, self-motivated, flexible, and reliable.

> Mercy Corps
> 3015 SW First
> Dept W
> Portland, OR 97201
> Tel.: (800) 292-3355 ext. 250
> www.mercycorps.org

Meridian International Center

Meridian International Center is a not-for-profit educational and cultural institution that promotes international understanding through the exchange of people, ideas, and the arts. For visitors from other countries, Meridian serves as a doorway to the United States through its programming and training services, including conferences and seminars. For Americans interested in global issues, Meridian provides a window on the world through lectures, briefings, educational outreach programs, concerts, and exhibitions. In addition, Meridian coordinates activities for its affiliate, The Hospitality and Information Service, whose volunteers assist Washington's diplomatic community.

Meridian has a staff of 100 employees. The annual budget is about $16 million.

> Meridian International Center
> 1630 Crescent Place, NW
> Washington, DC 20009
> Tel.: (202) 667-6800
> www.meridian.org

National Democratic Institute

The National Democratic Institute (NDI) was started with the National Endowment for Democracy. Its purpose is to teach democracy and the democratic process. The organization has field offices around the world. A recent focus has been on ways to broaden recruitment efforts of the organization.

Ideal candidates for positions at all levels of NDI should be knowledgeable in accounting, governance, development, political party structure, the parliamentary process, and be able to speak at least one foreign language. Resumés received at NDI are generally organized by region of familiarity and functional expertise. The position of program assistant is primarily administrative, providing full project support to program officers. About half of all program assistants possess master's degrees. Program officers survey missions abroad to monitor developments with local governments and help determine which projects are funded. A master's degree is required for this position. Regional directors, or senior program officers, are stationed abroad and oversee projects in the field offices in foreign countries.

> National Democratic Institute
> 2030 M Street, NW, Fifth Floor
> Washington, DC 20036-3306
> Tel.: (202) 728-5500
> www.ndi.org

The Nature Conservancy

With the accelerating loss of the Earth's biological heritage and the impairment of critical ecological processes that support life on the planet, the mission and work of The Nature Conservancy could not be more important or compelling. The Nature Conservancy provides the opportunity to conserve biological diversity on a global scale. As the world's leading private international conservation group, The Nature Conservancy has a fifty-year history of extraordinary success saving key natural areas throughout the United States and in twenty-eight countries around the world.

The Nature Conservancy's success depends on more than 3,000 staff members and numerous volunteers and colleagues. It has hired approximately 600 people a year for the last three years, many with international experience. It posts its staff positions and internships on the website and tries to attract men and women with a broad spectrum of backgrounds and experiences. The Nature Conservancy does not accept unsolicited resumés not linked to specific job openings.

International Headquarters
The Nature Conservancy
4245 North Fairfax Drive, Suite 100
Arlington, VA 22203-1606
Tel.: (800) 628-6860
http://nature.org/

Near East Foundation

The Near East Foundation, founded in 1915, is America's oldest voluntary agency devoted exclusively to programs of technical assistance in developing countries. It concentrates on community participation, utilizing appropriate technology, building local skill capacity, and providing cofinancing.

The provision of qualified specialists to assist with the transfer of technical skills and human resource development is the foundation's principal mode of operation. It assists only projects that have strong local support, and it actively seeks opportunities to extend its work through cooperation with other donor agencies. The annual budgets typically allocate more than $6 million for projects in Middle Eastern and African countries.

A small headquarters staff in New York provides support for field operations. An overseas staff of approximately 150 people includes resident specialists and local professionals. Preferred qualifications for specialist positions are a master's degree (or equivalent) with a development-related specialization and five years' relevant experience.

Near East Foundation
342 Madison Avenue
New York, NY 10173-1030
Tel.: (212) 867-0064 Fax: (212) 867-0169
www.neareast.org

Open Society Institute
The Open Society Institute (OSI) is a private operating and grant-making foundation that develops and implements a range of programs in civil society, education, media, public health, and human and women's rights, as well as social, legal, and economic reform. OSI is at the center of an informal network of foundations and organizations active in more than fifty countries worldwide that supports a range of programs. Established in 1993 by investor and philanthropist George Soros, OSI is based in New York City and operates network-wide programs, grant-making activities in the United States, and other international initiatives. OSI provides support and assistance to Soros foundations in Central and Eastern Europe and the former Soviet Union, Guatemala, Haiti, Mongolia, and parts of Africa.

The programs of the Open Society Institute fall into three categories: network programs, international initiatives, and programs that focus on the United States. Network programs based in New York include the Economic and Business Development Program, which assists the Soros foundations network in economic restructuring efforts, including micro-credit and small-enterprise development; the Children and Youth Programs, which aim to provide young people with opportunities and resources to help them become full participants in society; the English Language Programs, which provide English as a Foreign Language support and modern teaching methodologies to countries within the network; the Internet Program, which supports projects that develop e-mail and Internet services among the countries in the network; the Medical and Health Programs, which are aimed at improving public health care in Central and Eastern Europe and the former Soviet Union; the Scholarship Programs (based in Budapest), which provide academic exchange opportunities for students, scholars, and professionals from the countries of Central and Eastern Europe, the former Soviet Union, Mongolia, and Burma; and the Women's Program, which was initiated to support the Soros foundations network in dealing with women's issues.

New York–based programs with an international focus include the Burma Project, which promotes international awareness of the repressive military dictatorship in Burma and supports education and training for Burmese refugees. The Landmines Project, which supports efforts toward a comprehensive worldwide ban on landmines, is based at OSI's Washington, D.C., office.

The Open Society Institute-Budapest was established in 1993 to develop and implement programs in the areas of educational, social, and legal reform. Together with its sister organization, the New York–based Open Society Institute, OSI-Budapest provides administrative, financial, and technical support and establishes network programs to address certain issues on a regional or network-wide basis.

In addition, OSI-Budapest supports a variety of other initiatives throughout Central and Eastern Europe and the former Soviet Union, with a strong emphasis on projects in the areas of human rights, ethnic and minority issues, civil society, and women's issues. The OSI-Budapest is distinct from the Soros Foundation-Hungary, which funds activities exclusively within Hungary.

OSI has positions in the international programs at levels ranging from program assistant, program associate, program coordinator, and program officer to associate director. The academic and prior experience requirements for each position differ, depending on the responsibilities which will be performed, as described in the job description for the position. At the level of program assistant, an undergraduate degree and at least some prior office experience would be sufficient. Proficiency in a foreign language may also be necessary. The other positions may require graduate degrees, experience in working with an international program, firsthand knowledge of the region in which the program operates, foreign language fluency, and possibly experience working with NGOs or nonprofit organizations.

Open Society Institute
400 West 49th Street
New York, NY 10019
www.soros.org/osi.html

Open Society Institute-Budapest
Oktober 6 ut. 12
H-1051 Budapest
Hungary
www.osi.hu

Physicians for Social Responsibility

Physicians for Social Responsibility (PSR) is a national, nonprofit membership organization of more than 20,000 health professionals and supporters working to promote nuclear arms reduction, international cooperation, protection of the environment, and the reduction of violence. PSR was founded in 1961 and is the U.S. affiliate of International Physicians for the Prevention of Nuclear War, which was awarded the Nobel Peace Prize in 1985. PSR supports the downsizing of the nuclear weapons complex and cleanup of radioactive contamination at Department of Energy sites. In addition, PSR promotes an end to nuclear testing, the forging of new arms reduction treaties, a shift in federal budget priorities away from military spending and toward meeting human needs, preservation of the environment, and the reduction of violence and its causes.

PSR's activities include public education about the health impacts of nuclear weapons production and testing, the social costs of the arms race, and the links between pollution and public health. PSR's programs range from citizen advocacy with Congress, speaker tours, media work, and educational publications. A background or interest in nuclear weapons and security issues and related legislative policy, as well as an interest in PSR's goals, is sought in prospective hires and interns.

> Physicians for Social Responsibility
> Suite 1012
> 1875 Connecticut Avenue, NW
> Washington, DC 20009
> Tel.: (202) 667-4260
> Fax: (202) 667-4201
> www.psr.org/

Population Services International

Population Services International (PSI) is the world's leading social marketing organization, operating in fifty developing countries and in the United States. PSI works to create demand for essential health products through commercial marketing and advertising techniques and innovative communications campaigns designed to motivate positive changes in health behavior. On the supply side, PSI also makes critical health products and services for family planning, maternal and child health, and the prevention of AIDS, malaria, and other diseases easily available to populations at risk. The prices of its products and services are subsidized, so that they are affordable to those who need them most.

PSI operates in the private sector and exhibits a bottom-line orientation that is rare among nonprofits. For international program positions, PSI seeks candidates with at least two years of developing country work experience; fluency in French, Spanish, Portuguese, or Russian; and commercial sector work experience, preferably in marketing or sales and in a management capacity. Prior work experience in the public health field, as well as familiarity with the international donor community, is helpful.

Information about PSI's programs and current openings can be found at the website.

PSI Recruitment
1120 19th Street, NW, Suite 600
Washington, DC 20036
www.psi.org

Project HOPE

Project HOPE (Health Opportunity for People Everywhere) is a private international organization offering multidisciplinary assistance in health care education in the United States and abroad. It is the principal activity of the People-to-People Health Foundation, an independent nonprofit corporation. Project HOPE's principal objective is to teach modern techniques of medical science to medical, dental, nursing, and allied health personnel in developing areas of the world. Although immediate humanitarian assistance is often an element of activities, Project HOPE stresses long-term, systemic solutions to health care problems.

The basic requirement for employment in Project HOPE's international programs is licensure, or in some cases certification, within a health care profession. Because of the educational nature of HOPE's programs, most of their international staff have at least a master's degree and academic and/or clinical teaching experience. There were forty-one professional positions and job openings in the international field in recent years. Occasionally, internships are available to complement an existing HOPE program, provided the intern has outside funding.

Human Resources
Project HOPE
Millwood, VA 22646
Tel.: (800) 544-4673
Fax: (703) 837-9052
www.projecthope.org

Rockefeller Foundation

The Rockefeller Foundation, founded in 1913 to promote the well-being of peoples throughout the world, seeks to identify and relieve the underlying causes of human suffering and need. The foundation works in three broad areas: science-based development, arts and humanities, and equal opportunity. Its programs are carried out through grants and fellowships to institutions and individuals.

The Rockefeller Foundation's development program is of most interest to students of international affairs. This science-based development program has three divisions: agricultural sciences, health sciences, and population sciences. The program is designed to help developing nations, particularly in Africa, use modern science and technology in bringing food, health, education, housing, and work to their people by building partnerships between industrial and developing countries. Although the program is science-based, it also emphasizes factors such as local culture and values, equitable policy making, competent management, and production capability that can determine whether science and technology effectively contribute to the well-being of people in the developing world.

The foundation has a full-time staff of more than 130 people in New York. There are program officers and mid-level program associates in each division. Almost all professional positions are filled by people with extensive experience in the field and often who have published in the area of concentration of the position being filled. Employment opportunities with the foundation are limited.

> The Rockefeller Foundation
> 420 Fifth Avenue
> New York, NY 10018-2702
> Tel.: (202) 869-8500
> www.rockfound.org

Salvation Army

Founded in 1865 as a religious and charitable organization, The Salvation Army provides financial and personnel assistance in about 100 countries. Its programs embrace education (primary, secondary, vocational, technical, and teacher training), community centers, disaster relief, health and medical services, agriculture, and a range of community development projects. A major emphasis of the army's work is to administer spiritual guidance and aid wherever there is human need. It is an integral part of the International Salvation Army of London.

The overseas staff numbers about eighty to ninety, most of whom are administrators and have education and experience appropriate to their positions. U.S. staff numbers six to eight.

> The Salvation Army
> USA National Headquarters
> P.O. Box 269
> Alexandria, VA 22313
> Tel.: (703) 684-5500
> Fax: (703) 684-3478

Save the Children

Save the Children is a private, nonprofit, nonsectarian international organization committed to helping children through the process of community development. Program expenditures are directed primarily to community projects that attack interrelated problems of poverty: poor health, inadequate nutrition, low agricultural productivity, substandard housing, and the lack of education, skills training, and jobs, among others. The organization offers training, technical assistance, tools, and guidance for solving the problems of poor children around the world.

The organization employs more than 200 people in its Westport, Connecticut, headquarters with an equal number working in field positions in the United States and abroad. About five to ten professional positions are filled annually. Increasingly, successful candidates have master's degrees and some professional experience in community development.

> Save the Children
> 54 Wilton Road
> Westport, CT 06880
> Tel.: (800) 728-3843
> www.savethechildren.org/home.shtml

U.S.-Asia Institute

The U.S.-Asia Institute, founded in 1979, is a national nonprofit, nonpartisan organization devoted to fostering understanding and strengthening ties between the people and governments of the United States and Asia. Through conferences, congressional staff delegations to key Asian countries, policy research, symposiums, international exchanges, and consulting various East Asian embassies, the U.S.-Asia Institute promotes the examination of the economic, political, and cultural issues vital to U.S.-Asia relations.

The U.S.-Asia Institute currently has four professional staff positions and four staff interns. Employment opportunities are rare and competitive. The U.S.-Asia Institute also sponsors and coordinates professional internships for American undergraduate and graduate students as well as international young professionals. The U.S.-Asia Institute internship duties include assisting staff in organizing various programs; conducting policy research; and attending and disseminating congressional hearings, seminars, and State Department and NGO policy lectures.

Though academic training in the area of East Asia is certainly preferred, the U.S.-Asia Institute has hired individuals with economic, political science, public policy, and international relations backgrounds who have an interest in Asia. Successful applicants must have a minimum of a B.A. or B.S. and usually one to two years of international work experience. They must be well organized and able to communicate effectively in both written and oral form. It is vital that they recognize the importance of teamwork and be willing to do a variety of tasks.

U.S.-Asia Institute
232 East Capitol Street, NE
Washington, DC 20003
Tel.: (202) 544-3181
Fax: (202) 543-1748
www.usasiainstitute.com

Winrock International Institute for International Development

Winrock International Institute for International Development is a nonprofit organization that works with people in the United States and around the world to increase economic opportunity, sustain natural resources, and protect the environment. By linking local individuals and communities with new ideas and technology, Winrock is increasing long-term productivity, equity, and responsible resource management to benefit the poor and disadvantaged of the world. Winrock staff implement projects in more than sixty-five countries annually in leadership development, forestry and natural resource management, agriculture, clean energy, volunteer technical assistance, and policy. Winrock is headquartered on Petit Jean Mountain near Morrilton, Arkansas, and has offices in Arlington, Virginia; Salvador, Brazil; Beijing, China; Manila, the Philippines; and New Delhi, India.

Last year, Winrock utilized 111 consultants and recruited for forty-nine full-time positions for its domestic and field operations, twenty of which were professional openings in the program areas. The entry-level professional position for our various program units is program assistant, which requires a bachelor's degree that relates to the program area. Higher-level positions require at least a master's degree plus at least five years of related experience, including international experience.

> Winrock International
> 38 Winrock Drive
> Morrilton, AR 72110
> Tel.: (501) 727-5435, ext. 329
> Fax: (501) 727-5643
> www.winrock.org

Women in International Security
Women in International Security (WIIS) is dedicated to increasing the influence of women in the field of foreign and defense affairs and enhancing the dialogue on international security. WIIS offers a comprehensive set of programs designed to foster and promote women leaders in all sectors—government, business, think tanks, academia, and the media. WIIS members benefit from a worldwide network of valuable contacts in international security and related fields. Established in 1987, WIIS is a nonprofit, nonpartisan educational program based at the Center for Peace and Security Studies at the Edmund A. Walsh School of Foreign Service at Georgetown University.

In the past year, WIIS has had two open professional positions. Typically, WIIS has six internship openings per year (two per semester, as interns usually are undergraduate or graduate students). New recruits usually have a bachelor's degree in international relations or a related field and have overseas experience.

> Women in International Security
> Center for Peace and Security Studies
> Georgetown University
> 3240 Prospect Street, NW
> Washington, DC 20057
> Tel.: (202) 687-3366
> Fax: (202) 687-3233
> www.wiis.org

World Learning
World Learning is a private, nonprofit international educational institution committed to building a sustainable and peaceful world by fostering intercultural understanding and development. Since its founding in 1932, World Learning has built a reputation as one of the world's leading global education, development, and exchange organizations, with programs in more than ninety countries. Today, World Learning's programs provide life-changing learning experiences that lead to greater understanding and cooperation among people, communities, and nations drawn closer by the forces of globalization. World Learning has four major program activities:

- The School for International Training, in Brattleboro, Vermont, offers graduate degrees, intensive training, and undergraduate study-abroad programs, all designed to develop cross-cultural skills and build individuals' capacity to effect change.
- Projects in International Development & Training, World Learning's Washington, D.C.-based division, is a prominent nongovernmental organization that implements international development projects in more than thirty-five countries worldwide.
- World Learning Business Solutions, the organization's corporate practice area, builds the leadership, language, and intercultural skills of high-potential employees of global companies.
- The Experiment in International Living, World Learning's original program, provides cross-cultural summer learning experiences and international exchanges that have profoundly affected the lives of generations of high school students.

World Learning has about 1,000 employees in thirty domestic and overseas offices; most are nationals of the countries in which World Learning works. World Learning typically fills about twenty professional positions each year. These positions usually require international/intercultural experience (often country- or region-specific), and a combination of management and technical expertise, according to the particular project or activity. Position announcements are available from World Learning's Human Resources department.

World Learning
Kipling Road, P.O. Box 676
Brattleboro, VT 05302-0676
Tel.: (802) 257-7751
www.worldlearning.org

Youth For Understanding
Youth For Understanding (YFU) international exchange, an educational, nonprofit organization, prepares young people for their opportunities and responsibilities in a changing, interdependent world. With YFU, students can choose a year, semester, or summer program in one of more than thirty-five countries worldwide. More than 200,000 young people from more than fifty nations in Asia, Europe, North and South America, Africa, and the Pacific have participated in YFU exchanges. Each exchange is coordinated by a worldwide network of national YFU organizations and supported by more than 3,500 trained and dedicated volunteers. YFU has its International Center in Washington, D.C., five district offices throughout the United States, and more than forty national offices abroad.

YFU has a professional staff of about seventy working at the International Center, as well as ninety employed throughout the United States. Learn more about YFU programs, becoming a volunteer, or working at YFU by visiting the website.

> Youth For Understanding International Exchange
> International Center
> 3501 Newark Street, NW
> Washington, DC 20016-3199
> Tel.: (202) 966-6800
> (800) TEENAGE
> Fax: (202) 895-1104
> www.YouthForUnderstanding.org

Chapter 14

RESEARCH INSTITUTES

Careers in Research Institutes

JOSEPH CIRINCIONE

If you are looking for a fast track to a six-figure salary and a vacation home on the beach, you can safely skip this chapter. On the other hand, if you want an entry point to the international and security policy fields, if you want to do good while doing well, if you are willing to labor for a few years in assistant positions, or if you want a preview of one of the pit stops you will probably make during your career, read on.

Few people make a career solely at research institutes. But many get their start at one of the more than 100 think tanks in Washing-

> Research institutes come in all sizes and flavors, so it should not be difficult to find one that matches your particular interests and political leanings.

ton or the 1,000 research centers around the country. Many others cycle through institutes between government positions. It is common after elections, for example, for government officials and staff to take a job at a center, develop their expertise and influence policy with research projects, then reenter government at higher levels after the next change. George Stephanopoulos began his political career as an intern at the Arms Control Association before moving on to the House staff, the White House, and then ABC News. Richard Haas went from the staff of the National Security Council in the first Bush administration to direct foreign policy studies at the Brookings Institution and now serves as the U.S. State Department's Director of Policy Planning in the new Bush administration.

Joseph Cirincione, a 1983 graduate of the Master of Science in Foreign Service program, is director of the Non-Proliferation Project at the Carnegie Endowment for International Peace. He previously held positions as a senior associate at the Henry L. Stimson Center, on the professional staff of the House Armed Services Committee and the Government Operations Committee, at the U.S. Information Agency, and at the Center for Strategic and International Studies.

Research institutes come in all sizes and flavors, so it should not be difficult to find one that matches your particular interests and political leanings. There is considerable turnover at all levels, constantly generating new openings. Planning and persistence are critical, however, to locate a position at the precise time you need one. One of the best strategies for getting an entry-level position is to begin as an intern—paid or unpaid. From that position, you can establish a foothold that lets you search for a full-time position, learn the skills necessary to qualify for those positions, and have the satisfaction of doing work with a project that may have a real policy impact.

Fortunately, most institutes now have websites that provide information about the institution, employment openings, and application procedures. The Carnegie Endowment maintains an online listing of the major research organizations, with links to individual websites, at www.ceip.org/files/news/library/libtanks.htm. There are so many centers, however, that you should conduct your own web searches, or even better, pay attention when you are reading articles to see where a particular expert works, then follow up with a phone call or a visit, not just an Internet hit.

Positions are competitive at most centers. Those with bachelor's degrees can expect to be considered for administrative positions only. Some institutes, such as the Henry L. Stimson Center or the Carnegie Endowment, have special programs offering one-year positions for recent college graduates. These are highly competitive. With a master's degree, particularly from a prestigious school, applicants can expect to be placed at the top of the list for consideration for a research assistant position. Strong writing and oral communication skills are essential. Computer and web skills are a decided plus. Beginning salaries should range from the mid-twenties to mid-thirties, depending on the size and funding base of the institute. Work hours are usually nine to five, but researchers who come in early and stay late rise more quickly in the field. The work is often hard, but typically not repetitive, and even new researchers often find themselves on the cutting edge of international events with the opportunity to learn from and meet leading scholars and officials from around the world. Smaller institutes may pay less, but they are often engaged in direct advocacy work that will appeal to many, particularly in the environmental, human rights, and national security fields.

Expect to start off doing basic research work, working up to drafting sections of papers and articles as you demonstrate your writing skills. You can impress your boss by bringing him or her real books from the extensive libraries at many of the centers like Brookings, Carnegie, Center for Strategic and International Studies (CSIS), or Heritage. If you are at the right place working for the right person, you should expect that during your first year you will have the opportunity to author your own articles and begin to build your publishing credits. Most centers have a collegial atmosphere where you can make friends, develop your own personal career networks, play softball with the company team on the Mall, and find mentors that can guide your career advance.

Funding for research in international affairs over the past ten years has gone up, down, and now perhaps up again. With the end of the Cold War, many of the private foundations began shifting their grants away from the "old agenda." But the agenda did not go away; it just changed form.

Today, new threats, new international conflicts, and new transnational issues demand new solutions that governments are often unable to develop in the press of events and the stranglehold of bureaucratic interests. Path-breaking work, for example, identifying the new security threats and new government organizational imperatives, has come from several research centers and special commissions formed in cooperation with these centers. The independent nature of most of the major U.S. research institutes allows them to provide fresh ideas in a symbiotic relationship with government. Funding still remains high enough to keep most of the centers engaged (though with constant pressure to keep their work policy relevant).

Because most senior research positions require a Ph.D. or extensive experience in the field, research assistant positions will not lead directly up the career ladder at an institute. After two or three years, most people change jobs, go into government or commercial consulting firms, or go back to school for an advanced degree or to another program at a higher level. It is common to have five or six different jobs over a twenty-year period in Washington, with each one leading to new responsibilities, higher salaries, and more opportunities to make a difference in the world.

That, at least, has been my experience. My first job as a research assistant began at CSIS during my second year of graduate school. Now I am the one writing this essay. May your careers go as well.

Resource Listings

American Enterprise Institute

The American Enterprise Institute (AEI), founded in 1943, is a nonpartisan, nonprofit research and educational organization that sponsors original research on government policy, the American economy, and American politics. AEI research aims to preserve and strengthen the foundations of a free society—limited government, competitive private enterprise, vital cultural and political institutions, and a vigilant defense—through rigorous inquiry, debate, and writing. AEI is home to some of America's most renowned economists, legal scholars, political scientists, and foreign policy specialists.

AEI employs forty-five resident scholars, recruited mainly from colleges and universities. There are approximately twenty-four full-time research assistant positions in the disciplines listed previously, with four or five new vacancies filled, on average, throughout the year. Holders of bachelor's and master's degrees are eligible to apply.

American Enterprise Institute
1150 Seventeenth Street, NW
Washington, DC 20036
Tel.: (202) 862-5800 Fax: (202) 862-7177
www.aei.org

The Aspen Institute

The Aspen Institute is a global forum for leveraging the power of leaders to improve the human condition. Through its seminar and policy programs, the institute fosters enlightened, morally responsible leadership and convenes leaders and policymakers to address the foremost challenges of the new century. Founded in 1950, the Aspen Institute is a nonprofit organization with principal offices in Aspen, Colorado; Chicago, Illinois; Washington, D.C.; and on the Wye River on Maryland's Eastern Shore. The Aspen Institute operates internationally through a network of partners in Europe and Asia.

Total U.S. staff numbers about 150, with some temporary staff for summer activities and special projects. Overseas affiliates operate and hire staff independently from U.S. operations.

Human Resources
The Aspen Institute
1 Dupont Circle, NW, Suite 700
Washington, DC 20036-1133
Tel.: (202) 736-3856
www.aspeninstitute.org

Atlantic Council of the United States

The Atlantic Council is a nonpartisan network of leaders who are convinced of the pivotal importance of effective U.S. foreign policy and the cohesion of U.S. international relationships. The council promotes constructive U.S. leadership and engagement in international affairs based on the central role of the Atlantic community in the contemporary world situation. It does this principally by stimulating dialogue and discussion about critical international policy issues, with the intention of enriching public debate and promoting consensus in the administration, the Congress, the corporate and nonprofit sectors, and the media in the United States and among leaders in Europe, Asia, and the Americas, and by promoting educational and other programs for successor generations of U.S. leaders who will value U.S. international engagement and have the formation necessary to develop effective policies, building on U.S. leadership in the Atlantic community.

> The Atlantic Council of the United States
> 910 17th Street, NW, Suite 1000
> Washington, DC 20006
> Fax: (202) 463-7241
> www.acus.org

Brookings Institution

The Brookings Institution is a private, nonprofit, nonpartisan organization devoted to research, education, and publication in economics, government, foreign policy, and the social sciences. Its principal purpose is to bring to bear new knowledge on current and emerging public policy issues facing the United States and to provide an expanded body of knowledge to better inform scholars, decision makers, and the American public. Its activities are carried out through three research programs (economic studies, governmental studies, and foreign policy studies), the Center for Public Policy Education, an active website, and a publications program.

The institution's staff includes about 260 people. Most professional positions are senior fellows and fellows, numbering about fifty-five, fourteen of whom work on foreign policy issues. Senior fellows and fellows primarily hold doctorate degrees in a discipline relevant to a particular topic under research. Research assistants usually have a master's degree in international studies with fluency in a foreign language, primarily Arabic, Chinese, or Russian. Three or four research assistants are hired per year in the foreign policy area.

The Brookings Institution
1775 Massachusetts Avenue, NW
Washington, DC 20036
Tel.: (202) 797-6000
www.brookings.org

Carnegie Endowment for International Peace

An operating, as opposed to grant-making, foundation, the Carnegie Endowment conducts programs of research, discussion, publication, and education in international relations and American foreign policy. Although its program activities change periodically, emphasis has been on regional and country studies, including the Middle East, Central and Latin America, U.S.-Soviet relations, and South Asia. Recently, the endowment also has pursued a variety of projects concerning Eastern Europe. The organization also engages in joint programs with other tax-exempt organizations to invigorate and enlarge the scope of dialogue on international issues. *Foreign Policy* is the quarterly journal published as a public forum for its activities.

The endowment employs about sixty people, including about twenty senior associates as well as other professionals associated with research, administration, publications, and support activities. Almost all professional positions are held by well-known experts in particular fields of interest to the endowment. The endowment offers a one-year internship for graduating college seniors.

Carnegie Endowment for International Peace
1779 Massachusetts Avenue, NW
Washington, DC 20036-2103
Tel.: (202) 483-7600
Fax: (202) 483-1840
www.ceip.org

Cato Institute

The Cato Institute is a nonprofit public policy research foundation headquartered in Washington, D.C. Founded in 1977 by Edward H. Crane, the institute is named for *Cato's Letters,* a series of libertarian pamphlets that helped lay the philosophical foundation for the American Revolution.

The Cato Institute seeks to broaden the parameters of public policy debate to allow consideration of the traditional American principles of limited government, individual liberty, free markets, and peace. Toward that goal, the institute strives to achieve greater involvement of the intelligent, concerned lay public in questions of policy and the proper role of government. To counter what it sees as increasing government encroachment in individual rights, the Cato Institute undertakes an extensive publications program that addresses the complete spectrum of policy issues. Major policy conferences are held throughout the year, from which papers are published thrice yearly in the *Cato Journal*. The Institute also publishes the quarterly magazine *Regulation*.

For job opportunities at Cato, visit www.cato.org/jobs/jobops.html.

> The Cato Institute
> 1000 Massachusetts Avenue, NW
> Washington, DC 20001-5403
> Tel.: (202) 842-0200
> Fax: (202) 842-3490
> www.cato.org

Center for Defense Information

The Center for Defense Information (CDI) is an independent, nonprofit research organization founded by retired military officers. It is dedicated to providing up-to-the-minute, accurate information on U.S. and global security issues, free from ideological or special-interest bias. For that reason, the center accepts no U.S. government or defense industry funding—although CDI staff do seek to provide analysis and information to the public and policymakers alike. The *Defense Monitor*, the center's best known publication, is published ten times per year. Other publications include the *Military Almanac* of facts and figures regarding the U.S. defense budget and monographs on topics from nuclear weapons to small arms. CDI also produces television programming, including videos for educational purposes, as well as housing an independent documentary film production unit.

CDI staff includes retired U.S. military officers, former Pentagon officials, and civilian experts with background in a wide variety of international security issues. An internship program employs undergraduate students, graduate students, and recent graduates with strong interests in security affairs and related public policy questions. Interns can serve in research, television production, or web production positions.

> Center for Defense Information
> 1779 Massachusetts Avenue, NW
> Washington, DC 20036
> Tel.: (202) 332-0600
> Fax: (202) 462-4559
> www.cdi.org

Center for Strategic and International Studies

For four decades, the Center for Strategic and International Studies (CSIS) has been dedicated to providing world leaders with strategic insights on—and policy solutions to—current and emerging global issues. CSIS is led by John J. Hamre, formerly deputy secretary of defense, who has been president and CEO since April 2000. It is guided by a board of trustees chaired by former Senator Sam Nunn and consisting of prominent individuals from both the public and private sectors.

The CSIS staff of 190 researchers and support staff focus primarily on three subject areas. First, CSIS addresses the full spectrum of new challenges to national and international security. Second, CSIS maintains resident experts on all of the world's major geographical regions. Third, CSIS is committed to helping develop new methods of governance for the global age; to this end, CSIS has programs on technology and public policy, international trade, and finance and energy.

The Center for Strategic and International Studies is an equal opportunity employer. CSIS complies with the law regarding reasonable accommodation for handicapped and disabled employees. To search for opportunities at CSIS, visit www.csis.org/employment/index.htm. If you are interested in applying for an open position, forward a resume and letter of interest, including salary requirements to:

CSIS
1800 K Street, NW
Washington, DC 20006
Tel.: (202) 887-0200
Fax: (202) 775-3199
www.csis.org

Chicago Council on Foreign Relations

The Chicago Council on Foreign Relations is a diverse and growing foreign policy institute that sponsors both public education and more specialized professional activities. The council's membership consists of more than 7,000 individuals in the greater Chicago area, plus 125 corporate sponsors. Public lectures, corporate meetings, seminars, and study groups for the academic community and special research and publication projects are organized on a regular basis. The council has a continuing interest in public opinion and foreign policy, security, and defense issues and international economics. U.S. foreign policy, Europe, and Asia are areas of particular concern. Every four years, the organization publishes *American Public Opinion and U.S. Foreign Policy,* based on a nationwide survey conducted by Gallup. The council also publishes policy-oriented books on a range of international relations topics as well as occasional paper series. It administers the Atlantic Conference, attracting leaders from Western Europe and the Americas, and has close ties with the quarterly journal *Foreign Policy.*

The council has a staff of about seventeen people. Employment opportunities are extremely limited.

> The Chicago Council on Foreign Relations
> 116 South Michigan Avenue, 10th Floor
> Chicago, IL 60603
> Tel.: (312) 726-3860
> Fax: (312) 726-4491
> www.ccfr.org

Council on Foreign Relations

The Council on Foreign Relations, established in 1921, is a nonprofit and nonpartisan membership organization dedicated to improved understanding of American foreign policy and international affairs. As a leader in the community of institutions concerned with American foreign policy, the council conducts a comprehensive meetings program. The meetings sponsored by the council reflect the issues of current concern in international affairs and are led by top foreign policy officials and experts who are critical to the discussion of policy. The council's studies program examines key issues in U.S. foreign policy today through a combination of individual scholarly research, group discussions, and conferences. The council also publishes books and papers on international issues and since 1922 has published *Foreign Affairs,* the leading journal in the field. The council's research, editorial, and administrative staff are located at its headquarters in New York and in Washington, D.C.

The council provides excellent opportunities for recent graduates who are considering careers in international relations or political science through its entry-level professional position of staff assistant. Staff assistants can identify different career options in the field of international relations, as well as increase their knowledge of world events by taking advantage of the council's many resources. Those applying for staff assistant positions should possess a strong interest in international affairs and a willingness to assist with administrative work. Graduate degrees are not required. Positions generally are open from late spring to early fall.

> Council on Foreign Relations
> 58 East 68th Street
> New York, NY 10021
> Tel.: (212) 434-9400
> Fax: (212) 434-9800
> www.cfr.org

East-West Center
The East-West Center is an internationally recognized education and research organization established by the U.S. Congress in 1960 to strengthen understanding and relations between the United States and the countries of the Asia Pacific region. The Center helps promote the establishment of a stable, peaceful, and prosperous Asia Pacific community in which the United States is a natural, valued, and leading partner.

The Center carries out its mission through programs of cooperative study, training, and research. Professionals and students from the United States, Asia, and the Pacific study and work together at the East-West Center. As a national and regional resource, the Center offers an interdisciplinary research program, dialogue and professional enrichment programs, and educational programs.

The East-West Center offers visiting fellowships and short-term grants. Each year the center provides scholarships for graduate students from the United States and the Asia Pacific region who study at the University of Hawaii. The Center hires research fellows, usually on three-year contracts, for which it seeks Ph.D. or the equivalent in practical experience. There are other employment opportunities for research and program support positions and for technical and clerical work.

> Office of Human Resources
> East-West Center
> 1601 East-West Road
> Honolulu, HI 96814-1601
> Tel.: (808) 944-7975
> www.ewc.hawaii.edu

Foreign Policy Association

The Foreign Policy Association (FPA) was founded in 1918 as the League of Free Nations Association. It was formed by 141 distinguished Americans to support President Woodrow Wilson's efforts to achieve a just peace. The association was reconstituted in 1923 as the Foreign Policy Association with a commitment to the careful study of all sides of international questions affecting the United States. John Foster Dulles and Eleanor Roosevelt were among the incorporators.

The Foreign Policy Association is a national, nonprofit, nonpartisan, nongovernmental, educational organization founded to educate Americans about the significant international issues that influence their lives. FPA provides impartial publications, programs, and forums to increase public awareness of, and foster popular participation in, matters relating to those policy issues.

> Foreign Policy Association
> 470 Park Avenue South
> New York, NY 10016
> Tel.: (212) 481-8100
> www.fpa.org

Foreign Policy Research Institute

Founded in 1955, the Foreign Policy Research Institute (FPRI) is devoted to bringing the insights of scholarship to bear on the development of policies that advance U.S. national interests. FPRI conducts research on a broad range of issues, including U.S. policy toward Russia, China, and the Middle East. FPRI publishes a quarterly journal, *Orbis,* and a series of bulletins, both of which draw on the research findings of its scholars, Inter-University Study Groups, conferences, and seminars.

> Foreign Policy Research Institute
> 1528 Walnut Street, Suite 610
> Philadelphia, PA 19102
> www.fpri.org

Heritage Foundation

Founded in 1973, The Heritage Foundation is a research and educational institute—a think tank—whose mission is to formulate and promote conservative public policies based on the principles of free enterprise, limited government, individual freedom, traditional American values, and a strong national defense.

Getting Started at Think Tanks
KARLA J. NIETING

The first step I took was to search for internship opportunities. I was intrigued by the chance to work at the Carnegie Endowment but worried that the internship would not pay. Since most think tanks are nonprofit organizations, this was not unusual, but it was a major concern for me. Financial considerations nearly kept me from applying, but in the end it seemed to be a sacrifice worth making. I applied and was offered the internship.

The experience I had paid off in many ways. I used the time to learn and make many new contacts but also to observe how think tanks operate and ask questions about the opportunities available at them. Although no research organization is the same, most of them do function similarly: In general, there is an administrative layer at the top (executive, accounting, human resources, outreach); the research centers, programs, and projects in the middle (fellows, research assistants, program administrators); and a support structure on the bottom (technical assistance and other services such as a library or press). Most of

(Continued)

Heritage's staff pursues this mission by performing timely, accurate research on key policy issues and effectively marketing these findings to our primary audiences: members of Congress, key congressional staff members, policymakers in the executive branch, the nation's news media, and the academic and policy communities. Heritage's products include publications, articles, lectures, conferences, and meetings.

Governed by an independent Board of Trustees, The Heritage Foundation is a nonpartisan, tax-exempt institution. Heritage relies on the private financial support of the general public—individuals, foundations, and corporations—for its income and accepts no government funds and performs no contract work. Heritage is one of the nation's largest public policy research organizations.

Several professional positions are filled annually. The foundation also maintains a Washington Executive Bank (WEB) that places qualified conservative applicants in policymaking positions throughout the research-oriented positions lie in the middle and have titles such as junior fellow, research associate, and research assistant. Depending upon the organization, these positions will require a B.A. or M.A. The Carnegie Endowment, for example, has a one-year junior fellow program open only to those with a newly minted bachelor's degree. In contrast, the Council on Foreign Relations hires research associates with a master's degree for various lengths of time.

After graduation I accepted a nine-month fellowship in Germany. The fellows I had met at the Carnegie Endowment had encouraged me to avail myself of the opportunity and assured me that they would be willing to help me in my job search upon my return. The time I spent in Germany was well spent for many reasons, but I was particularly lucky to have made contacts with visitors to my German office from various think tanks in Washington.

My first move when I returned was to test the market for a job in European affairs at a think tank. I called many of the people I had met at Carnegie and in Germany and started my first round of informational interviews. At each interview, I tried to get as many names of new contacts as I could. Most

the administration and Congress. For more information on opportunities at the Heritage Foundation, visit www.heritage.org/jobbank/.

The Heritage Foundation
214 Massachusetts Avenue, NE
Washington, DC 20002-4999
Tel.: (202) 546-4400
Fax: (202) 546-8328
www.heritage.org

Hoover Institution

The Hoover Institution on War, Revolution and Peace within Stanford University is a public policy research center devoted to advanced study of politics, economics, and political economy—both domestic and foreign—as well as international affairs. Founded in 1919 by Herbert Hoover, the thirty-first president of the United States, the institution houses one of the world's largest private archives and major libraries on political, economic, and social change in the twentieth important, I did not forget to ask if they knew of a job opening at that organization or another one. Doing this, in fact, led to my first job interview.

By following these steps, I met most of the people at think tanks in Washington who work on European affairs. I quickly realized that it was important to meet people who were research assistants or senior fellows. Research associates/assistants tend to know about job openings at the entry level and they have numerous contacts at their level and above. More senior individuals, however, are able to pass your name along with more authority.

A job at a think tank has many advantages. Working with a scholar who is a recognized expert in his or her field opens many doors both academically and professionally. The ability to have an impact on policy debates is exciting. The networking opportunities are practically endless, and the job is relatively low stress. On the other hand, think tanks offer few opportunities for promotion unless you have a Ph.D. (The average life span for a research assistant position is two to three years.) Salaries are low in comparison with private- and public-sector jobs. However, the situation has improved in recent years. Much

century. The focus of the institution's international research is to identify and analyze major issues and potential crises that may face U.S. government policymakers in the future.

Research results are made public through a wide variety of books, journal articles, lectures, interviews, programs in the news media, seminars, conferences, expert congressional testimony, and consultative services.

Hoover Institution
Stanford University
Stanford, CA 94305-6010
Tel.: (650) 723-1754
Fax: (650) 723-1687
www-hoover.stanford.edu

Hudson Institute

Hudson Institute is a private, not-for-profit, public policy research organization headquartered in Indianapolis, Indiana, with offices in Washington, D.C.; Madison, Wisconsin; and Miami and Tampa, Florida.

of the job is dependent on the scholar with whom you work and how much actual research assistance he or she wants. The rest depends on you. Being at the junction of academia and policy in a Washington think tank is a unique and exciting position.

Karla J. Nieting is a 1996 graduate of the Master of Science in Foreign Service program at Georgetown University. Currently a research assistant in the Foreign Policy Studies Program at The Brookings Institution, she has been an assistant at the U.S. Peace Corps, an intern at the Carnegie Endowment for Peace, and a Bundestag Fellow in Germany.

The institute analyzes and makes recommendations about public policy for business and government executives, as well as for the public at large. Hudson Institute operates a Center for Central European and Eurasian Studies. Hudson's work on Eastern Europe, Russia, and the other states of the former Soviet Union focuses on identifying and analyzing the emerging economic, political, and security trends in this rapidly changing, often volatile region, and providing those governments and the U.S. government with specific, realistic policy recommendations for promoting the difficult transition to democracy and free-market economies.

Hudson also is examining the future of Japanese-U.S. relations, evolving relations between Taiwan and the People's Republic of China, Korea-Japan relations, emerging countries from the Balkans, and new transatlantic security arrangements.

Hudson Institute's staff of seventy includes thirty-four research professionals. Qualifications for entry-level research positions generally include advanced academic training and/or some professional experience in an area related to the institute's research interests. Excellent written and oral communication skills also are required.

Hudson Institute Indianapolis Headquarters
Herman Kahn Center
5395 Emerson Way
Indianapolis, IN 46226
Tel.: (317) 545-1000
Fax: (317) 545-9639

1015 18th Street, NW, Suite 300
Washington, DC 20036
Tel.: (202) 223-7770
Fax: (202) 223-8537
www.hudson.org

Institute for Defense and Disarmament

Founded in 1980, the Institute for Defense and Disarmament (IDDS) is supported by foundation grants, individual donations, and publication sales. The Institute for Defense and Disarmament Studies is a think tank for research and education on ways to reduce the risk of war, minimize the burden of military spending, and promote democratic institutions. The institute aims to multiply the numbers of individuals who have informed opinions on matters of war and peace and play an active role in shaping public policy on these matters.

The institute publishes studies of global military and arms control policies in three forms: reference works intended mainly for professional analysts and libraries, policy studies for all those concerned with international affairs, and free reprints for use in bulk by public interest groups and college and high school classes. IDDS Reference Works cover both armaments and arms control. The IDDS Database of World Arms Holdings, Production, and Trade gives an annually updated account of worldwide major weapon inventories, arms production, and arms trade. The *Arms Control Reporter* provides a day-by-day chronology of all arms control talks plus essential background material.

Institute for Defense & Disarmament Studies
675 Massachusetts Avenue
Cambridge, MA 02139
Tel.: (617) 354-4337
Fax: (617) 354-1450
www.idds.org

Institute for Policy Studies

The Institute for Policy Studies (IPS), founded in 1963, has been described as the first "respectable" offspring of the New Left. Through books, articles, films, conferences, and activist education, IPS offers resources for progressive social change locally, nationally, and globally. IPS seeks to create a more responsible society—one built around the values of justice, nonviolence, sustainability, and decency.

IPS's core programs are Peace and Security, the Global Economy, and Paths for the 21ˢᵗ Century, supplemented by several projects that address specific issues. The institute also houses three other networking programs: The Social Action and Leadership School for Activists (SALSA), the Letelier-Moffitt Human Rights Awards program, and the IPS Publications Program. Through its classes, SALSA teaches activists how to manage, organize, communicate, and strategize more effectively. The Letelier-Moffitt Human Rights Awards program annually honors outstanding human rights activists in memory of two IPS staff killed by a car bomb in 1976 under orders of the Chilean Secret Police.

IPS has a variety of opportunities for college students and recent graduates to get involved in its work through the internship program.

> Institute for Policy Studies
> 733 15th Street, NW, Suite 1020
> Washington, DC 20005
> Tel.: (202) 234-9382
> Fax: (202) 387-7915
> www.ips-dc.org

Institute of Peace, United States

The United States Institute of Peace is an independent, nonpartisan federal institution created and funded by Congress to strengthen the nation's capacity to promote international peace. The Institute works to expand basic and applied knowledge about the origins, nature, and processes of war; sponsors research by scholars and others who represent the widest spectrum of approaches to these questions; and elicits the personal reflections of practitioners of statecraft and international negotiations. The Institute then disseminates this knowledge and practical lessons from it to officials, policymakers, diplomats, and other practitioners in the United States and abroad. Finally, the Institute conducts and supports educational programs for the American public on aspects of international peace.

Candidates for positions with the United States Institute of Peace should have a background in international affairs and strong research and writing skills.

> United States Institute of Peace
> Suite 700
> 1550 M Street, NW
> Washington, DC 20005-1708
> Tel.: (202) 457-1700
> www.usip.org

Middle East Institute

The Middle East Institute (MEI) is a membership organization founded in 1946 to promote American understanding of the Middle East, North Africa, the Caucasus, and Central Asia. MEI is a nonprofit, nonadvocating resource center. It sponsors political and economic programs dealing with both current policy and historical issues. In addition, it conducts classes in Arabic, Hebrew, Persian, and Turkish; coordinates cultural presentations; publishes the *Middle East Journal;* and maintains a 25,000-volume library.

The MEI has a staff of sixteen, of whom half are professionals with extensive experience in Middle Eastern affairs.

The Middle East Institute
1761 N Street, NW
Washington, DC 20036-2882
Tel.: (202) 785-1141
Fax: (202) 331-8861
www.mideasti.org

The Population Council

The Population Council, an international, nonprofit, nongovernmental organization established in 1952, seeks to improve the well-being and reproductive health of current and future generations around the world and to help achieve a humane, equitable, and sustainable balance between people and resources.

The council conducts fundamental biomedical research in reproduction; develops contraceptives and other products for improvement of reproductive health; does studies to improve the quality and outreach of services related to family planning, HIV/AIDS, and reproductive health; conducts research on reproductive health and behavior, family structure, and function, and causes and consequences of population growth; strengthens professional resources in developing countries through collaborative research, awards, fellowships, and training; and publishes innovative research in peer-reviewed journals, books, and working papers and communicates research results to key audiences around the world.

Research and programs are carried out by the Center for Biomedical Research, the International Programs Division, and the Policy Research Division. Council headquarters and the Center for Biomedical Research are located in New York City; the council also maintains an office in Washington, D.C., and an international presence through its five regional offices and fifteen country offices. Council staff consists of more than 500 women and men from more than seventy countries, over a third of whom hold advanced degrees in medicine, public health, and the social sciences. Roughly 50 percent are based in developing countries in Africa, Asia, the Middle East, Latin America, and the Caribbean.

A listing of current job openings at the council, including instructions on how to apply, is available on their website. Ten job openings in the international field were posted last year (out of a total of ninety-six openings for professional and support staff at the council as a whole).

The Population Council
One Dag Hammarskjold Plaza
New York, NY 10017
Tel.: (212) 339-0500
Fax: (212) 755-6052
www.popcouncil.org

RAND

From its inception in the days following World War II, RAND has focused on the nation's most pressing policy problems. The institution's first hallmark was high-quality, objective research on national security, and it began addressing problems of domestic policy in the 1960s. Today, RAND's broad research agenda helps policymakers strengthen the nation's economy, maintain its security and improve its quality of life by helping them make the choices in, among other areas, education, health care, national defense, and criminal and civil justice.

RAND employs more than 1,500 full- and part-time staff; 85 percent of RAND's research staff hold advanced degrees. Most researchers work in RAND's Santa Monica headquarters, although a few others are based in Washington, D.C., or Pittsburgh, Pennsylvania.

RAND
1700 Main Street
P.O. Box 2138
Santa Monica, CA 90407-2138
Tel.: (310) 393-0411
Fax: (310) 393-4818
www.rand.org

Royal Institute of International Affairs

The Royal Institute of International Affairs is an independent, London-based organization founded in 1920 to encourage, facilitate, and inform the debate on international affairs. The institute organizes research by individual scholars and expert study groups; publishes books, periodicals, and pamphlets; arranges lectures and discussions; and maintains a specialized library of books and documents. The institute is responsible for the publication of the journal, *International Affairs;* the magazine, *The World Today;* and the *Chatham House Papers*. The Royal Institute has more than 3,000 members and associates and maintains a staff of about seventy people. Opportunities for careers are open to a very small number of individuals.

> Royal Institute of International Affairs
> Chatham House
> 10 St. James's Square
> London, SW1Y 4LE
> United Kingdom
> Tel.: (44) (0) 20-7957-5700
> Fax: (44) (0) 20-7957-5710
> www.riia.org

Woodrow Wilson International Center for Scholars

The Woodrow Wilson International Center for Scholars was established as a living memorial to the twenty-eighth president of the United States to commemorate President Wilson's lifelong commitment to uniting scholarship with public affairs. Through an annual fellowship competition, the center awards approximately twenty residential fellowships to individuals with outstanding proposals representing the entire range of scholarship, with a strong emphasis on the humanities and the social sciences. In addition, a number of shorter term scholars are also at the center on a rotating basis. Major thematic focus at the center is on three topics: governance, the role of the United States in the world, and the assessment of future challenges confronting the United States and the world. The center sponsors public meetings, generates publications discussing these various topics, and maintains an informative website at www.wilsoncenter.org. Activities are carried out under the structure of a number of programs including the Division of International Studies, which houses projects on Africa, the Middle East, conflict prevention, environmental change, security, and the Cold War History Project. Other regional studies programs include the Kennan Institute for Advanced Russian Studies, the Latin American Program, the Division of United States Studies, and the Asia Program. In addition to its fellowship competition for senior scholars, the center offers internships to outstanding undergraduate and graduate students.

The Wilson Center is administered by a staff of approximately 100 scholars and administrators, program specialists, and support staff.

> The Woodrow Wilson International Center for Scholars
> One Woodrow Wilson Plaza
> 1300 Pennsylvania Avenue, NW
> Washington, DC 20004-3027
> Tel.: (202) 691-4000
> Fax: (202) 691-4001

Worldwatch Institute

The Worldwatch Institute is a nonprofit, public policy research organization dedicated to informing policymakers and the public about emerging global problems and trends and the complex links between the world economy and its environmental support systems.

The Worldwatch Institute is dedicated to fostering the evolution of an environmentally sustainable society—one in which human needs are met in ways that do not threaten the health of the natural environment or the prospects of future generations. The Institute seeks to achieve this goal through the conduct of interdisciplinary, nonpartisan research on emerging global environmental issues, the results of which are widely disseminated throughout the world.

The Institute believes that information is a powerful tool of social change. Human behavior shifts in response to either new information or new experiences. The Institute seeks to provide the information to bring about the changes needed to build an environmentally sustainable economy. In a sentence, the Institute's mission is to raise public awareness of global environmental threats to the point where it will support effective policy responses.

> Worldwatch Institute
> 1776 Massachusetts Avenue, NW
> Washington, DC 20036-1904
> Tel.: (202) 452-1999
> Fax: (202) 296-7365
> www.worldwatch.org

Afterword

A Student's Reflections on the Job Search

LISA A. GIHRING

N ASA's External Relations Office. The Foreign Service. McKinsey Consulting. Freedom House. In the months I have spent editing *Careers in International Affairs*, I have found a wide range of agencies and organizations that appeal to me. And that is the problem.

Despite the forthright "Statement of Purpose" essays we wrote to gain admission to top graduate schools—with bold declarations of our determination to work with refugees or for U.S. interests at the State Department or negotiate trade agreements—many of my colleagues and I now find ourselves a year into graduate school and faced with innumerable work options and opportunities. We have so many options, we aren't sure where to turn and are quickly becoming paralyzed with indecision about a career.

And sure, maybe those bold declarations of purpose were intended just for the admissions committees. But at least when we started graduate school, we *had* a purpose—a comforting sense that we knew just what we wanted to do.

My statement said I wanted to view the world "with the wide-open eyes of a journalist," and I proceeded to focus on international media development. I was confidently planning to spend my career working with nongovernmental organizations dedicated to free-press issues and media development in Russia. However, my classes this year have led me into microfinance, community and civil society development, democratization and good governance, and public diplomacy—issues I never imagined would attract me. These new interests have encouraged me to explore fresh avenues. Suddenly, I find myself reassessing my career plans.

Lisa A. Gihring, the student editor of this volume, will graduate with a Master of Science of Foreign Service in May 2003. Prior to coming to Georgetown University, Ms. Gihring was a Fulbright Fellow in Russia. She also has worked as an editor and writer at regional newspapers in the Midwest. Ms. Gihring holds a B.A. in Russian and English from the University of Iowa and also has studied at Moscow State University.

After reading this book—with its more than 300 employer listings—you might be feeling the same way. But if you take the time to reread the essays and biographical sketches from the friends and alumni of the Master of Science of Foreign Service (MSFS) program, you will notice the circuitous paths some have taken to the positions they now hold. You might also notice that they emphasize flexibility in building a career. As Kelly Cesare, who wrote the introduction to the chapter on banking, states, "It is important to remember that your career is a progression. You will not be doing your first job (or any job) forever."

According to Maria Pinto Carland, the associate director of Georgetown's Master of Science in Foreign Service program, mine is a familiar dilemma. As one of the primary career counselors for MSFSers, Pinto Carland has for many years heard students agonize over what seems to be a life-defining moment: choosing a first job. However, as Pinto Carland says, "Choice now doesn't eliminate choice later. Today's graduates have such a range of skills and interests, they are faced with multiple opportunities to use them. Faced with so many possible doors to enter, they are often hesitant to choose just one. They need to know that while they can only open one door at a time, the other doors will never be locked, and they can go back and open them later."

> By keeping in mind that your first job after graduate school is just that—a first job, and not necessarily a lifelong career—you can look at your job search in a new, less stress-inducing light. Instead of finding the perfect career, you will be taking an interesting first step on your life's path. For me, this has been the lesson learned in editing this book.

Thus, the question becomes not "What is your career goal?" but "How do you want to get started?" By keeping in mind that your first job after graduate school is just that—a first job, and not necessarily a lifelong career—you can look at your job search in a new, less stress-inducing light. Instead of finding the perfect career, you will be taking an interesting first step on your life's path. For me, this has been the lesson learned in editing this book.

For me now, the job/career search is about seeking the commonalities among one's interests and finding organizations in which they will be appreciated and applied. I am looking at the world "with wide-open eyes" and see options of which I was previously unaware. This new view puts my job search into perspective. I have a clearer idea of what I'm looking at: not a single career-defining position, but rather a series of opportunities that will shape my professional life. My new career strategy is to develop skills, gain knowledge and experience, and remain flexible so that I can explore whatever unanticipated opportunities and options arise. My first work situations will allow me to keep learning, sample a variety of interests, gain experience, and make contacts. I'll get a good start, but I won't commit to a final destination now—if ever. Instead, my commitment will be to making a contribution and, one hopes, a difference.

Resources

Websites

www.brassring.com
www.brubach.com
www.career.com
www.careerkey.com
www.careershop.com
www.dice.com
www.flipdog.com
www.helpwanted.com
www.careerbuilder.com
www.hotjobs.com
www.idealist.org
www.jobbankusa.com
www.jobfind.com
www.jobhub.com
www.joblink-usa.com
www.jobtrak.com
www.jobs.com
www.jobsafari.com
http://jobstar.org
www.jobweb.com
www.journalismjobs.com
www.mediabistro.com
www.monster.com
www.rcjobs.com
www.salary.com
www.stepstone.com (jobs in Europe)
www.thingamajob.com
www.washingtonjobs.com
www.washingtonnetworkgroup.com/index.html
www.wetfeet.com

For legislative positions:
Roll Call (The Economist Group): www.rcjobs.com

For international organization positions:
United Nations: www.un.org/Depts/OHRM/

State Department, Bureau of International Organization Affairs:
www.state.gov/p/io/empl/

For international development positions:
UN/OCHA: www.reliefweb.int
USAID: www.usaid.gov/about/employment/

For human rights positions:
Human Rights Job Board: www.hri.ca/jobboard/index.cfm

Because the "dot.com" world is highly voluble and sites come and go quickly, be sure to check university career centers' web pages. These usually have up-to-date lists of job-hunting websites.

Suggested Reading

American Foreign Service Officer Exam. 2001. Philip J. Lane et al. Lawrenceville, N.J.: Peterson's.

Best Resumes and CVs for International Jobs: Your Passport to the Global Job Market. 2002. Ron Krannich and Wendy S. Enelow. Manassas, Va.: Impact Publications.

The Book of U.S. Government Jobs: Where They Are, What's Available, and How to Get One. 2000. Dennis Vamp and Samuel Concialdi. LaCrosse, Wis.: Brookhaven Press.

Capital Source. The National Journal Group. Look for it in your local library or career center.

Commerce Business Daily. Washington, D.C.: U.S. Department of Commerce. A good source for consulting leads. Includes information on unclassified requests for bids and proposals, procurements served for small business, prime contracts awarded, federal contractors seeking subcontract assistance, and upcoming sales of government property. Published daily.

Congressional Directory. Annual. Joint Committee on Printing. Washington, D.C.: U.S. Government Printing Office.

Congressional Staff Directory. Annual. Joint Committee on Printing. Washington, D.C.: U.S. Government Printing Office.

Consultants and Consulting Organizations Directory, 24th ed. 2002. Farmington Hills, Mich.: Gale Group. A listing of consulting firms by location, subject, and firm names.

Directory of American Firms Operating in Foreign Countries, 15th ed. 1998. New York: Uniworld Business Publications, Inc.

Directory of Foreign Firms Operating in the United States. 2002. New York: Uniworld Business Publications, Inc.

The Directory of Websites for International Jobs: The Click and Easy Guide. 2002. Ron and Caryl Krannich. Manassas, Va.: Impact Publications.

E-Resumes: Everything You Need to Know about Using Electronic Resumes to Tap into Today's Hot Job Market. 2001. Susan Britton Whitcomb and Pat Kendall. New York: McGraw-Hill Professional.

Encyclopedia of Associations. 2002. Farmington Hills, Mich.: Gale Group. A guide to national and international organizations. Gives names of chief officer, brief statement of activities, number of members, and publications.

Federal Jobs Overseas. Annual. Washington, D.C., U.S. Civil Service Commission.

Federal Resume Guidebook. 1999. Kathleen Kraemer Troutman and Michael Singer Dobson. Indianapolis, Ind.: JIST Works.

The Foundation Directory. 2002. New York: Foundation Center. Listing of various foundations and areas of interest.

How to Get a Job in Europe. 1999. Robert Sanborn and Cheryl Matherly. Chicago: Surrey Books.

How to Make it Big as a Consultant. 2001. William A Cohen. New York: American Management Association.

International Job Finder: Where the Jobs are Worldwide. 2003. Daniel Lauber. River Forest, Ill.: Planning Communications.

International Jobs, 5th ed. 1999. Eric Kocher and Nina Segal. Cambridge, Mass.: Perseus Books.

International Jobs Directory, 3rd ed. 1999. Ron and Caryl Krannich, PhD.s. Manassas, Va.: Impact Publications.

Jobs for People Who Love to Travel: Opportunities at Home and Abroad. 1999. Ron and Caryl Krannich. Manassas, Va.: Impact Publications.

Occupational Outlook Handbook. Annual. U.S. Department of Labor, Bureau of Labor Statistics. Washington, D.C.: U.S. Government Printing Office.

Overseas Employment Opportunities for Educators: Department of Defense Dependent Schools. 1999. Barry Leonard, ed. Darby, Pa.: DIANE Publishing Co.

Working Abroad: Using the Internet to Find a Job and Get Hired. 2002. Erik Olson and Jim Blau. Princeton, N.J.: Princeton Review Press.

Worldwide Chamber of Commerce Directory. Annual. Loveland, Colo.: Johnson Publishing Co., Inc. A complete list of chambers of commerce in principal cities throughout the world, and foreign embassies and consulates.

Yearbook of International Organizations. Annual. Brussels, Belgium: Union of International Associations.

Index